THE LANGUAGE OF THE CONSCIOUSNESS SOUL

THE LANGUAGE OF THE CONSCIOUSNESS SOUL

A Guide to Rudolf Steiner's "Leading Thoughts"

CARL UNGER

STEINERBOOKS | 2012

2012

STEINERBOOKS

An imprint of Anthroposophic Press, Inc.

610 Main Street, Great Barrington, MA 01230

LIBRARY OF CONGRESS CATALOGING-IN-PUBLICATION DATA

Unger, Carl, 1878–1929.
 [Aus der Sprache der Bewusstseinsseele. English]
 The language of the conscious soul : a guide to Rudolf Steiner's "leading thoughts" / Carl Unger.
   p. cm.
 Translated by Effie Grace Wilson.
 Includes bibliographical references.
 ISBN 978-1-62148-016-7 (pbk.) — ISBN 978-1-62148-017-4 (ebook)
 1. Anthroposophy. 2. Steiner, Rudolf, 1861–1925. I. Title.
 BP595.U4813 2012
 299'.935—dc23

                                                         2012017984

CONTENTS

ABOUT THE CONSCIOUSNESS SOUL

By allowing what is intrinsically true and good to come alive within us, we rise above the mere sentient soul. The eternal spirit shines into the sentient soul, kindling in it a light that will never go out. To the extent that our soul lives in this light, it takes part in something eternal, which it links to its own existence. What the soul carries within itself as truth and goodness is immortal. We will call this eternal element that lights up within the soul the *consciousness soul*.

We can speak of consciousness even in connection with the soul's lower stirrings; even the most mundane sensation is an object of consciousness, and to this extent animals must also be credited with having consciousness. But the very core of human consciousness—the "soul within the soul," so to speak—is what "consciousness soul" means here. The consciousness soul is different from the mind [or intellectual] soul, which is still entangled in sensations, drives, emotions, and so forth. We all know how to accept our personal preferences as true, at first. But truth is lasting only when it has freed itself from any flavor of such sympathies and antipathies. The truth is true, even if all our personal feelings revolt against it. We will apply the term "consciousness soul" to that part of the soul in which truth lives.

—Rudolf Steiner, *Theosophy*

ABOUT THE AUTHOR

This biographical sketch is based on a paper written by Carl Unger for Marie Steiner around 1925. He was describing the course of anthroposophic work in Stuttgart, and made some autobiographical statements for her to use as she wished. The quoted material is from those notes. Additions concern primarily the later years of his life.

Carl Theodor Unger was born on March 28, 1878, in Cannstatt near Stuttgart. He belonged to the family of a merchant with a scientific background. His grandfather, E. S. Unger, was Professor of Mathematics at the University of Erfurt and the founder of the first German Secondary School (*Realschule*). His father J. Unger was known as a collector of art.

As a child Carl Unger was distinguished for his musical ability and above all for his early interest in philosophy as well as for his scientific and technological talents. He received a secular education, and, from the age of fourteen on, he often visited the home of Adolf Arenson. The impressions those visits had on him were very important for his life. Although there was a difference of twenty-three years of age, he and Arenson developed a deep friendship.

When he was fifteen years old, Carl Unger was very impressed with Kerner's *Seer of Prevorat*—primarily by the objectivity of the book in terms of suprasensory experiences, which caused his "childish materialism" to fade away. When he reached seventeen, he asked Adolf Arenson about his view of the world. The question was almost unexpected. His friend presented him with the doctrine of reincarnation, "which, when extricating himself from spiritualistic experiences, he had already discovered for himself, and had found confirmed by Lessing." After that, this also became Unger's view.

He attended the humanistic *Gymnasium*, or high school, which includes classes in Latin and Greek. Later, he attended technical colleges in Stuttgart and Berlin-Charlottenburg and "took the usual examinations." He had studied mechanics and attained his diploma in engineering, as well as a Ph.D.

At the age of twenty, Unger's destiny brought him a strange interruption. During his military service—due to an unfortunate joke—he was shot by a comrade with a pistol, which, of course, was thought to be unloaded. The bullet went into his pericardium (the tissue surrounding the heart). For a long time he hovered between life and death, and it never became possible to remove the bullet. This experience made him conscious that his life had been given to him afresh by the spiritual world, and that it should devoted to serving that world (note the example by Unger in study 24).

Shortly before the twentieth century, during a conversation with an artist friend about reincarnation, Unger and Arenson were introduced to the Theosophical Society. They became members in 1902, when Rudolf Steiner was General Secretary of the German section of that society. In the autumn of the following year, Arenson, who was the first to become acquainted with Steiner, returned to Stuttgart deeply impressed by what he had heard in Berlin; but his impressions were received with skepticism.

By February 1904, Unger also wished to meet with Steiner in Berlin to express, among other things, the wish that more might be known of the society's German section. He describes this meeting:

> At the time, I had still not read one line by Dr. Steiner. On the occasion of this first conversation he was very silent, but he took me to Mrs. van Sivers, who, in his presence, pointed to the necessity of beginning the lecture journey, which had been long intended—especially now that Dr. Steiner's book *Theosophy* was ready to be published. Mrs. von Sivers invited me to a lecture by Dr. Steiner, which was to occur that evening; the lecture was on the passage from the Creed, "suffered under Pontius Pilate." This lecture immediately convinced me that this was a man to whose work I must dedicate my life. The strongest impression was this: Here is one who sees and *knows*.
>
> When I returned to Stuttgart, my enthusiasm was received, as was Mr. Arenson's, with skepticism. Some months later, Dr. Steiner began his lecture tours. Meanwhile, his book *Theosophy* was published, and I threw myself into it with the greatest enthusiasm, wrestling with it for months with every page, every sentence, and many words. When I had the foundation for a judgment, which I had somewhat carelessly expressed after my visit to Berlin, I would follow this man blindfolded. For now I had learned to follow with open eyes.

The time had come to focus the activity of the Stuttgart Group in terms of the work indicated by Rudolf Steiner. Unger made a proposal that was not carried; so he, Arenson, and some other friends resigned from that group to begin a new one on September 23, 1905. The intention of this work was, "through the experience of thinking, to go deeply into the human being and into the being of the world in order to encounter the Spiritual Science of Rudolf Steiner with a suitable activity." After 1905, Unger was a personal pupil of Rudolf Steiner.

In 1907, at Steiner's instigation, Unger presented a lecture at the Congress of the European sections of the Theosophical Society in Munich on the work accomplished by the Stuttgart group. As a result of this lecture, invitations came from numerous groups. Consequently, between 1907 and 1913, he gave hundreds of lectures to many groups in Germany and Switzerland.

This was made possible in this way: in the fall of 1906, with the help of his father, he had established a small machine factory with a definite intention of becoming completely independent. "This brought in its wake many business difficulties, but it also offered me the opportunity of an outer and, even more, an inner freedom. Indeed, I also gained some experience of life as a result of this."

That year brought him—immediately following his marriage to one of Arenson's daughters—another important conversation with Rudolf Steiner, who advised him to work in the realm of epistemology. This led to some writings that have appeared in part as books and articles. From that time on, Unger continued to work along those lines.

The Anthroposophical Society, founded in 1912, required an administrative body after 1913. Unger was then thirty-five and had belonged to its council from the beginning. In 1914, another task was added when Steiner—regretfully, as he said—was obliged to accept Unger's offer to oversee the work of building the Goetheanum, though it was also "anticipated that this would mean a loss to the work in the Society." It was possible only to continue this work until September 1915. After that, war conditions prevented journeys into Switzerland.

During the period immediately after World War I, Unger, together with others, devoted his strength to the many tasks that fell to the anthroposophic movement in every area of life. He paid particular attention, however, to the actual impulses of the Anthroposophical Society, while many became less conscious of them. This was owing to the necessity arising from Anthroposophy to work in the world in general—in education, medicine, and so on. His particular work during the last years of his life was his writing in relation to studying Steiner's leading thoughts.

Unger, however, was not simply a lecturer and independent worker in the Anthroposophical Society. When *Der Kommender Tag* was founded, there was an attempt, after World War I, to apply the ideas of the Threefold Social Order. Unger made his factory a part of that enterprise. When the enterprise failed, however, he was again obliged to assume independent ownership of his factory. This meant accepting the burden involved in an effort that proved a failure.

In the final years of his life, Unger toured to lecture publicly in addition to his work in the Society. On January 4, 1929, in Nuremberg, immediately before a lecture on one such tour, a bullet overtook him—this time fatal—for which an irresponsible person was the tool. The title of the lecture was "What is Anthroposophy?"

"After Rudolf Steiner had left us in the body, the gifts of the spirit that were offered by him in such overflowing measure could not continue. It must now happen that a community of human beings takes over the results of his spiritual research, taking them in such a way that they remain alive in the community. People must come together in anthroposophic work, united in such a way that Anthroposophy comes into its own."

—CARL UNGER (lecture in Stuttgart, Oct. 29, 1928)

INTRODUCTION

In the future, under the heading *Language of the Consciousness Soul,* we will find contributions in this periodical (*Das Goetheanum*). They will deal with anthroposophic activities as practiced in groups of the Anthroposophical Society in order to make the wealth of Rudolf Steiner's spiritual investigations increasingly accessible to individual experience. Steiner's work is available to the public, while transcripts of his lectures to Society members are gradually being published. It is becoming appropriate to look for broader circles in which to expose more individuals to this immense, far-reaching spiritual treasure. This exposure is not to convey a specialized explanation or apology but the impressions that can be gained by thinking, meditating, and vision.

In the final year of his life on Earth, Rudolf Steiner presented the entire body of Anthroposophy in a new language, as evidenced in his lectures to Society members at the Goetheanum in Dornach. The restriction of his activities to Society members had been provisional, and, since there is nothing essentially secret in his investigations, it seems obvious that, had there been more time—had his earthly life not ended prematurely—he would have given the substance of these lectures to the general public in an appropriate form (which, to a certain extent, he did).

The whole of Anthroposophy is also contained in the records of earlier lecture cycles; they are the imperishable gift of living spirit. In chapter 67 of Steiner's *Autobiography,* we read, "Aside from the demand of building up Anthroposophy and devoting myself solely to the results of imparting truths directly from the spiritual world to today's general culture, the demand also arose to meet fully the soul need and spiritual longing of the members." Further, "The written work for the public is the result of my own inner struggles and labors, whereas the privately printed material is the result of a joint struggle and labor with the society. I listened to what reverberated in the soul life of the members, and the perspective of each lecture arose in my living experience of what I heard."[1]

These earlier lecture cycles were given from time to time at particular places and dates and to a specific audiences. They exist in the various areas of the soul, as it were, within the spiritual life of our time. Anyone who studies those lecture cycles will search for these regions of the soul and unite

---

1   *Autobiography: Chapters in the Course of My Life, 1861–1907,* pp. 228–229.

with those soul needs, with the longing for the spirit struggling and working within; and knowledge of these soul regions will open before us.

We find, however, an epoch-making difference in Steiner's lectures at the Goetheanum in the final year of his life, after having united directly with and inaugurated the Anthroposophical Society. He no longer spoke there in the same sense out of the soul needs of his listeners. His words rang out of every soul region to all of humanity. New spiritual realities stood vividly before us at the threshold. If this is properly understood, Steiner's words presented an obligation to everyone with the capacity to awaken. Those present had been led there in freedom through spiritual longing, now able to listen to this new language.

Steiner emphasized this deep obligation in the *Anthroposophical Leading Thoughts*. They must be acted upon through an inner freedom that demonstrates the spiritual task of modern humanity. Steiner emphasized this for the Society in the leading thoughts, which he issued from the Goetheanum between February 17, 1924, and the last day of his earthly life, March 30, 1925. I am indebted to Mrs. Marie Steiner for permission to use the leading thoughts in these publications. The leading thoughts are the words of a new spiritual language. If they resound in human souls, the sounds of the language of the consciousness soul may take shape in inner experience. The leading thoughts can open worlds. The experience of the sounds indicates the inner renewal of the spiritual truths of these worlds. Because of this, work on the consciousness soul is needed. These sounds then become meditations of the consciousness soul.

STUDY 2

THE CONSCIOUSNESS SOUL

Within the entire body of Anthroposophy, we come to recognize the consciousness soul because of three important relationships. Rudolf Steiner presented in detail the essence of Anthroposophy in his book *Theosophy*.[1] By applying natural scientific methods, he begins by describing the human physical body, which connects us with the entire mineral kingdom. He characterizes the etheric and astral bodies and their relationship to the plant and animal kingdoms. These bodies are suprasensory organizations of forces and may be understood through natural scientific study, since they involve natural relationships between human beings and the world.

This method of observation, however, may be reversed when one's study moves from animal to human being. The organization of suprasensory forces that distinguishes human beings from animals is present in the one who is viewing, through an "I"-like experience. One may reexperience inwardly what was previously observed in the outer world, the other side of which is revealed to spiritual vision through suprasensory investigation. This experience may be compared with an awakening, and anyone who practices it gains an "I"-like connection between one's own astral, etheric, and physical bodies and the surrounding world.

The "I"-being's total experience of the astral body forms the *sentient soul*. It comprises the experience of the outer world in perception, sensing, and observation, but also one's reaction to it through immediate impulse, reflexive movements, and so on. As the "I" experiences the etheric body, the *intellectual soul* is formed; this shapes and preserves the otherwise transitory, more chaotic experiences of the external world through memories, representations, and thoughts; their counterparts are habits, passions, and temperaments. The most wide-awake "I"-experience arises as *consciousness soul* in relation to the physical body. Here the essential nature of being can be experienced, the substantially spiritual, as well as the impulse toward morality and free will, may be comprehended.

This is how contemporary human consciousness arises, and it leads us to the second important relationship through which Anthroposophy familiarizes us to the consciousness soul. From the fifteenth century on, humankind has

---

1   *Theosophy: An Introduction to the Spiritual Processes in Human Life and in the Cosmos.* For this and all following references to the works of Rudolf Steiner, see the bibliography.

lived in the *Age of the Consciousness Soul*. This time was preceded by the *Age of the Intellectual Soul*, reaching back into the eighth century BCE, which in turn was preceded by the *Age of the Sentient Soul*. In those times, which lasted until the third millennium BC, what today is the consciousness soul still hovered at two levels above ordinary consciousness. Anyone who could experience this could also rise two levels into the spiritual realm to become a great initiate and leader.

In ancient Eastern Mysteries, what is now available to general consciousness was cultivated with appropriate modifications. The power of human leadership still existed only in relationship to divine worlds and now began to pass through two stages of evolution to reach the human individual. That means that today individuals may learn to guide themselves—that is, freely work on the consciousness soul. In our time, therefore, it has become necessary that Anthroposophy make public the secrets of the ancient mysteries. Only to the degree that this evolution advances are human beings freed from direct spiritual guidance. Today, such leadership works only through fully self-aware individuals. This is the basis of the responsibility and obligation of the new language.

From the fifteenth century until our time, the consciousness soul has developed only on the side of nature. Consciousness reached down into the mineral kingdom, and led in our time to abstract knowledge and technology in the lifeless realm. A clamor reverberates there, not the sounds of a language. It rattles and clashes, gurgles and rumbles, whistles and hisses. This soulless world begins to master human beings themselves. The soul is in danger of losing itself unless it tries to save itself on the other side of nature. Yet something immensely important has been gained through this descent; humankind can now think and observe selflessly. This must also be preserved in the experiences of the soul and spirit so that we begin to hear the sounds of the language of the consciousness soul.

The third important relationship that, through the body of Anthroposophy, helps us to recognize the consciousness soul has to do with individual evolution in successive periods of life. These are abbreviated recapitulations of historical cultural epochs. In relation to education, Steiner repeatedly described the etheric body's liberation at approximately the seventh year and that of the astral body around the fourteenth year. These periods continue, though not as obvious in the physical body. Thus, the sentient soul is freed around the twenty-first year, the intellectual soul around the twenty-eighth year, and the consciousness soul, or bearer of consciousness, around thirty-five. This could be interpreted incorrectly to mean that one could assume the tasks of the age of the consciousness soul only after one's thirty-fifth year. One may observe, rather, that younger people also act, feel, and will as complete human beings. The principles of their being, however, are not yet fully impressed into the physical body. This takes place only in the thirty-fifth year and leads to a hardening of soul elements, unless Anthroposophy has actively helped to loosen and release them.[1]

With the addition of each new principle, the others are changed. For example, the plant has a physical body as does the mineral, but an etheric body is added to the plant, which in turn changes the physical body of the plant. In the same way, because the astral body is added to the animal, the etheric and physical bodies change. The situation becomes much more complicated in the human being. And this is also true of successive civilizations and stages of life. Thus, although the intellectual soul is the vehicle of consciousness from twenty-eight to thirty-five, it is different than it was during the time of the intellectual civilization, or so-called Greco-Roman period. It is changed by the force of the consciousness soul active in the impulses of our time. It is irradiated by the consciousness soul, which still hovers, so to speak, just above ordinary consciousness, reaching into and enclosed by the next higher world. This is the elemental realm that Steiner investigated suprasensorily.

Similarly, during early life, the consciousness soul extends into even higher realms. The consciousness soul is active in the impulses for knowledge and activity, but for younger persons it is still influenced by corresponding higher worlds, and its activities (*imagination, inspiration,* and *intuition*) are colored unconsciously by the quality of these realms.[2] By working on the consciousness soul, Anthroposophy opens the way to such higher forms of knowledge and thus to an experience of higher worlds.

---

1   For a detailed study of the stages of human development, see *The Child's Changing Consciousness: As the Basis for Pedagogical Practice.*

2   *Imagination, inspiration,* and *intuition* are terms that Steiner uses in a particular way. To denote this fact, they appear in italics throughout this volume. Their meaning should become clear through these studies; see also *The Stages of Higher Knowledge.*

STUDY 3

FUNDAMENTAL PRINCIPLES

The impulses of the consciousness soul tend toward isolation and separation if not practiced anthroposophically. This can be seen as a tragedy for humanity. Nevertheless, it is exactly this inner solitude of contemporary human beings that awakens a great longing for community. Anthroposophy needs to be experienced in the stillness of the soul, but it gives rise to community most significantly when, through the cooperation and unified efforts of many, something higher can take shape.

The *Leading Thoughts* presented to the members of the Anthroposophical Society by Rudolf Steiner from the Goetheanum in the last year of his life on earth are intended to serve such a purpose. They were intended for groups working together, and this is evident from his own advice concerning their use.

> Those who apply themselves week after week to these *Leading Thoughts* will find that they show how to penetrate more deeply the material in the lecture cycles, which they are meant to bring before the group meetings in a certain order.... The important thing, after all, is not that anthroposophic content is merely heard or read externally, but that the whole life of the soul absorbs it. It is essential to continue thinking and feeling what the mind has already understood. This is what the *Leading Thoughts* are especially intended to encourage regarding the material given in the printed cycles.... To continue with the anthroposophic content through thinking and feeling is also an exercise for training the soul. We find our way through seeing into the spiritual world when we treat this content as described.[1]

The leading thoughts appeared weekly in the *Nachrichten,* mostly in groups of three or four.[2] This arrangement is retained in the published work. The first group of leading thoughts follows:

> 1. Anthroposophy is a path of knowledge, intended to guide the human spirit to the cosmic spirit. It arises in humankind as a need of the heart, from the life of feeling. It is justified only to the degree that it can satisfy this inner need. Anthroposophy will be acknowledged only by those who

---

1 *Anthroposophical Leading Thoughts,* "How the Leading Thoughts Are to Be Used," p. 47.

2 Not to be confused with a Communist daily of the same name and era, *Nachrichten* was a supplement of *Das Goetheanum,* published by the Anthroposophical Society.

find in it what they feel impelled in their own inner Life to seek. Thus, in the same way that one feels hunger and thirst, only those who experience, as a basic life necessity, certain questions about human and cosmic matters can be anthroposophists.

2. Anthroposophy conveys knowledge gained spiritually. Yet, this is so only because everyday life and sense-based, intellectual science create a barrier along the path of life—a limitation where human soul life would die if it could go no farther. Ordinary life and science do not lead to this limit in a way that requires humankind to stop short there. At the very frontier where the knowledge based on sense perception ends, a further perspective into the spiritual world is opened through the human soul itself.

3. There are those who believe that the limits of knowledge derived from sense perception define the limits of all insight. Nevertheless, if they would carefully observe how they become conscious of these limits, they would discover in that very consciousness of the limits the faculties needed to transcend them. The fish swims up to the limits of the water, but must return since it lacks the physical organs to live beyond this element. Similarly, human beings reach the limits of knowledge attainable by sense perception. But they can recognize that, on the way to this point, soul powers have arisen in them, powers through which the soul can live in an element beyond the horizon of the senses.

Expressed here are grand, fundamental truths about all of Anthroposophy. Anyone who has thus far thought of Anthroposophy as a system or essence of a sect—or even as the dogma of some faith or a mere worldview in the ordinary sense—will do well to reconsider. In the preface to his book *Theosophy*, Steiner writes: "In certain respects, every page, even many sentences will have to be *worked out* by the reader. This has been an intentional goal." With these *Leading Thoughts* one feels that it would be good to continue this "working out" into the very word itself. The object of this book is simply to offer suggestions about how this may be done in the work of a group.

"Anthroposophy is a path of knowledge." This can be viewed as a key statement, a preface to the *Leading Thoughts* that serves to the very end. If this word resounds throughout this work, something has already happened that has an inner ability to decide; for "path of knowledge" means inner transformation. All knowledge transforms the one who knows. Indeed, this is true with every perception, experience, and observation, since they become a part of our being and enrich it. All knowledge signifies a conscious enrichment. Whatever the content of our minds may be at any given moment, we can ask questions that conform to that inner content. All knowledge changes this content, and then new questions may arise because we have changed. Contemporary human beings, out of ordinary, habitual viewpoints, have absolutely no desire for such change, but fear it.

Steiner spoke often of this fear in *Nachrichten*. It is the fear "of actually touching suprasensory worlds.... It disguises itself as a special kind of sense for truth, as a materialistic sense for truth."[1] This fear leads to passive thinking. "It is noticeable that, when people today speak of the spirit, they become defensive. What lives in their consciousness at those times does not mean much; but what lives in the subconscious, in the unconscious, is very important—that is an unconscious bad conscience. Fear keeps people today from rising from mere reflective to creative thinking."[2]

Someone like this who knows would like to understand the world, but remains a mere onlooker. Steiner observed that it has become more and more customary to disregard entirely the activity of thinking—the necessity of being present internally, inwardly active in thinking—only to surrender to successive events and then simply allow thinking to run on, but without activity in thinking.[3] Such passivity, however, paralyzes what is to be known; it limits, tabulates and labels what would be known. This makes corpses of knowledge and thoughts, which concretely form the boundaries of knowledge for this kind of knower.[4]

The question becomes very different when those striving for knowledge transform themselves in the act of knowing. When they experience knowledge in the course of their own developments, with each acquisition of knowledge, their boundary is extended. Steiner writes about how one overcomes the limits of knowledge in the corresponding chapter of *Intuitive Thinking as a Spiritual Path*.[5] But, even in fairly simple occurrences, decisive experiences can be gained. In what direction can we extend these limits? This cannot be a direction in the world, but only in human beings themselves. We ourselves ask the questions and limit knowledge through our own being. The very fact of making the effort for knowledge proves we cannot remain the same. If we were united with the world there would be no desire of the heart and feelings for knowledge. We feel cast out of this world. What we have in common with the world and what unites us with it can only be our own developing spiritual aspect. Thus, by saying "Anthroposophy is a path of knowledge," our experience continues in a way "that can lead the human spirit to the cosmic spirit." This expression in the first leading thought can, from its very first word, become the reality of our inner experience.

---

1   *Initiation, Eternity, and the Passing Moment.*

2   *The Karma of Materialism*, lecture 1.

3   *A Modern Art of Education.*

4   *The Forming of Destiny and Life after Death*, lecture 6.

5   "Are there Limits to Human Cognition?" pp. 104ff.

THE PATH TO THE LIMITS OF KNOWLEDGE

Anyone who has not consciously approached the cognitive boundaries of contemporary consciousness cannot experience reality. In this consciousness we feel torn from the world. All the efforts toward knowledge prove that we have not comprehended full reality, thus, the urge to reach the truth from which we were torn. The limit of our knowledge, therefore, is also the threshold of truth, which must be the threshold of the spiritual world. It is expressed in this sense in the third leading thought, "If they would carefully observe *how* they become conscious of these limits, they would find in their very consciousness of those limits the faculties to transcend them."

We will attempt to approach this boundary one step at a time. We can do this by withdrawing step-by-step from our ordinary consciousness. In one form or another, this is essentially true of all knowledge, but mostly it is completely unconscious. It is an abstract method, but here it is important that we take this path in a practical way, not theoretically. The realm of sense perception comprises the broadest range of consciousness from which we derive the substance for ordinary science. When we withdraw from it—that is, when we close the senses to perception—this realm is not obliterated from our consciousness. Inner impressions remain remembered images, or representations of the sense world. The next step also involves a withdrawal from the world of representation through closing our consciousness to the entry of such images, which is more difficult. But even when this has been accomplished, the outer world is not completely extinguished, since the relationships between those representations still remain. These relationships may be described as concepts; they also form an interrelated world. When we relinquish these concepts, conceptual relationships still remain, but they no longer contain anything of the external world.

This is the pure thinking spoken of by Rudolf Steiner in *Intuitive Thinking as a Spiritual Path*. Eventually, even pure thinking withdraws to the point where only the *potential*, or faculty, of thinking remains. A point still remains, like a nothingness; that, however, is the so-called "absolute I" of the classical idealist worldview. It is not difficult to see that all ordinary knowledge arises from this boundary of consciousness.

When we really pursue this to the boundary of ordinary consciousness—which appears here only as a theoretical abstraction—we usually fall asleep. Because of this, we do not even experience the boundary correctly. It follows, however, that by falling asleep every night, we actually cross the boundary of knowledge but lose consciousness. The kind of science looked at in the second and third leading thoughts, the science concerned only with percept, representation, and concept, is asleep at the boundary of knowledge. On the other hand, if we wanted to sink into the "I" in order to escape the "external" sciences, we would find ourselves in nothingness.

We can see, therefore, that something very different must happen. If the first leading thoughts are actively experienced inwardly (as indicated in the opening words), the content of the third leading thought is verified. When we observe how we become aware of the boundaries, we discover in that consciousness the ability to cross those boundaries. We can take the described path to the boundaries of knowledge as a soul exercise according to Steiner's advice, which he expressed numerous times—for example, in his book *How To Know Higher Worlds: A Modern Path of Initiation*.[1] It is not a matter of comprehending it once, however, but involves patient repetition. Standing at the boundary of knowledge and consciousness is nothing but the condition of meditation, the creation of inner stillness, but without falling asleep; it is the threshold of the spiritual world.

The boundaries of an individual human being are reached and crossed not just through knowing, but also, as we have seen, by the falling asleep each night. There, we leave behind in the outer world what we have stripped off, everything that belongs to our being; even the point, or spark, is extinguished. *We do not awaken from sleep due to our own efforts.* This kind of attitude toward the world arose through human evolution. Whereas waking and sleeping have emerged from a consciousness totally different from that of the present—one more interwoven with the spirits—unconsciousness has encompassed the experience of the threshold.

In a significant statement, Steiner describes ancient consciousness:

> We know that, during ancient times, human beings were endowed with direct [but not "I"-conscious] clairvoyance. They beheld, through their perceptual powers, not merely the world of the senses, but also the whole spiritual background of physical existence. This was possible because, for humankind of those times, there was an intermediate condition between what today is our waking and sleeping consciousness.[2]

All of human evolution from that time until now is like a path toward death, and we can realize that, according to Leading Thought 2, "the life of the human soul would die if it could not cross this boundary." If evolution, which has led to present-day consciousness, were to continue indefinitely

---

1   See also *Founding a Science of the Spirit*, lecture 12.

2   *According to Matthew*, lecture 3.

in the same direction, to the extent that human beings continue to separate themselves from the world, they would no longer be able to awaken from sleep.

Thus, we can experience inwardly that people cannot derive their being from surrounding nature, but that they have brought it with them out of the spiritual world from a distant past. This fact colors all human efforts to know. We seek "certainty of feeling…a strong unfolding of our will." Looking back from the boundary of all knowledge toward nature, which we have left, so to speak, it is clear that the natural world cannot give us an answer to the question of our own being. Nature can only destroy the human body, but the inner experiences of thinking, feeling, and the will show that they depend on it in many ways. The following leading thoughts address this subject:

4. Humankind needs knowledge of the spiritual world to gain certainty of feeling and a strong unfolding of the will. Regardless of how broadly we may feel the grandeur, beauty, and wisdom of the natural world, this world does not answer the question of our own being. Our being holds together the materials and forces of the natural world in the living and sensitive form of the human being until the moment we pass through the gate of death. Nature then receives this human form, and nature cannot hold it together but only dissolve and disperse it. Grand, beautiful, wisdom-filled nature does indeed answer the question: How is the human form dissolved and destroyed? But nature does not answer the other question: How is it maintained and held together? No theoretical objection can dispel this question from the feeling human soul, unless indeed we prefer to lull ourselves to sleep. The very presence of this question must incessantly maintain alive, in every human soul that is truly awake, the longing for spiritual paths of world knowledge.

5. Humankind needs self-knowledge in the spirit in order to gain inner peace. Human beings find themselves in their thinking, feeling and willing. They see how thinking, feeling and willing depend on human nature. In any development, they must follow health and sickness, bodily strengthening and weakening. Every sleep blots them out. Thus, the experience of everyday life shows that human spiritual consciousness depends, to the greatest degree imaginable, on bodily existence. People suddenly become aware that, in this realm of ordinary experience, self-knowledge may be completely lost, and our search for it hopeless. Then immediately, anxious questions arise: Can there be self-knowledge that transcends ordinary life experiences? Can we be at all certain about the true human I? Anthroposophy wants to provide an answer based firmly on spiritual experience. In doing this, it stands not on opinion or belief, but on conscious experience in the spirit, an experience in its own nature no less certain than the conscious experiences in the body.

COSMIC VIEW

Sleep extinguishes inner as well as outer conscious experience, and this shows us that, in the inner experience of ordinary waking consciousness and thinking, we cannot find a guarantee for the permanence and reality of our soul, spiritual being. Any philosophy that looks for reality in the experience of ordinary consciousness errs. Rudolf Steiner spoke at length on this subject:

> People disposed to philosophy recently thought they had found a certain path, which they expressed as follows: "What we call our individual 'I' remains one and the same being throughout our life from birth to death. I have always been the same as far as I can remember." I have frequently mentioned that, for any ordinary person, this is contradicted daily. One cannot know at all what befalls this "I," or Ego representation, between going to sleep and awaking. Really, one can speak of this ego only as it is experienced during periods of waking consciousness and must always imagine the chain as broken.[1]

The certainty spoken of in Leading Thought 4 is found on another path of self-knowledge, Anthroposophy. We can look at the fourth and fifth leading thoughts precisely in the sense of self-knowledge, and, like a secret hidden in the words, we can experience in Leading Thought 4 the whole human being as a question answered by Leading Thought 5. *It is a question of overcoming the death tendency of sleep by continuously shaping the soul.* This is the way of meditation. This does not imply that the proper claim of sleep on human beings should be removed. Meditation appears outwardly like sleep, but maintains full inner wakefulness while the consciousness rests on the object of meditation. Steiner advises that meditation should be practiced for only a relatively short time, although with the greatest possible regularity. The result of such exercises overcomes hindrances to the spiritual life, because thinking, feeling and willing are released from their bondage to the body (Leading Thought 5).

The path to the boundaries of knowledge is itself a steady release from ordinary consciousness and its physical bondage. In the retrospective view seen from the boundary, we experience a certain survey of the physical world, as though a cosmic view opens before us. Goethe demanded this of true scientists: "They should, as dispassionate and divine beings, so to speak, seek and examine what *is*, and not what gratifies." We refer again to the discovery of

---

1   *Aspects of Human Evolution*, lecture 7.

pure thinking in Steiner's philosophical works. They are excellent books of exercises for contemporary consciousness; they lead to the threshold of the spiritual world and provide the equipment for crossing it. Without pure thinking, even the least significant law of nature cannot be expressed. Indeed, it constitutes the basis of every science. It is also necessary, however, to acquire the capacity to breathe in pure thinking as such. In pure mathematics this is, of course, undeniable. Steiner repeatedly characterized breathing in pure thinking as the first, albeit a shadowy, clairvoyance.[2] It is the clairvoyance attainable by everyone out of ordinary consciousness.

Now, let us look at the following passage: "Truth is first truly perceived when people successfully form judgments in such a way that they are freed of the physical body—so that the etheric body is freed from the physical body. Now bear in mind the standpoint I have always assumed, which must be that of every spiritual scientist: initial clairvoyance is actually pure thinking. Those who grasp a pure thought are already clairvoyant, since a pure thought can be grasped only in the etheric body" (*The Bhagavad Gita and the West*). Such clairvoyance provides true concepts and ideas, such as those that live in the *Intuitive Thinking as a Spiritual Path*. To understand Anthroposophy, it is absolutely necessary to be fully at home in this area of the boundary between the physical and spiritual worlds. Steiner often referred to the task of Anthroposophy as the "spiritualizing of the intellectual." This is accomplished in the area of this boundary. In order to be accessible to contemporary consciousness, all knowledge—physical as well as spiritual—must be imprinted in the substance of this domain, the true concepts and ideas. This explains why Steiner said many times that, to investigate spiritual realms, one definitely needs the fully developed faculty of spiritual perception, but that the results brought down as knowledge (that is, the concepts and ideas) can be understood by everyone of good intention and free from bias. Indeed, he occasionally added that, to comprehend spiritual worlds, the spiritual investigator is in exactly the same position as those to whom the investigations are communicated.

Thus, in the boundary region mentioned, a remarkable meeting takes place in the etheric realm between the physical and spiritual worlds. For us, it is most important to rise into this world through pure thinking. Proper entrance requires an attitude of selflessness in seeking knowledge—in our time, the most beautiful fruit of the evolution of consciousness. *In this world, ideas and sight are of equal value.* Thus, for the etheric world, the conceptual presentation suffices in order to remain in reality. The distinction between concept and reality plays an important part in the following leading thoughts; it will become even clearer if we begin with the realm common to both.

---

2   *The Bhagavad Gita and the West*, lecture 2; *The Karma of Materialism*, lecture 9.

6. When we gaze on lifeless nature, we find a world full of lawful and orderly inner relationships. We look for these relationships and find in them the substance of natural laws. Further, we find that, by virtue of these laws, lifeless nature as a whole forms a connection with the entire Earth. We may proceed from this earthly connection ruling in all lifeless things and contemplate the living world of plants. We see how, from distances of space, the universe beyond the Earth sends in the forces that draw the living out of the womb of the lifeless. In all living things, we are made aware of an element of being that, by freeing itself from the mere earthly connection, manifests the forces that affect the Earth from realms of cosmic space. In the same way that, in the eye, we become aware of a luminous object that confronts it, also in the tiniest plant we are shown the nature of light from beyond Earth. Through this ascent in contemplation, we can perceive how the earthly, or physical, that holds sway in the lifeless world differs from the extraearthly and etheric that abounds in all living things.

7. We find human beings with their transcendent being of soul and spirit placed into this world of the earthly and the supraearthly. Inasmuch as we are placed into the earthly connection that contains all lifeless things, we bear with us our physical bodies. Inasmuch as we unfold within us the forces that the living world draws into this earthly sphere from cosmic space, we have an etheric, or life body. The tendency of modern science has been to ignore this essential contrast between the physical and etheric. For this very reason, science has given birth to the most impossible concepts of the ether. Fear of losing their way in fanciful and nebulous ideas has caused scientists to refrain from dwelling on the true contrast. But, unless we do so, we cannot attain true insight into the universe and humanity.

Goethe's archetypal plant is an etheric, living being and, at the same time, the *idea* of the plant. Steiner repeatedly reminded us of Goethe's conversation with Schiller, which led to their friendship. He described it in detail in the first chapter of his book *Goethe's Theory of Knowledge*. Schiller called Goethe's sketch of the archetypal plant an "idea." After a moment of surprise, Goethe was ultimately pleased. He believed he could now understand in his own concrete and visual manner what he could not understand when presented abstractly by Kantians as an "idea."

The relationship between thinking and seeing as presented here can be supplemented by the way Steiner characterizes thinking as applied in *Intuitive Thinking as a Spiritual Path* and in *Truth and Knowledge*. "These books are not written so that one thought may be taken and put somewhere else. Rather, they are written so that an organism arises; one thought grows from another."

Thus, we approach the intermediate kingdom from which humankind may cast a cosmic glance over the physical world. This is the gaze that is turned toward lifeless nature (Leading Thought 6). The relationships of law and order, the essence of natural laws that reveal themselves, can be cosmically understood from the archetypal ideas of the boundary region. Materialism has no desire to acknowledge this—but then, it denies the very ground on which it stands. "We may now proceed to contemplate the living world of plants," and if we apply a cosmic glance, the following part of this leading thought becomes a living reality, as both experience and thought. We can very consciously work toward a perspective that is different from ordinary scientific observation. Then we can see and think at the same time "how, from distances of space, the universe beyond Earth sends in the forces that draw the living out of the womb of the lifeless" (Leading Thought 6).

It is significant that light is presented here as a cosmic spiritual power. Goethe recognized this through modern consciousness and followed its sensible and moral effect into the depths of the human being. It is apparent from our language how closely allied light and thinking are. It very correctly speaks, in a cosmic sense, of something becoming clear to us. Language still belongs largely to the etheric boundary region.

In Leading Thought 7, the human physical and etheric bodies are described from the viewpoint of perceptive thinking, of Goethe's perceptive power of judgment. It is fundamentally important that it is possible and proper to comprehend, through pure thinking, the etheric body as Steiner developed it in his book *Theosophy*. This makes Anthroposophy accessible to modern consciousness as a science. Scientific comprehension of the etheric body is the only point in all of Anthroposophy where an element of metaphysics is in the right place. Metaphysics is the addition of something suprasensory in thinking to the facts apparent to the senses. In ordinary scientific theories and hypotheses, unauthorized metaphysical constructions are almost always involved. For example, atoms, which are used for explaining physical phenomena, are metaphysical phantoms. Only the etheric body may be understood as a metaphysical being, because pure thinking itself is an inner comprehension of the etheric body.

STUDY 6

CROSSING THE THRESHOLD

Anyone well acquainted with the boundary region, or the etheric realm of thought, may directly experience how our cosmic gaze (in the sense of these studies) is able to survey the mineral and plant realms of physical and etheric life, but cannot make the transition to the animal kingdom. We can see clearly why this is so. Goethe's etheric eye could perceive the archetypal plant and open the realm of the organic life to scientific investigation. Therefore, Steiner called Goethe the "Copernicus" and "Kepler" of the organic world.[1] But, Goethe wanted to go farther and investigate the animal kingdom in his studies in morphology. He did not achieve that, however; his etheric eye could not perceive the archetypal animal.[2] The human being cannot, as knower, confront the animal world with the same cosmic objectivity available through the forces of the boundary region in the case of plants. One becomes aware of being drawn into the stream of observation.

Goethe said that nature is a "wealth of creation so great that it makes a unity of the multiplicity of a thousand plants, one that contains all the others; and it makes of the multiplicity of a thousand animals one being that contains them all—the human being." Here the different method of observation is seen very distinctly, especially how humankind, in observing the animal, appears not only as knower, but also the goal of knowledge.

The animal is distinguished from the plant by its astral body, and it is significant how differently Steiner, in his book *Theosophy*, comes to terms with the astral and etheric bodies—the etheric body from without inward and the astral body from within outward. Thus, one might say that knowledge of the etheric body belongs more to natural science and knowledge of the astral body more to psychology. This same distinction is evident in the Leading Thoughts.

8. We may consider the nature of human beings insofar as it results from the physical and etheric bodies. We find that all the phenomena of human life that arise from this side of human nature remain in the unconscious and never lead to consciousness. Consciousness is not illuminated but darkened when activity of the physical and the etheric bodies is enhanced. Conditions such as faintness may be seen to result from such enhancement. Following this line of thought, we realize that something is active in the human being—and in animals—that is *not* of the same nature as

1   *Nature's Open Secret*, chapter 4.
2   *Goethe's Theory of Knowledge*, "Archetype of Animal Nature."

16

the physical and etheric. It become effective, not when the forces of the physical and etheric are active in their own way, but when they cease such activity. In this way, we arrive at the concept of the astral body.

9. The *reality* of this astral body is discovered when we rise in meditation from the thinking stimulated by the outer senses to an inner activity of seeing. To this end, thinking stimulated externally must be grasped inwardly and, as such, experienced intensely in the soul, separated from its relationship to the outer world. Through the strength thus engendered in the soul, we become aware of our inner organs of perception, which see the spiritual reality active in the animal and human being, right where the physical and etheric bodies are held in check to allow consciousness.

10. Thus, consciousness does not arise through further enhancing the activities of the physical and etheric bodies. On the contrary, the activity of these two bodies must be reduced to nothing—even less than nothing—to allow a space for conscious activity. They do not generate consciousness but only the basis for the spirit to produce consciousness in earthly life. Just as earthly humankind needs ground to stand, so also the spiritual, within the earthly realm, needs a material foundation on which to unfold. A planet in the cosmic spaces need no ground beneath it to establish its place. Similarly, when spirit, rather than looking into material with the senses, sees through its own power into the spiritual, a material foundation is unnecessary to bring its consciousness to life.

When observing any conscious process, one has the experience of being included rather than outside, as when observing natural processes. Therefore, observations of conscious processes linked to corporeality are only conditional. Corresponding facts must come from the other side—from spiritual investigation. Thus, one may say that Leading Thought 8 provides what appears to be a negative definition of the astral body, derived physiologically from the corporeal, natural aspect of the human being. We may certainly relate conscious phenomena with the nerves, but our conclusions are incorrect if we *begin* with the nerves. We need only recall the metaphysical construction of the so-called motor nerves, which Steiner often showed to be the essential error of physiology.[3]

"Motor nerves" do not exist; there are only *sensory* nerves. So-called motor nerves are sensory nerves; their purpose is to allow us to perceive muscle movement. It will not be very long before people recognize that muscle movement is not accomplished through the nerves, but through the astral body.[4]

It is a matter of suprasensory forces represented, in fact, by the nerves. These forces have an intimate, inner quality, with which human beings feel

---

3   *Human and Cosmic Thought,* lecture 4.

4   *Background to the Gospel of St. Mark,* lecture 8.

inwardly connected. The physiological considerations are extremely significant, since they fully confirm the suprasensory facts. There are physiological investigations into the life functions of the nerves that demonstrate less
recuperative capacity of the nerves representing higher levels of consciousness.
This lack of recuperative power points clearly to what Leading Thought 8
states—that the physical and etheric must cease their own activity before consciousness may determine its own activity.

In this way, we arrive at a negative definition of the concept of the astral
body. But, from the negative definition this concept turns toward the positive;
when it is comprehended it strives toward realization. This is proved in human
beings as they mature. The physical form reaches the point of completion,
growth ceases, the activity of the etheric body withdraws, and then the activity of the physical body begins to diminish. Consciousness, however, evolves
as the forces of growth lose strength.[1]

Development of consciousness does not necessarily end there; it may continue along the paths of meditative life, and in this way the concept of the
astral body strives toward reality.[2] This is shown in Leading Thought 9, where
there is an important transition. Thinking, otherwise aroused by the senses,
is given as content at the boundary of knowledge in meditative stillness, the
experience of itself separate from its relationship to external reality. Crossing
the boundary, in this case, done in such a way that the actual astral body
becomes conscious. The "inner organs of perception that see a spiritual reality" then arise. Recalling our considerations of the etheric body, we may say
that *concept and reality are still one for ordinary consciousness*; the reality of
the etheric body is still on this side of the threshold of the spiritual world. For
the astral body, however, the threshold lies between concept and reality. They
are united in cognition when the spiritual investigator carries supersensibly
explored reality into the world of pure thought.

This explains two points in Leading Thought lo, described entirely from
the spiritual perspective. First, new organs of perception are directed to the
earthly scene of action. They observe that the physical and etheric bodies "do
not generate consciousness" but furnish the foundation for the spirit to produce consciousness within earthly life. Second, the new organs of perception
may be directed to their own world. When it is not looking through the senses
into material, but through its own power into the spiritual, the spirit needs no
material foundation to enliven its conscious activity.[3]

This is a description realized by crossing the threshold of the spiritual world.
Since it is impressed into the world of pure thought, with such knowledge we

---

1   *The Bhagavad Gita and the West*, lecture 5; *Between Death and Rebirth*, lecture 7.

2   *The Apocalypse of St. John*, lecture 12.

3   *The East in the Light of the West*, lecture 12; *Initiation, Eternity, and the Passing
      Moment*, lectures 4 and 7.

can peek over the threshold, so to speak. Thus, as human beings we gradually become conscious of a world we otherwise enter only in sleep. Sleep is really a separation between the etheric and astral bodies. This is described in these leading thoughts as concept and reality in order that we may consciously cross the threshold. The philosophical form of this description allows us to recreate, through knowledge, this process of modern mysticism.

THE IMAGE AND REALITY OF THE HUMAN "I"

Previous studies showed that, for the etheric body, concept and reality coincide, whereas for the astral body concept and reality are separated by the threshold of the spiritual world. Now, what is the situation for the "I"-being, or fourth principle of the human being? In Rudolf Steiner's *Leading Thoughts*, a sharp distinction is made only for the astral body. There he speaks specifically about the concept of the astral body and its reality. This is unnecessary in the case of the etheric body, where the two unite, even on this side of the threshold of the spiritual world.

When we turn to the "I," we find that concept and reality also coincide in a certain sense, but now on the other side of the threshold of the spiritual world. This side and the other side are, of course, intended only in a limited way. it is a matter of a narrow strip, so to speak, that can nevertheless be surveyed and experienced through thinking. The descriptions provided by the spiritual investigator concerning experiences on the other side of the threshold are so radically different from our ordinary experiences that, when they are expressed in words of our earthly language, it becomes a matter of a reflection, or image, in the etheric world. This is the source of tremendous difficulties, particularly for any philosophy, and it creates endless misunderstandings.

No doubt, all true existence of the ordinary waking consciousness is experienced as "I." This is also the way we are used to expressing it. We do not say, "My body bumped the table," but, "I bumped the table." Likewise, we say, "I am hungry," and not, "My life processes require nourishment." Through all our experiences we also say, "I look at the world,"; "I remember"; "I think, feel, and will"; "I enjoy myself"; "I suffer." But there are more extreme examples: "I will sleep"; and "I have slept." What exists between, however, is withdrawn from consciousness and, with it, this whole world of experiences where the outer world is active but not the "I."

The contemplation of a center is instead an inference from our experiential external reality to something hidden. But, just as it is incorrect to build a world of philosophy of the "I" from "I"-representations engendered by the outer world (see Study 5), so it is equally incorrect to draw conclusions about something hidden in itself. That would be a metaphysical construction, which Steiner finally cleared away in *Truth and Knowledge* and *Intuitive Thinking As a Spiritual Path*. It is correct, however, that in these processes the outer world is experienced through the subjective organism and that, in a certain sense, one can properly look for a transcendental "I" beyond ordinary consciousness.

In the first of eight meditations in *A Way of Self-Knowledge*, Steiner shows, with particular penetration, that the "I"-like experiences of a mentally pictured external world do not belong to our true being.

> When the soul is plunged into the phenomena of the outer world by means of physical perception, it cannot be said—after true self-analysis—that the soul perceives these phenomena or that it actually experiences the things of the outer world. For, during the time of surrender, in its devotion to the outer world, the soul knows in truth nothing of itself. The fact is rather that the sunlight itself, radiating from objects through space in various colors, lives or experiences itself within the soul. When the soul enjoys any event, at the moment of enjoyment, it actually is joy insofar as it is conscious of being anything. Joy experiences itself in the soul. The soul is one with its experience of the world.

On the other hand, our search for the experience of our own being must be a path of knowledge. This helps us to understand Leading Thought 11, which follows apart from its group.

> 11. The consciousness of self summed up in "I"-being emerges from the sea of consciousness. Consciousness arises when the forces of the physical and etheric bodies disintegrate these bodies, and thus allow the spiritual to enter the human being. Through the disintegration of these bodies, the ground is prepared for the unfolding of conscious life. To avoid destroying the organism, however, such disintegration must be followed by reconstruction. Therefore, when a process of disintegration has occurred for conscious experience, what has been destroyed will be rebuilt. The experience of "I"-consciousness rests in the perception of this building-up process. The same process can be observed with inner vision. We then experience the awareness is led into "I"-consciousness by our *creating out of ourselves* an after-image of mere consciousness. The image of this mere consciousness is in the emptiness produced, as it were, within the organism through disintegration. It passes into "I"-consciousness when the emptiness has been filled again from within. The being capable of this "fulfillment" is experienced as "I."

Mere consciousness indicates for us our being surrendered to the world. That is one side of primitive soul life. "The soul is one with its experience of the world." That, however, signifies at the same time a penetration of external reality into the corporeality. This is thereby injured, or disintegrated, so to speak. Thus, the eye arose from injuries, as ulcers generated by the light. By resisting the outer world, the soul creates organs through pain. The body would be completely destroyed if it were subject only to the law of the outer world— which indeed does happen after death. Consciousness arises from disintegration. But healing originates from deeper forces, physically represented by the blood. These are the "I"-forces that remain hidden behind the surrender of our primitive soul life.

Steiner presented detailed descriptions of this from his spiritual investigations. They constitute a wonderful beginning for a physiology of these processes.

> Eons ago, there were two places on our head particularly sensitive to the Sun's rays. At the time, we still could not see, but whenever the Sun rose its rays must have caused pain at these two spots. The tissues would be destroyed, and this was certain to cause pain. This had to continue over the long ages, and the healing took the form of eyes at these two points. It is true that our eyes visualize the beauty of the world of color, and it is likewise true that they have arisen only on the basis of the injury caused by the Sun's heat in places especially sensitive to light. Nothing that provides happiness, pleasure, or bliss has arisen from anything but the foundation of pain.[1]

> When we stand before a colored object, we are certainly affected by it. But a process of destruction in the human organism plays a role between the colored object and the human organism. It is a miniature death, so to speak, and the nervous system is the organ that continually processes this destruction. These processes that continually occur in our organism due to outer influences are balanced by the influence of the blood.[2]

The disintegration of the physical and etheric bodies is experienced as consciousness, whereas perception of the rebuilding is experienced as "I"-consciousness. This is where our resistance to surrender is revealed; the substance of this resistance receives the "imprint" of the destroying external world. These are the after-images of mere consciousness. In this way, the image, or representation, of the "I" is formed. In order to attain the reality of the "I," a continuation practice of meditation is necessary. Human beings must recreate an after-image of the merely conscious out of themselves.

> 12. The reality of the "I" is discovered when inner vision (through which the astral body is known and grasped) is carried a stage further. Thinking that has come to life in meditation must now be permeated by the will. First, we simply surrendered to this new thinking without active will. Thus, we enabled spiritual realities to enter this thinking life, just as color enters the eye, and sound enters the ear, through outer sense perception. Through an act of will, we must now reproduce what has been thus far enlivened in consciousness through a somewhat passive devotion. When we do this, perception of the "I," or one's self, enters into this act of will.

---

1   *The Karma of Materialism*, lecture 3.

2   *Anthroposophische Lebensgaben* ("Anthroposophic Life Gifts"), lecture 10 (CW [The Collected Works of Rudolf Steiner] 181), unavailable in English.

Perhaps it is appropriate to clarify this process by which this initially unconscious inner activity forms, through meditation, organs of suprasensory perception. Goethe compares the human soul to water; that is true mystery language. Just as water takes on any form that a vessel offers it, so the soul is stamped with the form of every impression. Therefore, no soul perception arises in this way. Even in the world of the senses, perception arises only because the body resists outer impressions. The body places its own life form in opposition to impressions. Therefore, when perception begins to arise between soul and soul realm, the soul must be able to oppose its own established form to the soul effects of the soul realm. This inner firmness of soul is developed through the personal experiences gained through meditation.

We may now carry the analogy of soul and water even farther; water may take the form of any vessel, yet its very mobility still has another tendency. At its boundary with the air, it forms a level surface parallel to the surface of the Earth and at perpendicular to the zenith of the heavens. There it forms a mirror into which the heavenly phenomena look down: Sun, Moon, stars, and clouds. Then the wind—the soul's destiny—may ruffle the mirror of the lake, but again it becomes the true mirror and portrays the heavens. In this way, the spiritual heaven reflects its image in the soul; that is "I"-consciousness.

> O human soul,
> How like to the water,
> O human destiny,
> How like to the wind.
> —GOETHE

THE "I" AND MEDITATION

One's experience of "I"-experiences is meditative in character and, inversely, the practice of meditation may be derived from "I"-experience. The coincidence of the "I" as idea and reality in the spiritual world may be understood in precisely this way. The "I" is characteristic of every experience of reality, because a standard for reality is attained only through the "I." Natural science applies this standard as well. Natural scientists cannot speak of anything as more real than themselves. Thus, knowledge of nature does not become subjective, nor is it objective but beyond both. We call what we seek "the absolute," but we really mean "spiritual reality." Therefore, in all knowledge there is an ability to flow freely at the threshold of the spiritual world, and in such mobility, apparent contradictions are solved in various ways, because when they are adhered to inflexibly they are experienced as contradictions.

In Rudolf Steiner's little book *Philosophy and Anthroposophy*, we find the following words:

> The "I" lives within itself in that it produces its own concept and lives there as reality.... As a theory of knowledge, we may formulate as a fundamental axiom the following: In pure thinking, a certain point may be reached where the real and the subjective converge completely, and one experiences reality.[1]

It is important that we are, to begin with, only concerned with a point. We found this point on the way to the boundary of knowledge. It was said in our fourth study that, ultimately, even pure thinking withdraws so that only the *possibility*, or faculty, of thinking is present. One point remains as a zero point, or the classical idealist's so-called absolute "I." It's not difficult to see that "all ordinary knowledge originates at this boundary of consciousness." We are concerned here with the reality of the "I," but only at a certain point— the threshold of the spiritual world. From there, turning back to ordinary consciousness, everything becomes picture, or "after-image" (as in Leading Thought 11). We take with us, however, the imprint of our experience of reality and, from that, gain a standard for knowledge.

---

1   *Philosophie und Anthroposophie*, p. 51.

This approach to the boundaries of knowledge is not something that happens once and for all, where one comes to know something once and then knows or has it forever. It reveals its secrets only through patient, rhythmical repetition. In the first of eight meditations in *A Way of Self-Knowledge*, Steiner says: "This withdrawal is not merely a process that happens only once. Rather, it is merely the beginning of a pilgrimage into previously unknown worlds." This thinking—which has been experienced and, through further practice, permeated with will—forms in meditative stillness at the boundary of awareness. Leading Thought 12 describes this as a process of offering oneself to thinking without the will, in which a spiritual element enters thinking just as color enters the eye.

Steiner repeatedly describes this process (in *How to Know Higher Worlds*, for example). It is a matter of choosing and maintaining, in the most vivified way, a specific image in one's empty, stilled awareness and not falling asleep. Thinking may then be transformed into the faculty of *imagination*.[2] This process is exactly the opposite of our ordinary experience of knowing as we approach the boundaries of knowledge. For ordinary knowledge, perception is followed by *representation* (the image) and concept, and then by the initial "I"-experience. Now, however, we begin with the "I"; it places a freely chosen image at the center of awareness, not taken from the sense world, but one having a conceptual quality. Other free images then unite with it. These are individual *imaginations*; they are like a reversal of representations, or a wakeful dreaming.

The intervention of the will is seen distinctly in this process. Willed activity becomes independent and self-directed. What Leading Thought 12 says becomes clear at this point. A percept of the "I" itself arises in the willed act. In leading thoughts that follow, such perception of living being is termed *inspiration*. It is the spiritual counterpart of perceiving an individual object with the senses; this relationship is the same as that between *imagination* and representation.

Thus, we see that entrance into spiritual experience does not lead beyond the world.[3] We come back to the world we had apparently left on the path to the threshold; but the other—the spiritual side of the same world—now becomes visible. The spiritual world is all around and within us, permeating everything. The complete coalescence of the "I" with the living being in the spiritual world is called *intuition*. Through it, the beginning and end of this way insert themselves as though in a spiral, one above the other. (See drawing on the next page.)

In this whole process, therefore, the "I" goes through many forms as a picture. Leading Thought 13 describes this aspect of spiritual investigation.

---

2   *Rosicrucian Wisdom*, lecture 14.

3   See *Founding a Science of the Spirit*, Rudolf Steiner Press, London, 1976, lecture 1.

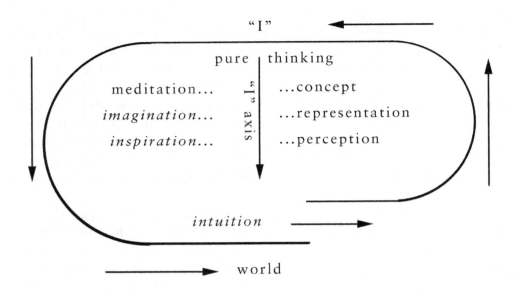

13. On the path of meditations we discover (aside from the "I"-being's form in ordinary consciousness) three more forms. 1) In the awareness that takes hold of the etheric body, the "I" appears as a picture, yet this picture is simultaneously an *active being*, and as such gives the human being substance, shape, growth, and the formative forces that create the body. 2) In the consciousness that takes hold of the astral body, the "I" manifests as a member of a spiritual world from which it receives its forces. 3) In the consciousness just indicated, as the last to be achieved, the "I" reveals itself as a self-contained, spiritual being, relatively independent of the surrounding spiritual realm.

The "I" appears in four conditions, which may be described briefly as: the "I" in the physical body, *ordinary consciousness*; the "I" in the etheric body, *imaginative consciousness*; the "I" in the astral body, *inspirational consciousness*; "I" in itself, *intuitive consciousness*.

Since primeval times, however, "I"-forces have been unconsciously connected with the development of the human sheaths. In *An Outline of Esoteric Science*, Steiner describes the great epochs of the world evolution as demonstrated by the principles of humankind. We must refer to these descriptions in order to understand Leading Thought 13. From such principles we see how the human "I"-being—still without self awareness—was connected with the creative beings of the hierarchies (spoken of in later leading thoughts), when the human physical body was created on *ancient Saturn*, the etheric body on *ancient Sun*, and the astral body on *ancient Moon*. On Earth, this cosmic process was recapitulated, but in such a way that all the principles of humankind were transformed through the addition of the "I."

Thus the "I" permeates all other principles. The "I" caused the transformation of the physical, etheric, and astral bodies on Earth, and in this way cosmic impulses are transformed into those of earthly humankind. Thus, today's human soul principles were fashioned and the ground prepared for the spiritual existence of the "I." So far, these impulses have not entered human consciousness to a very large degree. In Leading Thoughts 14 to 16 they will be substantiated from the perspective of spiritual knowledge.

14. The second form of the "I," or self (the first of three more forms mentioned in the previous section), appears as an image of the "I." When we become aware of this pictorial character, we can also see the quality of thought where the "I" appears before the ordinary consciousness. With all kinds of reflections, human beings have searched this consciousness for the true "I." Nevertheless, earnest insight into the ordinary conscious experiences is enough to demonstrate the absence there of the true "I." Only a vague representation is able to appear—a shadowy reflection, not even a picture. We are struck even more by the truth of this when we progress to the "I" as an image, which lives in the etheric body. Only now are we properly kindled to search for the "I," the true human being.

15. Insight into the form in which the "I" lives in the astral body leads to the proper feeling for the relationship between human beings and the spiritual world. In ordinary consciousness this form of the "I" is buried in the dark recesses of the unconscious, where humankind connects with the cosmic spirit through *inspiration*. Ordinary consciousness feels only a faint echo of this *inspiration* from the vast expanse of the spiritual realm that holds sway in the depths of human souls.

16. The third form of the "I" offers insight into the independent being of humankind in a spiritual realm. It causes us to experience, through the nature of our physical senses, how we stand before ourselves as mere manifestations of our true being. This is the beginning of true self-knowledge. The self that forms true human nature is revealed to us as knowledge only when we progress from the thought of the "I" to its picture, from the picture to the creative forces of the picture, and from the creative forces to the spiritual beings who sustain them.

With a little attention, we find in Leading Thought 14 the origin of thinking; in Leading Thought 15 the origin of feeling; and in Leading Thought 16 the origin of willing. Thus, we also find that the "I," in thinking, feeling, and willing, is the forerunner of *imagination*, *inspiration*, and *intuition*.

STUDY 9

THE "I," NOTHINGNESS, AND LIGHT

It always makes an impression to place before the soul the fact that all knowledge comes from threshold experience. Ordinary knowledge comes about because the "I" approaches the threshold unconsciously and turns back again. In spiritual knowledge the "I" crosses the threshold consciously and while returning transforms spiritual experience into ordinary forms of consciousness. The way across the threshold, however, leads through experiences that, from the times of the most ancient Mysteries, were always made to connect directly with the experience of death.[1] Secret societies that trace back their cults to the old Mysteries have traditionally preserved something of them. However, they possess only the outer symbolism: Death's Head and Coffin, Burial and Resurrection. Rudolf Steiner has spoken of this several times.[2] But we must recognize with deep reverence that the conscious crossing of the threshold in initiation is today likewise a passing through death.

> One can enter the spiritual world through three gateways, so to speak. We may call the first the "gate of death." It has been spoken of since primeval times, whenever Mystery truths were discussed earnestly. We can reach the gate of death only when we try to do so through what is known as meditation.... Such entry into the spiritual world has been called the gate of death because it is truly deeper than physical death. In physical death, human beings recognize that they lay aside the physical body. When entering the spiritual world, however, we must in fact decide to set aside our concepts, images, and ideas, allowing our being to be built anew.[3]

Such are processes of soul experience. Falling asleep each night is simply an unconscious image of this death.

In our approach to the boundaries of knowledge, we found a narrow portal, and experienced the "I" as a point. Compared to the actual experiences at the threshold, however, this mode of expression is abstract. In *How to Know Higher Worlds*, for example, Steiner describes the experience of the "Guardian of the Threshold" as a tremendous act of most formidable self-knowledge.[4]

---

1   *Initiation, Eternity, and the Passing Moment*, lecture 1.

2   See *Gegenwaertiges und Vergangenes im Menschengeiste* ("Present and Past in the Human Spirit"), lecture 6 (CW 167); and *Welt wesen und Ichheit* ("Cosmic Being and "I"-being"), lecture 3 (CW 169); neither are available in English.

3   *The Destinies of Individuals and of Nations*, lecture 8.

4   *The Effects of Esoteric Development*, lecture 8.

We must struggle through this otherwise being of evil, hidden within himself. Fear in the presence of this real experience causes ordinary efforts toward knowledge to turn back at the threshold. Ordinary knowledge, however, is also related, to a certain extent, to the tradition of knowledge of ancient times, and so-called unbiased science too often proves illusive.[5] It may be observed that this tradition exists only because initiates throughout past ages have taken this path of death.

Thus, we can say that *all knowledge is taken from death*. Throughout the leading thoughts, the appearance of the death experience becomes stronger. Experiences of the old Mysteries became history through the cosmic Mystery of Golgotha. This event overcame the spiritual death of humankind, which the old Mystery wisdom saw approaching, and the tasks of the old Mysteries entered the souls of all human beings.[6] In *Christianity as Mystical Fact*, Steiner magnificently outlined those historical facts, creating a point of departure for all his later investigations into the Mystery of Golgotha.

Our studies on the "I" may at first seem abstract, but behind them is a feeling of this grand cosmic event. Genuine abstraction is a training for approaching reality; it frees us from ordinary consciousness, as a word indicates in its meaning. Thus, in our seventh study, concept and "I"-being coincide on the other side of the threshold. Therefore, when approaching the boundary, we leave the world of individual concepts behind, and only the potential for thinking remains. At the threshold one can, in fact, no longer speak of a single concept, but only about the infinite totality of all the possibilities of thinking. This is experienced as a point, however; it is the outlet for *all* conceptual possibilities from the spiritual world. The reality of the "I" exists within it as a last (or first) representative of all that can be comprehended in concepts, the only source of our consciousness. This is how we may understand the union of concept and reality of the "I" in the spiritual world.

The path of training leads almost to "nothingness." This is the nothingness of Mephistopheles to which Faust courageously replies, "In your 'nothingness' I hope to find the *all*." Steiner said of this:

> The scene depicted so marvelously by Goethe in *Faust* is continually reenacted in humanity as a whole. On the one hand, we see Faust searching for the way into the spiritual world; on the other hand, Mephistopheles describes that world as "nothingness," because it is in his interest to represent the sense world as everything. Faust responds with what every spiritual investigator would use in a similar situation: "In your 'nothingness'

---

5   *Anthroposophische Legensgaben* ("Anthroposophic Life Gifts"), lecture 10; and *Gesunder Blick fuer heute und wackere Hoffnung fuer morgen* ("A Sound View for Today and Genuine Hope for the Future"), lecture 20 (CW 181); unavailable in English.

6   *The Karma of Materialism*, lecture 5.

I hope to find the *all*." Only when we recognize that there is spirit in the smallest particle of matter and that matter is represented as a lie—only when we recognize Mephistopheles as the corrupting spirit in our views of the world—will the outer world present itself to us in its true aspect and help humankind evolve.[1]

Steiner, however, has also shown how the "I" (*Ich*) is connected, even in the placement of the letters, with the central mystery of humanity, and how in true imagery, the disciplined path of knowledge is filled with life.[2] Thus, we may conclude this study with the following image:

> At the boundary of existence, the cross of the *I* appears erected, and on either side are the malefactors: the *N* as ahrimanic denial, and the *T* (or Tao with serpent) as luciferic seduction: N-I-T, or "nothingness." Then, however, in working properly toward the reality of the cosmic "I," this picture is changed, and beyond the threshold appears the spiritual world— what humanity seeks on the paths of death: L-I-T, or "light."[3]

Anyone familiar with the language of eurythmy feels the widespread surging of the world in the *L*, and in the *T* the force that encloses us from above as human personalities. When the bandage falls from our eyes, light will belong to humankind. This may occur in every bit of knowledge, even the most modest. These are the real letters in the language of the consciousness soul; by transforming images, they create reality.

In the sequence of leading thoughts, numbers 17 and 19 begin a new tone. It begins anew concerning human beings as body, soul, and spirit:

> 17. Human beings unfold their life in the middle, between the regions of two worlds. Through bodily development, they belong to a lower realm. Through their soul nature, they constitute a middle realm. And through the faculties of spirit, they constantly strive toward a higher realm. We owe our bodily development to everything that nature has provided. We carry the being of soul within us as our own portion. And we discover within ourselves spirit forces as gifts that lead us beyond ourselves to participation in a divine realm.

> 18. The spirit is creative in these three areas of the world. Nature is not void of spirit. Even nature is lost from knowledge, however, if we fail to recognize spirit within her. Nevertheless, in the existence of nature, we find the spirit sleeping, as it were. Yet, sleep has a task in human life; just as the self, or "I," must sometimes sleep in order to be more awake at other

---

1   *The Gospel of St. John and Its Relation to the Other Gospels*, lecture 5.

2   *Necessity and Freedom*, lecture 5.

3   This imaginative analogy works better in the original German, in which the letters come closer to the words meaning "nothingness" and "light."

times, so also the world spirit must sleep within nature in order to be more awake elsewhere.

19. In relation to the world, the human soul is like a dreamer if we fail to pay attention to the spirit at work within us. Spirit awakens the dreaming soul from ceaseless weaving within our inner life to active participation in the world where our true being originates. When dreaming we close ourselves off from the surrounding physical world, and we entwine ourselves into ourselves. Similarly, if our ears are deaf to the spirit's awakening calls within us, the human soul loses its connection with the world spirit through whom we originate.

BODY, SOUL, AND SPIRIT

People begin cosmological study with the phenomena of the natural, mineral world, in accordance with modern methods of science and education. If, however, we could imagine a fully developed man arising from nothing, he would certainly not begin with the mineral realm, but with himself, finding himself as an enclosed unity. The myriad variations of the world and his own being would then be revealed to him.

In Rudolf Steiner's works, we find many presentations of the human being, and the most varied analyses result according to the perspective from which we review such relationships. All categorization and analyses have in some form or another a methodical basis. Nothing is sillier than opponents perpetually harping about the sevenfold nature of the human being. An essential quality of Steiner's presentations is his refusal to allow his investigations to become rigid. Instead, he frees them again and again to become living forms. In his works, there are descriptions of the human being as a unity and as a duality; there are triads in every possible sense. Human beings also appear with four, five, seven, nine, and twelve principles; even a presentation based on fifteen can be justified.[1]

When we try to understand ourselves as a unity, we realize immediately that we can do so only in opposition to everything else. When we assume that we exist, we also assume the world's existence. There is no unity, therefore, except in opposition to the existence of something else. The more we desire to remain a unity, the more our own being vanishes into the *other*, the world, until a mere point—as through nothing—is left. This is the tragedy of the "I." Any attempt to balance it with the world becomes dualistic in every way. The essential dualism is that of inner and outer worlds.

We can try to grasp the outer world from the inner world, or the inner world from the outer world. In either instance, the object being considered is withdrawn. If we begin with the soul and look for a connection with the outer world, we arrive at a boundary, because every connection of this type is interrupted by sleep. As we direct our attention to the outer world more intensely, we become increasingly tired and, in sleep, the object of our attention is withdrawn. But when we try, from the outer world, to understand the human being, we discover that the forces of the surrounding world—if they become

---

1   See Carl Unger, "Mathematik als echte Symbolismus," *Die Drei*, Stuttgart, Sept. 1927, vol 7, no. 6.

active in the human being—destroy the body as the bearer of the inner realm. This may be seen in a corpse; death is the other boundary where the object is withdrawn. These are only suggestions that may be used in myriad ways.

The essence of the matter has nothing to do with the immediate inner world or the outer world, but is concerned with a third aspect that is active as a common factor, permeating both. Thinking unites these opposites. The polarity of the two opposites generates the third element. Let us take, for example, the basic phenomenon with which Hegel began. A given unity already contains its opposite as a second element, and these two generate a third that unites them: *thesis, antithesis,* and *synthesis.* Hegel formulated this as a final abstraction: *being* (thesis), *nothingness* (antithesis), and *becoming* (synthesis). Rather than placing it where it first appears: *I* (thesis), *not I* (antithesis), *knowledge* (synthesis).

In keeping with our considerations, we may develop such thinking as follows: *inner world* and *outer world* are united by a third, higher principle, or *thinking,* which appears inwardly; there it is given initially. But only the form of its appearance belongs to the inner world as subjective. Its being, or essence, does not belong to the inner world, but detaches itself from the mode of presentation; it is absolute. My inner world and my own efforts are necessary, so that the Pythagorean theorem becomes apparent in me. This theorem, however, is not my own, but remains the same whether it manifests in me or in another. It is independent of the mode of manifestation. Something that is an absolute experience in my own inner world may also be applied to the outer world. This does not mean that the Pythagorean theorem would now belong to the outer world, since it cannot be perceived anywhere, but it can be applied to the outer world. In relation to the outer world, it is also absolute.

When we understand how something experienced inwardly fits the outer world, we experience a spiritual reality. At the beginning of the age of the consciousness soul, notable men experienced this as a powerful revelation. Kepler, the great astronomer, experienced this and described it in his works.[2] When we observe humankind externally, we are concerned with the bodily entity. The inner realm is experienced as a soul entity. In both instances, the observer is the spirit, which embraces the outer and inner worlds equally. Thus, when speaking about the human spirit, one must always remember that we are not speaking of an enclosed spiritual entity, but that the spiritual manifests in the human soul as an absolute entity.

This is presented specifically in *Theosophy,* where Steiner speaks of body, soul, and spirit.

By *body* is meant the means by which things in our environment...reveal themselves. The word *soul* designates the means by which we link these

---

2   *Manifestations of Karma,* lecture 1; *The East in the Light of the West,* lecture 8.

things to our own personal existence.... By *spirit* is meant what becomes apparent in us when...we look at the things of the world.[1]

We can well observe that, in the case of *body* and *soul*, it says "the means by which," but in the case of the *spirit* it says "what becomes apparent in us." When reading Steiner's books, it is indeed necessary to note every single word; that is very different than swearing by it. Understood in this sense, the change from *by which* to *what manifests* expresses that human beings have definite bodies and souls, but that human beings contain only as much spirit as manifests in them. This is true also for our time, when the human spirit is still weak and shows little definite form. Human beings are open to the spiritual realms, just as nature is.

We have in this a direct link with Leading Thought 17, and we can acknowledge that we properly attend to the *word of the master* when we work to realize it inwardly. Leading Thought 17 says, "Through bodily development, they belong to a lower realm. Through their soul nature, they constitute a middle realm. And through the faculties of spirit, they constantly strive toward a higher realm." There is the same distinction, as quoted from *Theosophy*. Thus we read that human beings unfold their life between two world spheres.

Again, we find something significant in the words themselves. The words are formed from world spheres themselves: physical *evolution*; soul *being*; and spirit *forces*." Only as a soul does humankind have being. Through physical evolution, nature is stirred up. And through spirit forces, a higher world works into human beings. We are faced with the grand, universal polarity of *macrocosm* and *microcosm*. In Leading Thought 18, spirit is described as *sleeping* in nature; but the human being is awake through the union of soul and body, through which nature is stirred within. Working into humankind from the upper realm, spirit is awake in its own sphere, but in regard to spirit, the human being is asleep—indeed, precisely during the state of physical, waking life. The aspects that now open up will be reviewed throughout the leading thoughts.

The soul's dream (in Leading Thought 19) is a mixture of waking and sleeping. Moreover, the dreamy state of the soul is not confined to the boundaries of waking and sleeping, but pervades the whole human waking state. Broad areas of Steiner's spiritual investigations cover waking, dreaming, and sleeping states of consciousness. He could never describe such tremendous discoveries in their entire relationship simply because there was not enough time. He gave the public purely introductory communications, whose tremendous significance could not be understood in this form by the world. An infinite amount remains to be done, since they are not merely flashes of thought, cast out lightly, as the superficial reader of our time may think, due to their

---

1   *Theosophy: An Introduction to the Spiritual Processes in Human Life and in the Cosmos*, p. 24.

somewhat aphoristic nature. After years of careful testing, using all the means of contemporary science, he became absolutely certain of his investigations; only then did Steiner offer them to the public. In *Riddles of the Soul*, he speaks directly and plainly about such discoveries. Amid the chaos of the [First] World War, however, they were simply ignored by the public. We will have to return to this again in our studies.

Only one comprehensive passage shall be quoted for our purpose.

Thus we see that, in the truest sense of the word, we are truly awake only in relation to our sense perception and in our life of representations. Even during the waking state, in our feeling life, we are really asleep and dreaming. Regarding the life of will, we are always completely asleep. Therefore, the sleeping state extends into our waking state.

Let us picture how we pass through the world. With our waking consciousness, what we experience is only the perception of the sense realm and our world of representations. Embedded in this experience is a world where our feeling and will impulses float—a world surrounding us like the air. But they do not enter ordinary consciousness at all. Those who approach the matter in this way will, in fact, not be far from recognizing a so-called suprasensory world around them.[2]

---

2   *Earthly Death and Cosmic Life*, lecture 3.

STUDY 11

THE SPIRIT'S CALL TO AWAKE

The spirit's call, resounding throughout the world, can dissolve the dream of the human soul only through our own unbiased self-observation. Thus, it is important to delineate the way this state of dreaming reaches from night consciousness into day consciousness. Outer sense perceptions penetrate the picture realm from which we emerge when we awaken in the morning. Rudolf Steiner often spoke of the image world of true dreams represented by symbols.[1] This transition however, seldom occurs with a jolt. It is usually gradual and, with some practice, can be extended in awareness; the necessary time amounts to mere seconds. We may observe this passage when, for example, such symbolic imagery covers physical objects while the soul is still linked to the laws of the world of imagery.

Early morning dream consciousness and the slow decrease in the curve of fatigue are well known. Less well known is the faculty of association of representations available before noon. This is why memory is more reliable in the morning. It is obvious, therefore, that the waking life is by no means uninterruptedly, continually surrendered to the external world; rather, a different world—the world of representations and recollections—shines continually into our waking life as a real picture world with its own laws. The laws that govern image association constitute a broad field for investigation. Everyone, however, may have observed the way some representations stay with us and cannot be dispersed; and whereas we seek others through strenuous concentration, they maliciously hide and do not allow themselves to be found. Often, they arise at inopportune times when they might lead to unpleasant situations.

Another experience may easily happen. Someone goes into the forest just for the pleasure of it, to enjoy the beauty. Then, gradually, that person begins to dream, losing self-awareness. Suddenly, there is a shot. The shock has a waking effect, and, with sufficient awareness at that moment, the place from which this person is recalled may be realized—perhaps the banks of the Brahmaputra. One's wandering into far distances through mental pictures can then be retraced.

Such an awakening during what seems like a waking state is an important experience; for, in fact, it is the spirit that awakens. The wake-up call of the spirit

---

1   *Founding a Science of the Spirit* (previously *At the Gates of Spiritual Science*), lecture 12; *Rosicrucian Wisdom* (previously *The Theosophy of the Rosicrucians*), lecture 8; *Man in the light of Occultism, Theosophy and Philosophy*, lecture 7.

always sounds in the dreaming soul (Leading Thought 19). To hear it in reality requires us to overcome dreaming while awake. This occurs through constant practice, which, at certain times, silences the laws of the dream world of images. As soon as someone begins to struggle against them, however, such mental images are strengthened. One may then immediately evoke the surrounding witches' revel, and the images begin to assume an impish, even demonic, quality. They are really like mischievous beings who have slipped out of the elemental world through the portal of ordinary waking into day consciousness.

Memory is certainly connected with such beings, but for it to be of any value to us those beings must be morally controlled. Even here there are important experiences. When I want to overcome some passion, I must not fight it; this will only strengthen its temptation. Rather, I must turn my consciousness away from that passion—consciously forget it and bring other images into the field of consciousness. This is also the way of proper meditation, where we must ward off intruding imagery, practice conscious forgetting, and bring an entirely willed representation into consciousness.

Such soul exercises sharpen the inner ear for the spirit's wake-up call. They also bring us to the following leading thoughts:

20. Proper development of the human soul life requires that human beings work from the spiritual sources in their being in full consciousness. Many who hold a modern scientific worldview are also strongly biased in this sense. They state that a universal causality dictates all world phenomena and that those who believe they can cause anything by their own means are merely deluded. Contemporary natural science always attempts to follow observation and experience faithfully, but a bias concerning the hidden causality of inner human resources leads it to violate its own principle. Free activity, directly from inner human resources, is an essential experience of self-observation; it cannot be argued away. We must instead harmonize free activity with our own insight into universal cause within the natural order.

21. The greatest hindrance to spiritual knowledge is a failure to recognize the spiritual impulse active in human life. Indeed, to think of our own being as merely a part of the natural order diverts the soul's attention away from our own being. And we cannot penetrate the spiritual world unless we first comprehend the spirit where it is directly given to us—in clear, unbiased self-observation.

22. We may begin to observe spirit through self-observation. In fact, this can be a proper beginning, because if this is true we cannot possibly stop there, but must progress to the world's spiritual essence. Just as the human body wastes away when it lacks physical nourishment, those who observe themselves properly will experience the "I" as becoming stunted if forces are not seen working into it from a creative spiritual world.

Steiner gives the spirit's wake-up call, which rings clearly in the soul world of modern human beings. It is correct to say that he has sounded this wake-up call since the turn of the century. He describes the human being as *body, soul,* and *spirit.* Indeed, the words *and spirit* are significant. Let us recapitulate briefly what Steiner often presented.

In ancient cultures, the trichotomy of body, soul, and spirit was experienced naturally. In 869, at the Eighth General Council in Constantinople, *spirit was eliminated.* Thereafter, it could only be taught that the human being is made up of body and soul, and that the soul merely possesses certain spiritual qualities. The prevailing conditions of that time make it obvious that this dogma was generally accepted. This teaching was then sustained without further ado in Western science, so that even contemporary psychology finds only body and soul.[1] Science certainly considers itself to be unbiased, but in fact it is based in the tradition of the Catholic Church, which established her power through the very decision of that Council. Since then, anyone who attributed spirit to human beings was considered a heretic. Steiner spoke of this and its context. In his final lectures, he spoke incisively about the time around 869 and its significance for the earthly and spiritual realms.[2] We will encounter the results of this in later leading thoughts. Here we need only approach it from one particular aspect:

> The time drew near when humanity would gradually become free. Just before closing the door, the Catholic Church established the dogma that eliminated the spirit. Human efforts were thus directed toward the physical body, which was surrendered in order to free science. The human soul, on the other hand, was claimed with great success as the exclusive domain of the Catholic Church. Since then, the human spirit has been sleeping. Nevertheless, it is active.

> Science, now assigned to the body, ultimately became "materialism." In materialism, spirit works in a self-negating way, where it nevertheless becomes a new force in the world.[3] Now there is a danger of repeating the whole process in relation to the soul. In a not too distant future, we can imagine a general council of scientists and doctors, who will resolve that, from now on, the human being should be considered only a body, merely

---

1   *Earthly Death and Cosmic Life,* lecture 3; *Building Stones for an Understanding of the Mystery of Golgotha,* lecture 2. The situation has since declined to the point where contemporary behavioral and cognitive psychologies view the physical body and its electro-chemical functions as the entire human being, eliminating completely the soul, or *psyche,* from human psychology.

2   *Gesunder Blick fuer Heute und wackere Hoffnung fuer Morgen* ("A Sound Outlook for Today and a Genuine Hope for the Future"), lecture 20 (CW 181); unavailable in English.

3   *The Karma of Materialism,* lecture 6.

possessing certain soul qualities; this would be the dogma that eliminates the soul. Anyone who taught otherwise would be considered a heretic— not burned at the stake but locked in a mental institution.[4]

Thus, loss of soul is a threat, and the content of Leading Thoughts 19 and 21 must be taken with extreme seriousness.

> If our ears are deaf to the spirit's awakening calls within us, the human soul loses its connection with the world spirit through whom we originate.... Indeed, to think of our own being as merely a part of the natural order diverts the soul's attention away from our own being. [But the soul arises through its inherent forces against this threatening fate.] Freedom of activity, directly out of human inner resources, is an essential experience of self-observation. (Leading Thoughts 19–20)

Steiner's call to awaken resounds in the souls of those who feel something of this threatening fate in dreams. Indeed, this wake-up call is not at all a moral preaching, nor does it contain the slightest gesture of sectarian prophecy; it simply allows the true name of humanity to ring out. When I wish to awaken someone who is sleeping, I call that person's name. Thus, Steiner calls people by their proper name, which is expressed in the knowledge of body, soul, and spirit. The whole significance of this is precisely in the words *and spirit*. This is not just a teaching firmly supported by every means of knowing that the human being has three aspects—body, soul, and spirit; it is an act of knowing that bears fruit in the physical and spiritual realms. Because of this, the primal experience of body, soul, and spirit has tremendous cosmic importance.

---

4   *Building Stones for an Understanding of the Mystery of Golgotha*, lecture 1;
     Aspects of Human Evolution, lecture 1.

STUDY 12

CONCERNING FREEDOM

The primary experience of body, soul, and spirit forms the basis for an introduction to the nature of the human being as Rudolf Steiner presented it, for example, in his book *Theosophy*. The question may arise as to why he chose another method in the leading thoughts, where the essential triad of body, soul, and spirit—from which all other triads in Steiner's works can be derived—does not appear until Leading Thought 17. We may notice intimate differences and how everything depends on the description given.

The awakening call of the spirit that rings out in *Theosophy* sounds powerfully in the ordinary consciousness of contemporary human beings as their true name (see study 11). One of the most important aspects of this book shows how the sense for the freedom in ordinary consciousness is preserved from beginning to end. In this way, the truly decisive first steps can arise from our very own being. This sense of freedom finds its proper range precisely in the sense for truth; the appeal is made only to this sense. Unprejudiced thinking and good will are joined to this feeling. When the will is activated in knowing, the feeling for truth leads thinking to further questions. We can deeply commit ourselves in freedom only when self-knowledge leads to a path of knowledge (this was discussed in our first study). This fact dominates the language of the leading thoughts.

In this way, the being of freedom is not ignored in any sense, but raised to a higher level. The initial approach to Spiritual Science is an act of freedom in ordinary consciousness. While progressing in this work, it is essential that the being of freedom be activated on the way to spiritual knowing. *Anthroposophy is a path of knowledge* (Leading Thought 1). The ordinary sense of freedom attempts to understand itself; the being of freedom on the higher level seeks an understanding with beings of the spiritual realms. As the leading thoughts proceed, we find clear proof of this; at the very beginning of the leading thoughts, we are led immediately into cosmic spiritual spheres. Thus, the body, soul, and spirit (as presented in Leading Thoughts 20 to 22) acquire cosmic significance.

The phrase *understanding with itself* arises from Steiner's earlier books, before his works specifically on Spiritual Science. His Ph.D. dissertation entitled *The Fundamental Question of the Theory of Knowledge with Special Reference to Fichte's Scientific Teachings* (1891) was published a year later with the title *Truth and Knowledge*. Its original subtitle was *Prolegomena* to an *Understanding of the Philosophizing Consciousness with Itself*. *Truth and Knowledge* is now subtitled *Introduction to a Philosophy of Spiritual Activity*. Then in 1894 came *Die Philosophie der Freiheit* (*Intuitive Thinking as a Spiritual Path: A Philosophy of Freedom*), subtitled *Fundamentals of a Modern Worldview: Some Results of Soul Observation in Conformity with the Method of Natural Science*.

An understanding of consciousness with itself and the establishment of freedom as a result of human self-observation (Leading Thought 20) began Steiner's wake-up call of the spirit. It is an impulse that pervades all his works, because freedom is not simply a matter of a single pronouncement concerning whether or not a human being is free; it is a process of freeing the human spirit.

Intuitive Thinking as a Spiritual Path begins by demonstrating that the question of human freedom is always stated incorrectly. It is comprehended only by going more and more deeply into one's own being, where it reveals itself as related to the nature of thinking. This, however, immediately points beyond itself and brings us into an evolution through which we release ourselves from bondage to the body. We free ourselves from our original connection with nature and its *necessity*. To investigate freedom is to conquer freedom. We are thus placed before the spiritual world as we previously stood before nature.

Throughout his later years, Steiner continually referred to *Intuitive Thinking as a Spiritual Path*, and he clearly shows in his *Autobiography* how this book stands on the same spiritual foundations as everything that appeared later. We read, "In my *Intuitive Thinking as a Spiritual Path* ... it is emphasized that human beings become free when they achieve the possibility of drawing impulses from the spiritual world. In one passage, it is even expressly stated that impulses of free will come from the spiritual world."[1]

Intuitive Thinking as a Spiritual Path is a book of initiation. It provides a path where the understanding of the consciousness through itself is transformed into an understanding of consciousness through the new world into which it leads. Steiner gave this new understanding from the other side as Spiritual Science. The great question before us leads us again to Leading Thoughts 20 to 22, which show the vast nature of the task Steiner took up. His task was to arouse modern human beings to awareness of the path of knowledge, so they would be able to proceed on it with increasing freedom. We will outline this problem more closely; it is insoluble to ordinary consciousness and, thus, one of the most difficult.

Ordinary consciousness encounters the necessity of nature, or *unbroken causality*. Self-observation reveals free activity within the human being. These two experiences must be harmonized (Leading Thought 20), since they completely contradict each other. The strong feeling inherent in this contradiction

---

1   *Necessity and Freedom*, p. 79.

drives ordinary consciousness to a transformation on the path of knowledge. Life's contradictions are to be solved only through inner development. Besides his other references, Steiner devoted an entire lecture cycle to this question.

> What we think of as *necessity* is the past within us. We must have passed through something, and what we passed through must have stored something in our souls. It remains to work on in the soul as necessity.... We all carry the past within us; thus, we bear necessity within us. What belongs to the present time does not act as necessity, otherwise there would be no free act in the immediate present. The past, however, works into the present, and it is linked with freedom. Because the past continues to work, necessity and freedom are closely knit together in a single act.[1]

This view is then applied to nature—not as analogy or theory, however, but as exact spiritual investigation.

This is something that provides spiritual scientists with an important perspective. They realize the connection between the past and necessity, begin to investigate nature, and discover necessity in nature. While investigating natural phenomena they see that everything discovered in nature by the natural scientist as necessity also arises from the past. Whatever we can observe in nature today as necessity, existed at one time in a state of freedom—a free act of the gods. It appears to us as necessity only because it is past. If we could see what is happening now in nature, it would never occur to us to see necessity there—we see only what is left behind in nature; we do not see the spiritual now taking place in nature. (Ibid.)

One can speak in this way only through an understanding of the spiritual realm. An inner method of development frees the inner being from nature's necessity. Through pure thinking, it leads to an independent spiritual experience. From such a perspective, nature—which has been left behind—can be comprehended by a new natural science that understands nature as spirit. In his works on natural science, Steiner dealt with this problem as a *theory of knowledge*, and he dealt with it in every detail from the perspective of Spiritual Science.[2] Spiritual knowledge exists on the other side of nature. When spiritual investigators encounter spiritual beings, they recognize themselves as like them.[3] To the degree we develop and maintain our free being, we continue to penetrate higher hierarchies. How do we now view nature and its necessity? As the place where spirit *sleeps* (Leading Thought 18). Nature is the other side of spirit.

Such statements point to a complete change of outlook. They also help ordinary consciousness understand why the other side of spirit appears to

---

1   Ibid., lecture 2.

2   *Goethe's Theory of Knowledge.*

3   *The East in the Light of the West*, lecture 5; also *Spiritual Beings in the Heavenly Bodies and in the Kingdoms of Nature*, lecture 2.

human beings as necessity—it is because, compared to nature, we are awake. Through such a change of outlook, a kind of exchange occurs between willing and thinking. We can understand natural laws as *willing*, which is so exalted that it foregoes all arbitrary action. Ordinary human consciousness contains only a representation of the will of those spiritual beings behind nature; they appear to sleep, because they have renounced arbitrary action. But this is human thinking. It must renounce partiality in order to understand the laws of nature. Nevertheless, by rising to the spiritual world, thinking is permeated by will (Leading Thought 12). Through pure willing—which is higher freedom—spirit beings reveal themselves to human beings. In the review of nature seen from the spirit, it appears as the thinking of these spirit beings. That is creative thinking. Therefore, to paraphrase a sentence from ancient occult science: *Human consciousness thinks things as they are; things are as spiritual beings think them.*

FREEDOM AND DEATH

Rudolf Steiner presented a new aspect in the Leading Thoughts. When we try to understand how this method of presentation differs from that of his earlier works, we gain a significant insight into the leading thoughts. Bearing in mind the sequence of his fundamental books, we see in particular the direction he wanted to give to the whole anthroposophic movement. It is also alarming to realize the infinite loss due to the short time he had to work with this new impulse.

When Steiner first sounded the wake-up call of the spirit, beginning with natural scientific methods, he appealed to the impulse of freedom in everyone. He did this in *Intuitive Thinking as a Spiritual Path: A Philosophy of Freedom* (as discussed in study 12). From there, we can turn to his book *Theosophy*, which begins with a presentation of the human being as body, soul, and spirit, through which the impulse to freedom acts as an aspect of knowledge, leading to spiritual investigation. In *An Outline of Esoteric Science*, Steiner's presentation is extended from the human being to cosmic being. The sequence of these books corresponds to the soul attitude of contemporary humankind, at a time when materialism began to overreach itself to destroy its own foundations.

Comparing that with the sequence of leading thoughts up to this point, we see its arrangement is methodically reversed. It begins immediately with cosmic perspectives; what it has to say about the physical, etheric, and astral bodies is from a cosmic and spiritual perspective. The presentation then progresses from the twofold cosmic and human "I"-being to a differentiation of body, soul, and spirit. Only then do we encounter aspects of human freedom. This method of presentation appeals to a more advanced consciousness, which can in fact be grasped directly by spiritual impulses. Through true self-observation, human beings will find that they cannot merely remain with observing the self, but must continue on in search of a spiritual world essence (Leading Thought 22).

Following a presentation of the nature of freedom (Leading Thoughts 20–22), we find a description of conditions after death (23–25). This is important; *the strongest argument against freedom is death—it is the bitter necessity of earthly life.* "Many who hold a modern scientific worldview are also strongly biased in this sense. They state that a universal causality dictates all world phenomena" (Leading Thought 20). "If the soul cannot create a picture

44

beyond the physical world—of the realm to which the physical body returns following death—then it will see itself only as a void after death."[1] According to Leading Thought 20, however, if we desire freedom "directly from inner human…we must instead harmonize free activity with our own insight into universal cause within the natural order"; we must take care to become acquainted with the nature of death from the spiritual side. Within the experience of earthly consciousness, the anthroposophic path of knowledge leads to an understanding of what happens in terms of everything relating to the soul after death. The German mystic Angelus Silesius said that those who do not die before they die perish when they do die.

> 23. When passing through the gate of death, we go out into the spiritual realm. We experience, falling away from us, all the impressions and substance of soul that we received during earthly life through the physical senses and brain. Thus, consciousness is confronted with an all-embracing panorama, the entire content of life. Such content entered during our earthly sojourn as pictureless thoughts into memory, or, unnoticed by earthly consciousness, it nevertheless made a subconscious impression on the soul. After a very few days, these pictures dim and fade away. When they completely vanished, we know that we have also laid aside the etheric body, since we recognize the etheric body as the bearer of these pictures.

Study 5, "Cosmic View," considered the boundary of ordinary consciousness. *"In this world, ideas and sight are of equal value.* Thus, for the etheric world, the conceptual presentation suffices in order to gain a footing in reality." The cosmic view, which shows us the etheric body as a cosmic picture, is formed when, through practice, we are emancipated from ordinary consciousness and its bondage to the physical. Added to this is what we found in study 9 related to experiences at the threshold: *"All knowledge is taken from death."* These are the elements necessary for understanding the events related to the etheric body after death. All knowledge—especially the ascent to spiritual knowledge—anticipates the experiences brought about by spiritual laws after death.

It can be said that, with pure knowing, the etheric body is freed somewhat from its bondage to the physical. At the moment of death, the etheric body frees itself entirely from the physical body and follows its cosmic tendencies, returning to its source. Therefore, the etheric body's experiences between birth and death are widened to the cosmos. What constituted our inner world during life becomes the outer world—an environment of memories. Through the death experience, we are turned inside out. Steiner often spoke of this process.[2] Any description of this process shows that, even during life, the etheric body does not deny its cosmic origin and, after death, reveals it.

---

1   *A Way of Self-Knowledge,* "Second Meditation."

2   See *Forming of Destiny and Life after Death,* lecture 4; and *An Outline of Esoteric Science,* chapter 3.

Steiner spoke of the duration of the life tableau (mentioned in Leading Thought 23 as a few days):

> We can maintain it under normal conditions as long as we have the power to stay awake in the physical body. It does not depend on how long we once remained awake in life under unusual conditions; it depends on the power within us to keep ourselves awake.[1]

This is understandable when we remember that falling asleep is usually accomplished by freeing the astral body and "I" from the physical and etheric bodies—a separation of the etheric and astral bodies. After death, this process is effected more radically, though it may be compared to falling asleep. During life, we fall asleep in such a way that first the astral body is freed from the physical body but remains united with the etheric body; this is the ordinary dream state. After death completely inverts everything, the cosmic "superdream" of the life tableau arises instead. Once the etheric body has been disposed of after death, a corresponding cosmic "supersleep" arises that indicates a higher state of wakefulness. This comparison with ordinary sleep is valid; after death, or separation from the etheric body, the astral body recapitulates the sleep contents of the past earth life, whereas the etheric body recapitulates dream experiences in the life tableau, inasmuch as they represent day experiences.

> 24. After laying aside the etheric body, the astral body and "I" still remain as the members of our being. The astral body, as long as it remains, brings to our consciousness all that was unconscious in the soul during earthly life while resting in sleep. This content includes judgments instilled into the astral body by spirit beings of a higher world during sleep—judgments that remain hidden from earthly consciousness. We now live through this earthly life a second time, but now in such a way that the content of our soul judges our thought and action from the perspective of the spirit realm. We live through it in reverse—first, the most recent night, then the previous one, and so on.

> 25. This judgment of our life, which human beings experience in the astral body after passing through the gate of death, lasts as long as the entire time spent asleep during earthly life.

After death, our sleep experiences are lived through in reverse, and this leads our understanding back to what was brought out in our fifth study. Let us recapitulate briefly.

The threshold of the spiritual world exists between concept and reality of the astral body. The concept of the astral body therefore has a kind of negative quality; it strives unconsciously during sleep toward its reality, but consciously when entering spiritual knowing. As long as the astral body is connected to

---

1   *The Inner Nature of Man and the Life Between Death and Rebirth*, lecture 5.

the physical and etheric bodies, it is at the opposite pole to its reality, since it essentially belongs to the spiritual realm. We can also call it the "moral world," a world of spiritual beings.

Thus, true knowledge of the astral body is an inner, moral process. The astral body's ordinary functions in the physical world contradict this. Turning inside out through death reverses all relationships. We found concept and reality on this side of the threshold in the case of the etheric body. As a result, everything accomplished in the etheric body before *and* after death may be understood in the same way. In the case of the astral body, however, everything is reversed, since its reality exists on the other side of the threshold.

It is the astral body that passes judgments in us. Such judgments are expressed in ordinary consciousness as sensation, feelings, impulses, and passion. All such processes are like injuries to the spiritual realm; they are experienced in the astral body when it returns during sleep to its own realm, the spiritual world. We may refer to this as judgment in the spiritual world. All of these processes are experienced in reverse after death. The laws of the etheric and astral bodies will have to engage our attention in the studies that follow.

STUDY 14

DEATH, MORALITY, AND TIME

It is not until Leading Thought 24 that Steiner specifically refers to spiritual beings of a higher world who, during the night, judge human soul experiences. After death, awareness of such judgment is unhindered. This addresses a potent cosmic moral process, toward which we need a new approach in regard to the question of freedom. In progressing from the ordinary conscious experience of freedom to a higher experience of freedom, our *understanding with ourselves* changes to an understanding with beings of the spiritual world (study 12). Thus, investigation into conditions after death is a spiritual conversation—true *inspiration*. What, for the spiritual investigator, constitutes a gain toward free being, is law for the ordinary human being.

In ancient Mystery tradition, the experience in the astral body after death is illustrated by Moses' appearance showing the dead a record of their sins and, at the same time, pointing to *hard and fast law* or holding before him the tablets of the Law.[1] A glass window in the first Goetheanum, now destroyed, showed the reversed life after death, and the gigantic tablets of the law are shown above at the starting point. In other worldviews, similar descriptions are preserved—for example, in the Egyptian concept of meeting the judges of the dead. Thus there is a necessity in addition to that of nature—its other side, which is morality, or the picture of the true human being as seen by spiritual beings.[2]

Each night we stand before the law of this vision. We can picture their effects even when awake. In this sense, we may add to some earlier psychological observations (study 10). The dreamy mood immediately after awaking reflects in a certain sense our night experiences—it continues their effect. We are averse to being spoken to immediately after awaking; it's like being slightly out of tune. And, when we practice observing the impressions of the spiritual world, we notice a very distinct mood of a bad conscience, which can spread to the experiences of the entire day. This is the voice of our own true being, which, during the night, stood before a vision of its home. What constitutes law for ordinary consciousness in this sense, or necessity for the moral world, is achieved in freedom on the path of initiation. Thus, it is said that one must take three steps in morality before taking one in spiritual knowledge.

---

1   *From Jesus to Christ*, lecture 3.

2   See *Anthroposophy and the Inner Life*, lectures 8 and 9 (previously titled *Anthroposophy: An Introduction*).

Leading Thought 24 touches on another problem, the most difficult of all—that of time. After death, time runs backward in the experiences in the soul realm, contrary to time between birth and death. We are not very concerned about the ways philosophy and science have struggled unsuccessfully with the problem of time. Even the distinction between objective and subjective time interests us only insofar as it gives us a shining example of how we may overcome the illusion of the "objective" by transforming the "subjective" into the spiritual. It is especially characteristic of the path of spiritual knowledge that something higher will overcome the distinction between subjective and objective by transforming the subjective.

Ordinary scientific consciousness recognizes only one direction of time— that the essential distinction between time and space is that the direction of time cannot be reversed. This is a completely one-sided judgment, arrived at from the perspective of *objective* time. Even the inner experience of time related to ordinary consciousness demonstrates a variation in flow, depending on whether it is tedious or amusing—time sometimes creeps, at other times it races. Ordinary consciousness, however, also shows indications of time running in reverse.

An incorrigible thinker (and, indeed, that is today's scientist) knows only time that flows from the past into the present. This is because thinking is directed toward the past, but the will is directed toward the future; it belongs to the opposing stream flowing from the future into the present. The present is not time; outwardly it is space, inwardly it is feeling. We can understand space as having fallen out of time, in the sense that the present attains duration. This points to an equilibrium, or mutual damming, of the two streams of time. Language understands something about the spatial quality of the present: The exhibition was opened in the presence of the Secretary of State.

At the same time, it is only indicated here that time may also be understood as having fallen out of causality, from beyond space and time. Natural scientific method uses it in precisely this way, classifying phenomena in terms of cause and effect. It can be seen that concrete investigation runs contrary to the objective flow of time, moving from present phenomenon, understood as *effect*, to an earlier *cause*, which is further assumed to be the effect of a cause even farther back in time, and so on. This is the method of investigation; if its results are presented as a system, one progresses forward in time from some starting point and offers explanations that go from causes to effects. This, in fact, follows the direction of the will. We will look at these relationships in later studies.

In accordance with Spiritual Science, it may be said that time runs its course in cycles, which reveal only one side to ordinary consciousness; Steiner points to the other side. From birth to death, we travel in one direction; in the soul world after death, we travel in the other direction, returning to our birth in the spiritual realm. According to Steiner's interpretations, the return to the spiritual realm is what it meant by becoming *as little children*.[1] Then we enter the *timeless*, or spiritual, from which we were born. Seen from the spiritual perspective, we dive down into time and return again out of time.

By overcoming the concept of time in this way, we also gain knowledge of repeated earth lives. Now, one could argue that *objective* time from one earth life to the next runs on as it does in sleep; we reach the timeless and return. Nevertheless, we can also understand that cosmic rhythms and cycles relate to a consciousness greater than our day, greater than our earthly life, greater than our whole sequence of Earth lives. These cycles have yet another side where they arise from time again. In *An Outline of Esoteric Science*, as well as other places, Steiner speaks of cosmic days and cosmic nights, even cosmic years. We have also found an image in miniature for this—*nature*, which reveals objective time, found where spirit sleeps (Leading Thought 18).

26. We enter the spiritual world only after the astral body has been laid aside, when the conscious judgment of life has ended. There we stand, similar to beings of purely spiritual nature, just as on Earth we were similar to the beings and processes of nature. In spiritual experience, everything that constituted our outer world on Earth now becomes our inner world. We no longer merely perceive it, but its spiritual being, which was hidden from us on Earth, is experienced now as our own inner world.

27. In the spirit realm, human beings as they are on Earth become an outer world. We see them just as on Earth we see stars, clouds, mountains, and rivers. Nor is this "outer world" any less rich in essence than the glory of the cosmos as it appears in earthly life.

28. *Forces*, born of the human spirit in the spirit realm, continue to shape earthly humankind, just as our actions in the physical realm continue to act as substance for our soul in the life after death.

---

1   See *Founding a Science of the Spirit*, lecture 3; and *Background to the Gospel of St. Mark*, lecture 6.

EXERCISE IN THOUGHT

Anthroposophy, as a path of knowledge, leads away from the illusion of one-sided time. According to the results of our earlier studies, we may describe it by saying that the past being of thinking is changed into the future being of willing. We must seek spirit along paths of the future; in ancient times, spirit was sought along the paths of the past. When we consider the change of places by thinking and willing (see Study 7), we can realize, by passing into the spiritual world, how the understanding of relationships by ordinary consciousness is completely reversed. Descriptions of the entry into spirit country after death (Leading Thoughts 26–28) will also become understandable. There is certainly a much more radical interchange of functions, so that the phrase *turning inside out* becomes increasingly justified. Transitions there make this way of being possible for the dead. Rudolf Steiner described these transitions in *Theosophy*. It will be found that this concerns thought exercises through which those inverted laws can be understood. It is simply a matter of forming correct concepts of spirit country.

Concepts are the spirit country's conscious participation in ordinary consciousness. Concepts arise, however, in relation to a sense-perceptible environment, and it is good to practice comprehending the relation between concepts and corresponding percepts. Steiner repeatedly mentioned this—for example, in *Intuitive Thinking as a Spiritual Path*. Suitable exercises may be found in *Theosophy* and in *How to Know Higher Worlds*. Thought exercises—in an earnest, spiritual sense, not merely entertaining thoughts—are unappreciated today, particularly in circles that seek a mystical approach to higher worlds. But, to understand the way of knowledge indicated in the Leading Thoughts, such exercises are indispensable. If a person embarks on them in view of an earnest approach to life, thought exercises afford great joy and genuine inner warmth.

In the chapter "The Essential Nature of the Human Being" in *Theosophy*, Steiner characterizes the human being as a citizen of three worlds, insofar as we are body, soul, and spirit. He speaks of three worlds in relation to three fundamentally different human principles. Under the subheading "The Spiritual Nature of the Human Being," thinking is presented as a standard for the spiritual. A later chapter, "The Country of Spirit Beings," says, "this spiritual world is woven out of the 'substance' that constitutes human thought" (p. 123). Thus, when the archetypes primal forces of spirit country are mentioned in this connection, we have the opportunity to ask how their shadowy images live in human thoughts.

In *Theosophy*, the passage that describes the first region, or "continental mass" of spirit country, uses the comparison of spatial cavities that may be imagined by thinking away the substance of things in physical space. The activity of the archetypes plays between these cavities (pp. 127–128). In other connections Steiner once said, "If we look at the spiritual aspect of things, their qualities appear around them. If we observe the way thoughts are connected with things—from their appearance penetrate to their real being—we find this description to be absolutely correct: the qualities appear in the surroundings."[1]

An example will help to clarify this. Take a crystal of common salt—a cube, transparent, sharp to the taste, fairly soft and sticky to the touch, and so on. These are qualities of the senses, even though instruments can observe and specify them more precisely. But that is not the essential aspect toward which thinking is directed. This approach observes only something finished, or complete, as a phenomenon; the crystal has really been emptied of its essential being. How different it is when we consider its coming into being. Out of a saturated solution, out of liquid, it takes form from six directed forces of cosmic space. There it is, pushed out of the mother liquor. If we wish to find the essential forces, we have them in this solution—that is, in their true environment. In this way, thoughts can begin to work, even if they are mere shadows of spiritual realities.

Thus, as a practice, we can completely invert the method of observation in ordinary consciousness. We can also extend this to other things and, in this way, attain genuine exercises of spiritual sight. For example, we can try to feel our way into the plastic negative of a human being. By doing this, something of that person's spiritual aspect enters the field of vision—for example, how strongly an important person stands in space, or the way a nose sticks out into the air. It will become apparent that we would be wise to look for spirit in our surroundings.

It then becomes a matter of applying these exercises of the negative image to the moral element and to the question of destiny. In the highest sense, the first Goetheanum (now destroyed by fire) could shape the soul. Its supple forms originated from the spirit of true beauty to become constant spirit meditations. We may also become aware of this spiritual influence in the way the forms of capitals and bases, and especially the architraves, rose and sank as a kind of spiritual breathing, forming arches and hollows. And we can experience the correspondence between protruding forms in one place and receding forms in another. One form became the spiritual reality of another. Steiner sometimes spoke of such sculptural correspondences in the old Goetheanum.

---

1   The source of this quote is unknown.

Through such means, we can approach what was said in Leading Thoughts 26–28, and something else may become clear. This applies to thinking specifically when it wishes to comprehend not only the spiritual in itself (thinking) but also thinking in the spirit country. We learned from previous studies how thinking transforms itself into willing. Something else takes place along with this, and we must consider it in a continuation of what was said about the reversal of time. In the physical realm, space provides the given, soul projects into it as time, and spirit acts as causality.

Causality as a factor of law has a definite flow, just as time has in the physical realm. In spirit country, however, its direction is exactly reversed. This means that, considering such a process in the light of time or if a spiritual element of this region is revealed in the physical, we must deal with causality in its higher regions going in the opposite direction; effect precedes the cause. Therefore, in *Theosophy*, the upper region of the spirit country is called the "Region of Intentions" (pp. 129–130). *Intent* refers to the fact that effects are thought of as prior to causes.

Through such exercises we can familiarize ourselves with how the outer world is experienced as the inner world after death in spirit country (Leading Thought 26). What was outer world approaches the realm of intentions from which it had flowed before birth. Likewise, the inner world becomes outer when one expands to the cosmos (Leading Thought 27). Leading Thought 28 shows the tremendous significance and consequences of outer and inner destiny. The midnight hour of existence is the powerful turning point that transcends causality, and it is the last great reversal for the "I"-being in the entire after-death experience of spirit country. Steiner spoke of the mysteries of this turning point in the sequence of experiences between death and rebirth. He did so only after his mystery plays had awakened a deep feeling for this mystery in those who took part in their performances in Munich.[2]

It is evident from Steiner's writings how, in the mysteries after death, we gradually withdraw from our last incarnation, and a new perspective opens before us.[3] Thus, we review earlier earthly lives and view those of the future, becoming able to see into their karmic relationship. This happens according to the ruling hierarchies of spiritual beings. In our work on the leading thoughts, we approach a description of destiny and the relationship between humankind and the hierarchies. Therefore, we must fulfill a few preliminary conditions, and a series of leading thoughts will help us in this way.

> 29. What lives as soul and spirit in the inner life of human beings is at work in evolved *imaginative knowledge*. It fashions the physical body in its life and unfolds human existence in the physical world on its bodily founda-

2   See *The Souls' Awakening*, Steiner's fourth mystery play.

3   See *Secrets of the Threshold*, lecture 1; and *The Inner Nature of Man and the Life between Death and Rebirth*, lecture 2.

tion. In contrast to the physical body, whose substances are constantly renewed through metabolism, we arrive at the inner human nature, which continually unfolds itself from birth (or conception) until death. Facing the physical body in space, we come to a body in time.

30. What we experience in a spiritual environment between death and a new birth lives in the form of pictures as *inspired knowledge*. Here, without the physical and etheric bodies we use to go through earthly life, what we are in our own being is revealed in relation to cosmic worlds.

31. In the *intuitive knowledge* we become aware of how former earthly lives work into the present. As they evolved, previous lives were divested of past connections with the physical world. They became the purely spiritual core of the human being and, as such, are active in the present life. In this way, they are also an object of knowledge—the *knowledge* that results through further unfolding of *imagination* and *inspiration*.

THREEFOLD ORGANIZATION AND MORALITY

In the German periodical *Anthroposophie* (vol. 8, no. 4), a series of my articles appeared entitled "A Debt of Honor to Rudolf Steiner." Their subject was the threefold organization of the human being, one of Steiner's groundbreaking discoveries and one of the greatest spiritual acts of all time.[1] It supplies the indispensable unifying bond between natural and Spiritual Science. In his *Autobiography* Steiner speaks very modestly of this discovery, which is decisive for broad areas of spiritual life. After unsuccessful attempts to build a new social order on this discovery—the threefold commonwealth—during Christmas 1923, Steiner used it as the basis for reestablishing the Anthroposophical Society.

The threefold structure of the human being can be summed up as follows:

> The physical counterparts to the soul element of mental representation may be seen in the processes of the nervous system that radiate into the sense organs on the one hand, and into the inner organization of the body on the other. [Feeling must be brought into relationship] with the life rhythm centered in the activity of breathing, with which it is connected.... [Indeed, this] must be followed into the outermost periphery of the organism.... In regard to the will, we find that this depends in a similar way on metabolic processes. Again, we must take into consideration everything that plays a role in the branching out and ramification of the processes of metabolism in the whole organism.[2]

Steiner shows that, in regard to the consciousness of these soul processes and their basis in the body, that "fully conscious experience exists only in the act of mental representation conveyed by the nervous system." Everything of a feeling nature has only the strength of consciousness "characteristic of dream images." And the will has only the very dull consciousness "that exists in sleep."

In addition to this there are the relationships "that the soul element of ordinary consciousness carries into the life of the spirit." The "spiritual reality that forms the basis for representation in ordinary consciousness [can] be experienced only through knowledge that arises from sight." It reveals itself in *imaginations*. Feeling flows from the spiritual side, "out of a spiritual essence

---

1   Carl Unger, "The Necessity of an Anthroposophical Movement and the Work of Rudolf Steiner."

2   *Riddles of the Soul.*

found through anthroposophic research using the methods characterized in my writings as *inspiration....* Willing streams from spirit for the seeing consciousness through what I call true *intuitions*."[1]

Riddles of the Soul (chapter 4) indicates the ways of physiological research and their hindrances. Contemporary science offers an excellent basis for the fact that representations must be based in the nervous system. In order to recognize that the rhythm of breathing forms the basis for feeling, physiological research must be followed up in a very unusual way. Biases exist even there, because people allow only the soul qualities related to nerve processes. Feeling is treated, therefore, as a mere characteristic of representation. Willing is omitted entirely—it is not even seen as a characteristic of representation. Clear thinking in this area requires that physiological and psychological investigations be directed toward the interaction of nerve activity, the rhythm of breathing, and metabolic activity.

The discovery of the human threefold structure is, as a free act, created out of spirit and placed into the world of sense observation. In this way, it is handed over to the developing freedom of humankind; they can do with it as they wish. The *Age of the Consciousness Soul* has truly arrived; the determining factor for centuries emanates from the ordinary consciousness of individual human beings.

> What is necessary for the future must arise from human beings as individuals. We cannot wait for a cosmic message, which humanity would then follow. Such a message will never come. What can come from the spiritual worlds, however, will be able to shine forth in every individual soul.[2]

Events after the fifteenth century were merely a prelude. First there were great discoveries in the mineral realms, in physics and chemistry. They did not remain in the realm of science, however, but were carried into ordinary life by the consciousness soul; thus, modern technology arose. Natural science and technology, as they have arisen in our time, carry with them no moral responsibility—they are amoral; they can be used as a blessing or a curse. The same activity of consciousness can build a bridge or a murderous weapon. Traditional morality, which constrained souls to some extent, is rapidly disappearing.

> Natural science attempts to eliminate morality altogether from its consideration, and morality begins to come to terms with the fact that no physically supporting forces dwell within it. The dogmatism of certain religious beliefs tries to form ideas that are a sort of compromise with natural science, inasmuch as the scientist points out that a sharp line should be

---

1   Ibid.

2   *Anthroposophische Lebensgaben* ("Anthroposophic Life Gifts"), lecture 4 .

drawn between what is moral and what is physical, chemical, geological, and so on.[3]

There, decisions are ripening of a kind that can only be turned to the good by souls spiritually conscious, and herein lies one of the most important tasks of Anthroposophy.

The discoveries of modern times arise from ordinary consciousness; questions of morality become infinitely more important with the discovery of the human threefold organization. It must indeed be noted Steiner's presentation of this in *Riddles of the Soul* is entitled "How the Human Being Depends on the Physical and Spiritual." In this way, it addresses a duality, because the soul's experience exists between bodily and spiritual reality, where it finds the path to freedom.

Let us imagine that we were robbed of this discovery by Steiner—that the moral foundation in the twofold activity of the soul were lost or destroyed. Add to this the fact that not only is there a tendency to abolish the spirit but to consider the soul a mere characteristic of the body. Let us observe that Theodor Ziehen, in his *Physiological Psychology* quoted by Steiner, finds no reason to assume the existence of a special faculty of will. He speaks of tones of feeling only as qualities, or characteristics, of sensation and representations. Then we can be clear that Steiner's discovery presents us with an extraordinary danger. In other words, only one side—the soul's dependence on the three bodily organizations—is physiologically and psychologically investigated; the other aspect, spirit, is completely ignored. In that case, an unheard-of misuse of that discovery will occur. Humankind will even discover a definite means to control thinking by working on the nervous system, control human feeling by working on the rhythmic system, and control the human will by acting on the metabolic system. That would then be the third act of the threatening tragedy of humanity (mentioned in Study 11 as the abolition of spirit and soul). Materialistic doctors of medicine will then completely dominate humankind. There is already a novel of the future describing this domination by Doctors as a complete enslavement in every domain; it is a harrowing description of physicians' intoxication with power.

This enormous danger arises, because Steiner's work has been handed over to human freedom. And there is only one protection from this danger; the Anthroposophical Movement must nurture the other side—the discovery of the spiritual aspect. This requires that the way of knowledge shown by Steiner—thinking, feeling, and willing—be freed from subordination to the physical organism; thus, the means mentioned for the enslaving of the soul cannot work. Due to the evolution of modern times, thinking has already reached a high degree of selflessness. If we can take the step to pure thinking as outlined in *Intuitive Thinking as a Spiritual Path*, thinking frees itself from

---

3   *Building Stones for an Understanding of the Mystery of Golgotha*, lecture 4.

domination by the body, or nervous system. The force of *imagination* grows from this.

The next step is much more difficult: to transform feeling into *inspiration* by making it equally selfless. Selfless feeling is *love*; it shows the characteristics of *inspiration* within ordinary consciousness and leads to mutual understanding between human beings. Love, as an inspirational force of knowledge, frees feeling from its slavery to the body's rhythmic system. This third step leads to selfless willing, transforming it into *intuition*. Selfless willing is devotion and sacrifice. This leads to entering the being of others, and it reveals even in ordinary consciousness, when possible, the characteristics of *intuition*. Devotion, as an *intuitional* force of knowledge, frees the will from subjugation to the body's metabolic system.

Pure thinking, love, and devotion constitute the path to freedom for humanity.

TRANSFORMATIONS

Leading Thoughts 29 to 31 present the relationship of higher stages of knowledge to the principles of the human being and the experience of passing from one earthly life to another. If we do not avoid the difficult task of following this relationship in detail, important anthroposophic knowledge can develop. It is immediately apparent that *imaginative* knowledge is related to the etheric body, *inspired* knowledge to the astral body, and *intuitive* knowledge to the "I." Similarly, if we take a step back, we can see that the knowledge of ordinary consciousness must be based on the physical body. This must not be confused with materialistic ideas about brain functions. Rudolf Steiner gave much attention to this problem.

> The brain is a part of the physical body, and nothing related to our essential life of thinking—nothing brought about by the knowledge-producing activity of our soul—reaches as far as the physical body. This occurs, instead, in the three higher principles of the human entity, from the "I," through the astral body, down to the etheric body.... Superficially, of course, contemporary philosophers and psychologists point to the fact that certain processes occur in the brain during the act of discernment.... In terms of what actually happens in the soul when we visualize and think, brain activity has precisely the same significance as a mirror in which we look at ourselves. When the brain is active, the three higher principles of the human organization become spiritually active. In order for this to be perceived by the individual concerned, the brain becomes necessarily as a mirror so that, reflected in it, we perceive what we are spiritually.... If, as an earthly being of today, humankind did not have this reflective bodily organism—especially the brain—we would indeed think thoughts, but we would know nothing about them.[1]

Without higher principles there would be no human consciousness and no knowledge at all. Experience of the higher principles of the physical body brings about ordinary consciousness. We can also say that an unconscious *imaginative*, *inspired*, and *intuitive* knowledge forms the basis of ordinary knowledge; it is colored, however, by the physical body. In our first study, we already noted how these appear in the various stages of growth in the human being. We also find a connection with previous studies in another sense. The physical body itself appears as the "boundary of knowledge," which Steiner

---

1   *Wonders of the World, Ordeals of the Soul, Revelations of the Spirit*, lecture 7.

speaks of in Leading Thought 2. And, according to Leading Thought 3, when we again and again become conscious of standing at this boundary, we also realize from our last study what it means to free ourselves from bondage to the physical body. Little by little, thinking, feeling, and willing are thus transformed into *imagination, inspiration,* and *intuition.* And, at the same time, we become conscious by means of the etheric body, the astral body, and, eventually, the "I." In this way, the soul—thus far dependant on the physical organism—acquires spiritual support, as Steiner pointed out in *Riddles of the Soul,* mentioned in our last study.

Steiner often spoke of yet another transformation. The "I" takes hold of the three lower principles of human beings—the physical, etheric, and astral bodies—thus creating sevenfold beings and transforming them into *spirit self, life spirit* and *spirit body.*[1] The whole process may be presented as follows, but this should not be seen as an abstract diagram, for it concerns human beings; the surrounding lines may be viewed as the sheath of the "I."

ORDINARY CONSCIOUSNESS

BODY	physical body	etheric body	astral body
SOUL	willing	feeling	thinking
SPIRIT	Spirit body	Life spirit	Spirit self

IMAGINATIVE CONSCIOUSNESS

BODY	physical body	etheric body	astral body
SOUL	willing	feeling	thinking
SPIRIT	Spirit body	Life spirit	Spirit self

INSPIRATIONAL CONSCIOUSNESS

BODY	physical body	etheric body	astral body
SOUL	willing	feeling	thinking
SPIRIT	Spirit body	Life spirit	Spirit self

INTUITIVE CONSCIOUSNESS

BODY	physical body	etheric body	astral body
SOUL	willing	feeling	thinking
SPIRIT	Spirit body	Life spirit	Spirit self

Leading Thought 29 mentions some functions that characterize the essence of *imagination* in relation to the physical body. These functions are expressed in the physical body's growth and when this essential being

---

1   See note on the term *spirit body* at end of this study.

unfolds inwardly as consciousness.[2] Thus, *imaginative* knowledge is the "I"-being's activity that becomes conscious in the etheric body. In ordinary consciousness, the essence of higher knowledge comes up against the physical body. Likewise, *inspired* knowledge is the "I"-being's activity that becomes conscious in the astral body; and *intuitive* knowledge indicates the "I"-being becoming self-aware.

This developing consciousness at various stages signifies, at the same time, experience of the world at increasingly higher levels, or entrance into the worlds of higher beings. From this, it becomes clear that it is the essence of this higher knowledge that has shaped humankind on the physical plane. For this reason, human beings, too, cannot understand their own being merely through facts of the physical world; we are not of this world.

Furthermore, Leading Thought 29 shows how what is constant between birth and death in the human being confronts the physical body, which is constantly renewed by the metabolic processes. This points to the nature of the etheric body. The physical body, in itself, has no reality, only form in a certain sense. Steiner gives us descriptions of the highest importance about the human and about the illusory character of the physical.[3] What is physical in humankind belongs to the external physical world, which, according to its laws, can only destroy the physical body. Only what possesses permanence between birth and death is the reality of human beings. The etheric body is referred to as a *time body*, as opposed to the *space body*. The etheric body, as shown in Study 13, gathers the experiences of the waking consciousness and holds them together. The etheric body provides continuity amid change; it forms the human physical body and memory. As far as memory extends, human beings have inner form.

We experience the events of waking life between birth and death as passing time; the etheric body gives them a permanent cohesiveness. This is a kind of synchronization. The experience of time passing does not arise from the etheric body; we shall soon see its source. The etheric body's characteristic realization of permanence is always present. *Imagination* knows it and, after death, it arises as a panorama of life. It already existed, however, before death and contains all at once the experience of waking life going back to birth, though it could not be perceived by ordinary consciousness. *Imagination* sees it as a whole before death; but ordinary consciousness sees only a wavering shadow of it as memory. The physical body is designated as a "space body"; it falls away at death. At that point, the etheric body becomes space. What we experience as time before death appears as space

---

2   See *The Bhagavad Gita and the West*, lecture 7; and *The Being of Man and His Future Evolution*.

3   See *Man in the light of Occultism, Theosophy, and Philosophy*, lecture 5; and *Background to the Gospel of St. Mark*, lecture 5.

in the life panorama surrounding the human being after death; *imagination* transforms time into space.[1]

EDITOR'S NOTE: Rudolf Steiner's term *Geistesmensch,* translated literally, means "spirit human being" or, as in previous translations, "spirit man." In theosophical language, and in the earliest editions of *Theosophy,* it is called Atman (as the spirit self is called Manas and the Life Spirit is called Budhi). *Geistesmensch,* or "spirit human being," is the physical body transformed by the "I," and "spirit body" is the least ambiguous and confusing translation. Cf. *The Spiritual Hierarchies and the Physical World,* p. 47: "Outwardly the physical body appears a physical body, but inwardly it is completely controlled and permeated by the 'I.' At this stage, the physical body is both physical body *and* Atman." See also, Rudolf Steiner, *The Gospel of St. John:* "[The human being] will finally reach the point where, by means of the 'I' he [or she] will transform the physical body also. The part of the physical body that is transformed by the 'I' is called Atman, or spirit man" (p 36); and: "The physical body will be so greatly metamorphosed that it will, at the same time, be as truly a spirit man, Atman, as it is now a physical body" (p. 116).

---

1   *Earthly Death and Cosmic Life,* lecture 3.

THE ART OF THINKING

Rudolf Steiner has often spoken of the lack of a true art of thinking in our age. He pointed to Scholasticism; its instrument of thought was very subtly ground to sculpt fine concepts that could understand spirit and penetrate the boundary, on the other side of which were the revelations of Christian tradition.

> In the time of the Scholastics—the Thomists and so on—philosophers who expressed concepts as a fine conceptual art were in contact with the spiritual world.... People will be able to appreciate Scholasticism only when, by reexamining it, they are taught how a finer, more highly organized way of thinking can be developed than is practiced today.[2]

In lectures at the Goetheanum in January 1924, Steiner referred to Aristotle, who established Western thought and natural science. Before his time, thinking was still a kind of cosmic perception that, to a large extent, was part of the etheric world (*sublunary sphere*). The transition to the Middle Ages included the belief that thinking is a product of the inner human being. Steiner showed this in the relevant chapter in *The Riddles of Philosophy*.[3] In modern times, thinking threatens to vanish into subjectivity. It is necessary, therefore, to permeate thinking with willing, so we can form it into *imagination* as an active organ of knowledge for the etheric realm. It will then become an authentic human element of cosmic processes in the future. We will consider this in later leading thoughts related to the mission of Michael.

Aristotle's logic created and trained independent thinking. He gave the essential training for thinking in his *Categories*, which molded the primeval wisdom of the Mysteries into ideas. In our time, these Categories have degenerated into lifeless ideas; one cannot imagine anything more abstract. In the lectures mentioned, Steiner warned that we should revive these lifeless ideas in humankind. This can be done through working on the consciousness soul, where ideas become cosmic again. Step by step, Steiner's efforts show the path on which thinking can live again, so that it can finally follow his spiritual researches by recreating them. In this way, however, he has left us the task of *securing his investigations through eternal thoughts*. He laid the foundations everywhere by shaping entirely new concepts. We are

---

2   *The Karma of Materialism*, lecture 7.
3   *The Riddles of Philosophy*.

called on to weave them into a new art of thinking, as Scholasticism did for Aristotle's efforts. We can point to this task in many of the leading thoughts and find the path leading to it.

Such new concepts underlie, for example, the terms *etheric body, astral body*, and so on, which Steiner used to make the corresponding spiritual facts available to ordinary thinking. We must successfully transform the rigid Categories into living thoughts; we must again make them flexible and mobile within us, so that concepts such as *imagination, inspiration,* and *intuition* are the result. Once this is done, we have taken a step forward in continuing Steiner's work.

This kind of stimulation can arise from Leading Thoughts 29 to 31; thus, at the end of our previous study, we arrived at the statement: *Imagination transforms time into space.* This is an attempt to loosen the Categories and show how we can lead one fundamental state of thinking to another, saving it from rigidity and leading it to *becoming.* The phrase itself may sound familiar (as in Wagner's *Parsifal*); but its significance is neither symbolic nor, indeed, abstract, since what must be expressed, depends on how such exercises are practiced. When he speaks of the first experiences after death, Steiner refers to this statement:

> It is just as Wagner expressed it out of a deep intuition: *Time becomes space.* The past is certainly not past for spiritual experience, but exists just as, for physical human beings, natural objects exist in space.[1]

It is characteristic of the shortsighted thinking of our time that we do not think matters through to the end. Such a statement is certainly present, but it is necessary to follow it farther. This is indicated in Leading Thoughts 30 and 31. *Inspired knowledge* gives an insight into the experience of the astral body both before and after death. In the foregoing Study, the question arose: What is the origin of the realization of time's flow? According to studies 8 and 14, we can easily see that it arises from the astral body. However, we must be definite about the difference between *being* and *experience*.

Human experience is always connected with the "I"; but, according to the entity where experience occurs, something else manifests. When this is expressed through thinking, corresponding concepts arise. Leading Thought 29 describes the etheric body as a *time body*; its being is essentially *time*. Its essence, however, is not realized in ordinary consciousness but, as we have seen, produces the experience of *space*.

We must make the same distinction in relation to the astral body; it produces the experience of *time*—flowing forward between birth and death and backward after the spatial experience of the etheric body ebbs after death. What is its essence, or basic nature? There is an expression that may be added

---

1   *The Destinies of Individuals and of Nations*, lecture 7.

as a third element—an extension of space and time: causality, the concept of *one because of another*, just as time is a concept of *one after another*, and space the concept of *one next to another*.

The relationship between cause and effect is only an inadequate and one-sided expression of what we are calling *causality*. By this, we mean something living and linked to motives and impulses—an activity.[2] We tried to show in Studies 8 and 14 how judgment may be attributed to the astral body, which is judged during sleep (Leading Thought 24). This does not contradict the fact that we are referring to the astral body's essential nature as "causality." Living judgment unites motives. In logic, it is said that, for every judgment there must be sufficient cause. We imagine cause and effect by looking one-sidedly at the phenomena we inwardly call "reason" and "consequence." This activity is essentially what we mean by the word *causality*.

Between death and rebirth, we find ourselves in a world whose substance forms our astral body.[3] One side of this is our experience of being judged again and again during the night in such a state. There is another side, however, that is not completed by looking back at our past earthly life and being judged. The other side of our experience of the astral body between death and new birth can again be compared with a judgment. This, however, does not work like the judgment between birth and death, which mainly refers to something finished; rather, the future earth life is being shaped through this judgment. When we speak of destiny, we concretely approach the living essence that reveals itself abstractly as *causality*. Thus we can say: experience communicated by the astral body is *time* flowing forward between birth and death and backward after death, once the etheric body has been laid aside. The living essence of the astral body is causality. Inspiration is the astral body's way of knowledge leading from experience to being: Inspiration transforms causality into time.

Now we must consider a third step. Leading Thought 31 points to the kernel of the human being, the "I." Again we may ask: Who presents us with the experience of causality? It is the "I"-being, the bearer of destiny from one earthly life to another. The "I"-being, however, belongs to a sphere that requires an even higher conceptual form in the series of space, time, and causality. This fourth form does not appear in a table of Categories, yet only it can conclude this series, beyond which it cannot continue. Only by the living concept of *through itself* can follow the concepts of *one beside another*, *one after another*, and *one because of another*. This may be called *permanence of being*. Spinoza was aware of this when he spoke of *its own cause*, or a

---

2   In *A Psychology of Body, Soul, and Spirit*, Steiner emphasized that the word *judgment*, when used in relation to the astral body, has the quality of the verb *judging* (see "Aspects of Soul Life," lecture 1 of "Psychosophy").

3   See *Earthly and Cosmic Man*, lecture 7.

being that exists in and of itself. It constitutes in human beings our pure spiritual kernel (Leading Thought 31). *Intuition* is the way of knowledge for the "I"-being, the "I" who passes from one life to another. According to what has been said, we may add: *Intuition* transforms permanent being into causality.

SPIRITUAL-SCIENTIFIC COPERNICANISM

We are accustomed to regarding our way in the world from the perspective of earthly life; initially that is what we are given. By working
on the consciousness soul, however, we gradually shift our perspective to the
spiritual world, where we can partake in the life between death and rebirth. If,
in Copernicus, there was something great and daring, it was the transmittal
of his mathematical perspective from Earth to the Sun, even though it went
against the experience of the senses. This was an act of thinking, independent
thinking from his own being.

Thus, human thinking became free of traditional, earthly bondage. This
occurred at the beginning of the age of the consciousness soul. Thinking rose
above the Earth, even became selfless—but only in order to begin to master
the Earth in the succeeding age, in order to serve the lowest human needs. The
beings who guide humanity led human beings to Earth; ancient spirit and soul
life consisted in the knowledge of this fact, and in the future, humankind must
again look to the cosmos.[1] This is the task of Anthroposophy in its work on
the consciousness soul.

When we understand through ordinary consciousness the nightly entry of
our astral body and "I"-being into the cosmos and how we return after death
to our primeval home, we begin to overcome the gravity of the earth, which
has enabled humankind to gain independence and freedom. By understanding
the significance of higher states of knowledge—*imagination, inspiration,* and
intuition—we gain the capacity to comprehend the meaning of earthly life
arising from cosmic impulses *sub specie aeternitatis,* or as an aspect of eternity. Anthroposophy, as Spiritual Science, teaches us to understand human
cosmic being through earthly consciousness; Anthroposophy, as evolution of
the soul, leads us to shape earthly lives out of the cosmos.

In previous studies, our transformation, or interpretation, of the
Categories related to human beings growing out into the cosmos and the
return of human beings to their primeval spiritual home.[2] The return journey,
however, is just as important—from the cosmos into a new earthly life. This
follows the same direction as the activity of creation in the past, through
which Earth and humankind were formed. In the leading thoughts that fol-

---

1   See Rudolf Steiner, *The Gospel of St. John,* lecture 6; also *The Gospel of St. John in
     Relation to the Other Gospels,* lecture 2.

2   See *Life Between Death and Rebirth,* lectures 2, 5, and 10.

low, we will see that this is the how the Categories came about, through a similar transformation. Human beings repeat this process with every new incarnation and, in the future we will increasingly find it our task to continue the work of creation in conjunction with the hierarchies of the creative spiritual beings. This demonstrates the way our perspective can change through work on the consciousness soul.

Out of divine creation, it is our human heritage to experience the human soul as thinking, feeling, and willing, based on the human threefold organism and sustained in a tripartite way out of spirit (Study 16). It is the talent entrusted to us, and we should use it well; it the light we should not hide under a bushel. In the following leading thoughts, the head, the limb and metabolic system, and the rhythmic system are shown to be the result of creation as the human soul enters its field of activity. These leading thoughts may be seen in terms of this shift in perspective:

32. The physical organization and the spiritual individuality of the human being are impressed, or manifested, in the human head. The physical and the etheric aspect of the head are expressed as complete, self-contained images of the spiritual. Beside these, existing independently as soul and spirit, is the astral and "I" aspect. Thus, the human head expresses the development of a relatively independent physical and etheric, on the one hand, and the astral and organization, on the other.

33. In the human limbs and metabolism, the four members of the human being are intimately related to one another. The "I" and astral body are not present next to the physical and etheric aspect. They are within them and vitalizing them, affecting their growth, faculty of movement, and so on. It is precisely because of this that the human limb and metabolic system is like a germinating seed, forever attempting to unfold—continually striving to become a head, and equally prevented during a human earthly lifespan.

34. The rhythmic organization exists in between. Here the "I"-being and astral body alternately unite with and free themselves from the physical and etheric aspect. The breathing and blood circulation are the physical impression of this alternating unification and loosening. The process of breathing in portrays the union, breathing out the loosening. Processes in the arterial blood represent the union, and those in the venous blood portray the loosening.

When we look at these leading thoughts in terms of the change in perspective, we get a living feeling that the human being, by descending into incarnation, has shared in the development of this threefold organization. Physiologists must certainly investigate these matters scientifically, but such investigation should be done thoroughly from an anthroposophic viewpoint in such a way that it is a kind of continuation of prenatal impulses. This becomes truly divine labor on the temple of humankind. Steiner's courses on natural science offer a wonderful example of this.

For general anthroposophic work with a certain philosophical tendency (as we try to develop it in our studies), it is important to create forms of thought and feeling that offer methodical help to the souls of those engaged in scientific investigations. Such investigators can then bring their results into general anthroposophic life.

We can gain significant knowledge merely by comparing Leading Thoughts 32–34 with one another. It happens that the human head is a finished work, the rhythmic system is half finished, and the system of limbs and metabolism is in embryo. This shows that the entire physical organization is scarcely more than half finished, and, as a result, we can definitely say that the other half of this creation is up to human beings themselves, who indeed shape the soul being as individuals. This brings us to one of the greatest revelations of Rudolf Steiner. In various places, he has explained human evolution in this way: *The destiny of humankind is to rise from created being to creator.*[1]

If we observe these three leading thoughts consecutively, we find new aspects that clarify our previous studies. The polarity between the head and the metabolic, limb system is clearly illustrated. We find, at the same time, the contrast between *within* and *side-by-side*, or between spirit and nature. The *within*, as expressed in Leading Thought 33, can be clearly experienced as what was called, in our previous study, the essence of *causality*. The *side-by-side* in Leading Thought 32 reveals the essence of *space*. The rhythmic element in Leading Thought 34 shows how the essence of *time* reveals the appearance and disappearance of the eternal.

In study 10, we saw that waking life is not simply defined, but continually interwoven by dreaming and sleep. It can be seen that the astral body and "I"-being unite with the physical and etheric bodies to different degrees. This points to the important fact that consciousness is asleep precisely where the astral body and "I"-being are active entirely within the physical and etheric bodies (specifically in the system of limbs and metabolism). On the other hand, consciousness is awake in the head, where the two groups exist side-by-side. And, just as dreaming is a mixture of waking and sleeping, so the rhythmic organization alternately shows the *side-by-side* and the *within*.

---

1   See *The Spiritual Hierarchies and the Physical World: Reality and Illusion*, lecture 9, especially pp. 138ff.

STUDY 20

ENTERING THE INNER BEING OF NATURE

Since *Riddles of the Soul* was first published, Rudolf Steiner has continually enlarged on his far-reaching discovery of the three principles of the human organism—particularly, their relationships with one another through repeated earthly lives. The head forms the completion of evolution. It is the result of the prenatal work of the I—its experience of the cosmos as reflected in the head.[1] Thus, the head forms a sphere.[2]

The sense organs are concentrated in the head, and because of them the cosmos is able to see physically and etherically into the human being during earthly life. But again, each individual sense organ is, in all its details, a copy of the whole human being.[3] In one lecture, for example, Steiner showed how the various parts of the ear represent an entire human being in miniature. In the head, the etheric body corresponds almost entirely with the physical body. The complete entry of the etheric body resulted during the course of human evolution in the possibility of self-awareness.[4] Because past evolution is portrayed in the head, and because the "I" has imprinted its being there, the head serves internally as a physical and etheric mirror for the "I"-being between birth and death, just as it does externally for the cosmos.[5] "I"-awareness arises through the reflection of consciousness and the other principles of the head.

The Leading Thoughts that follow contain profound words for understanding the physical out of the spiritual.

> 35. We understand the physical nature of the human being only when we view it as an image of soul and spirit. By itself, our physical substance is incomprehensible. Nevertheless, it is a picture of the soul and spirit in different ways in its various aspects. As a perceivable image of soul and spirit, the head is the most perfect and complete. Everything related to the system of metabolism and limbs is like an unfinished, or unformed, picture; however, it is still being worked on. And finally, everything related to the

---

1   See *The Spiritual Guidance of the Individual and Humanity*, pp. 62ff.

2   See *Earthly Death and Cosmic Life*, lecture 2.

3   For a thorough discussion by Steiner concerning the formation and activity of the senses, see *Anthroposophy (A Fragment)*, chaps. 2 and 7.

4   See *Rosicrucian Wisdom*, lecture 12; also *Cosmic Memory: Prehistory of Earth and Man*, chapter 18.

5   See *The Effects of Esoteric Development*, lecture 2; and *Human and Cosmic Thought*, lecture 4.

human rhythmic organization—the relationship of soul and spirit to the body—exists between these opposites.

36. When we contemplate the human head from this spiritual viewpoint, we find that it helps us to understand spiritual *imaginations*. In the forms of the head, *imaginative* forms are coagulated, as it were, to the point of physical density.

37. Similarly, when we contemplate the rhythmic aspect of the human organization, it helps us to understand *inspirations*. The character of *inspiration* is demonstrated by the physical appearance of the life rhythms—even presenting a sense-perceptible picture. Finally, in the system of the metabolism and the limbs, when we observe the full activity of its necessary or possible functions, we have a picture—suprasensory yet sensible—of pure spiritual *intuitions*.

The physical world is all surface to us. We try in vain to penetrate physically the inner being of an object. If we break it apart, we only create new surfaces that again obstruct entry. *The inner being is always spiritual.* When we emerge from sleep into physical consciousness, we often notice that dreams, as free-floating images—especially colors—spread over objects of the physical world and form their surface.[6] Likewise, we can experience, when falling asleep, how the surface of the physical world frees itself from objects. Wherever there is surface, the inner corresponds to the outer; surface constitutes the boundary.

Mathematics makes it easy to picture this phenomenon. Let us imagine a mathematical sphere; its surface forms the boundary between inner and outer. Before the sphere's boundary was established, inner and outer formed a whole; thus, according to the law of the sphere itself, every point, every form of what is within, must have a corresponding form outside. Projective geometry addresses this matter.

Through detailed spiritual scientific investigation, Steiner demonstrated that the inner aspect of Earth becomes increasingly spiritual as we approach its center. He showed how this corresponds exactly to what happens as we move away from the Earth's surface into the cosmos.[7] There is a sphere that helps us to recognize this immediately—the head. We must not, however, cut it open to see what it contains, since we would discover only more surface. If we remove the brain, we see that its essential feature is *surface*. We must instead experience our own head in a living way; in this way, we can recognize that sense perceptions are external, that thoughts are internal, and that they may correspond precisely with each other. When we transform thinking as described in Study 16, we find the *imaginative* world around us in place of the

6   *Founding a Science of the Spirit*, lecture 2.

7   Ibid., lecture 14 addendum.

sense world. The head forms a boundary shaped by thoughts internally, and shaped by sense perceptions externally; the boundary is common to both of these. This is *imagination* in the sense of Leading Thought 36.

The situation is different in the metabolic and limb system. Certainly we could also open it up and look at its contents, but this would reveal even more surface than the head. Of course, these remarks are not in the least intended to imply anything derogatory toward anatomy or surgery. We should just be clear that such manipulations relate only to the outer and do not penetrate the essential nature. The formative forces in the head have come to an end; they are at rest. Because the head is the imprint of the forces of the "I"-being, the "I" can acquire self-awareness in this being side by side; the "I" can use the head as its instrument.

The metabolic, limb system is not completely whole nor at rest like the head; on the contrary, its very nature is movement. It continually works to become head, and during our life on Earth it is constantly prevented from doing so (Leading Thought 33). After death, however, it pursues this effort unhindered and, influenced by the cosmos, it truly becomes head in the next incarnation—as far as the connection of forces is concerned, while the physical aspect is newly added. From his investigations, Steiner presented concrete details in his lectures about this connection between earthly lives. To become head signifies a release from formative forces. When the "I" is active in the head, the head remains at rest. If the "I"—or indeed the astral body—is active in the metabolic and limb system, this system is carried along and begins to move. Thus, the "I" cannot become self-aware in this region.

The "I" thinks in the head and wills in the limbs. This willing is a truly magical act; in the movement of the limbs, there is magic; in the metabolic processes, there is alchemy. The spirit works directly upon the physical. The metabolic, limb system is surface only for the ordinary waking consciousness, the magic of the will works within and, for this reasons is unconscious. The inner region is always spiritual; here, we are spiritually active in matter, but we do not know how. *Intuition* is a spiritual being within, spirit in spirit; in the metabolic, limb systems we have a sensible/suprasensory picture of the purely suprasensory *Intuitions* (Leading Thought 37). But it is expressly said, "If we observe it in full action, in the development of its necessary or possible functions." This is really a mobile concept; the sum of all possible actions is contained in this picture of the *intuitive*. Eurythmy forms in their totality fulfill these possibilities.

In Leading Thought 37, the rhythmic portion of the human organism is spoken of in relation to *inspiration*. It derives its name from breathing. Leading Thought 34 shows how breathing and the blood represent an alternating union and separation between "I"-organization and astral body on the one hand, and physical and etheric on the other. This a wide field for physiological research. In inner experience, it is like a continual setting of boundaries and withdrawing them again, a continual awakening and falling asleep (dreaming), a to-and-fro, an up-and-down between head and limbs, like a conversation between the inner and outer being of the spiritual as recitation is to eurythmy. True *inspiration* is a spiritual conversation, the rhythmic system is its image.

With regard to the descriptions of the rhythmic system in Leading Thoughts 29 to 34, attention may be drawn briefly to some facts that have so far obviously been unnoticed by physiologists in spite of the fact that they are easily observable. This will be a help for the understanding of the rhythmic system. Between two senses that are active in breathing, namely smell and taste, the following relationship exists: when we breathe in, we can smell; this is known to everyone. But with inhaling, the sense of taste, as far as it relates to aroma, is extinguished.

Conversely, when we breathe out, we can taste and, thereby, the sense of smell is interrupted. Therefore, if we wish to smell something, we must breathe in; if we wish to taste, we must breathe out. Each sense cancels out the other. If we hold our breath, breathing neither in nor out, we can neither smell nor taste.

The functions of both senses lie in their relationship to the sensory, nervous system and to the metabolic system. By breathing in, the "I"-being and astral body unite with the physical and etheric bodies (Leading Thought 34). The rhythmic system approaches the metabolic system and thereby withdraws from the nervous system. But it leaves behind a watchman for the latter—the sense of smell. It takes care that the sensory, nervous system comes to no harm as long as the rhythmic functions are turned to the metabolic system, for there are smells that are harmful to the sensory, nervous system, such as those that lead to fainting, narcolepsy, dimming of consciousness. Conversely, the rhythmic system turns to the sensory, nervous system in the process of breathing out and leaves the sense of taste behind as a watchman for the metabolic system so as to protect it against poisoning.

This whole subject is worthy of profound scientific study.

STUDY 21

CONCERNING MORALITY

The leading thoughts we have already considered led to a greater understanding of higher forms of knowledge—*imagination, inspiration,* and *intuition*—in relation to the human being. Once we have gained a certain comprehension of these evolutionary stages, we also establish a new relationship with the world. We can learn to comprehend spirit even with ordinary consciousness. The attitude toward life that arises from this may be properly referred to as *moral.* This leads to the creation of a new foundation for morality, since our old foundations for moral conduct in life have crumbled and fallen apart. No morality can be based only on the phenomena of the sense world. Consequently, natural science, which has no desire to enter the spiritual sphere, consciously maintains an amoral approach.

Let us look at what Rudolf Steiner said about this:

> Natural science attempts to eliminate morality completely from its investigations. Thus, morality begins to lose out, because for science there are no inherent physical forces that support morality. Even the doctrines of certain religions attempt to cultivate ideas that form a kind of compromise with natural science, since scientists insist that anything related to the moral element must be clearly separated from anything physical, chemical, geological, and so on.[1]

Nevertheless, if we delve beneath nature's surface as mentioned in our previous study, we come to realms where matters must be considered very differently than in the case of physical facts. In the physical world measure, number, and weight must have a specific value externally. In the higher worlds, measuring, weighing, and counting have inner value; they are moral standards.

Through our inner life, we participate in the spiritual worlds, but we must activate ourselves inwardly to make this participation gradually more conscious. Knowledge of the spiritual realm gives us a moral attitude, and this alone makes it possible to enter the spiritual world legitimately. Steiner stated that a foundation for morality in our time—having experienced the amorality of natural science—would be found only through forces related to life before birth in the spiritual world.

Traditional morality, which often appears complacent and satisfied, was, in terms of ecclesiastical impulses, based on a life after death; therefore, it could

---

1   *Building Stones for an Understanding of the Mystery of Golgotha,* lecture 4
     (compare study 16).

never be free of egoism. The driving forces were fear of damnation and anxiety over continued personal existence. Only a Spiritual Science free of egoism can investigate life before birth. Before penetrating prenatal life, everything related to life after death must be overcome by the spiritual investigator during earthly life. Otherwise, the danger of egoism arises again with even greater danger, because, behind the prenatal life, even earlier incarnations will arise. Consequently, Steiner elevated his investigations of this sphere to a moral pinnacle. He raised individual karma to the sphere of a soul exercise. Previous earthly lives can be viewed without danger only by those who are able to observe their own destiny with the kind of calm approach found in natural science.

One of the most difficult problems is gaining an adequate concept of the spirit's activity in the physical regardless of the laws of nature. Such representations must be correct, however, in order to understand destiny and freedom. Contemporary science understands the physical world only as a continuous (mineral) causality. To get beyond this idea, we saw that we should investigate the difficult matter of introducing *imagination*, *inspiration*, and *intuition* into the transformation of the Categories (Study 18). Steiner appended a letter to Leading Thoughts 35 to 37. It contains exercises that help us to incorporate the genuine morality of higher knowledge of the human being into our experience. The studies that follow are based on these exercises.

The foundation of modern thinking is an affront to the human being. Although we will address this matter in other studies, it was already touched on in Leading Thought 7. Since the consciousness soul has been approaching since the fifteenth century, we should keep in mind that natural science could have included the whole sphere of the etheric. If this had in fact occurred, history—especially social history—would have taken a very different course. Goethe and his adherents were on their way to gaining a proper appreciation for a spiritual understanding of nature.[2] The forces of materialism, however, gained the upper hand once again. Steiner's appearance in the world was needed so that humankind might be able to correct this error.

> Contemporary natural science is merely a phase. Despite all its value and great accomplishments, it is only an interlude that will be followed by another. Only then will it be recognized again that there is a higher way of looking at the world, one that sees nature and morality as two sides of the same being.[3]

When the etheric realm and the etheric human body are made available to natural scientific inquiry, the great disparity in the world between the physical and the spiritual realms becomes apparent.[4] We see this disparity expressed

---

2   Ibid., lecture 5.

3   Ibid., lecture 4.

4   See Günther Wachsmuth, *The Etheric Formative Forces: The Etheric World*;

in human beings, since we often feel that the physical and etheric bodies must be placed on one side and the astral body and "I"-being on the other. This is where waking and sleeping separate, where after-death experiences turn away from the earthly to the cosmic, where thinking and the will—past and future—separate and unite. This also suggests the difference between natural and moral laws as seen in our studies. Only by clarifying these distinctions can we understand the union of opposite forces.[1]

Leading Thoughts 35–37 help us to contemplate an image that can be taken very literally. Through it, we are inspired to see the various attitudes of soul when we consider a finished picture, the artist at work on the picture, or the future image still carried in the artist's soul. While we are absorbed in a finished picture, we experience a spiritual activity of the past expressed in the physical. We do not need to know who the artist is—that person may be forgotten or long dead. The artistic attitude active in the soul corresponds to *imagination*; the word itself implies "image," or "picture."

I can, for example, exchange views with an artist at work, while the picture is in the process of becoming. I must, however, be an artist myself and have some understanding of painting in order to offer advice. The artist can also communicate to me the intended image. If I want to take part intelligently in another person's creative effort, I must have the capacity to put myself in the place of the other. That is the soul attitude that corresponds to *inspiration*—harmony in breathing and in the heart.

If the artist has not even begun to paint, however, I will comprehend the future image only by uniting completely with the artist's soul. I must, in my very being, *become* the artist who carries the image in the will; this is pure spirit experience. This attitude of soul corresponds to *intuition*. If I consider only the painting materials, however, my only concern has to do with the mineral aspects, whether the picture is finished or only the materials exist. In that case, perhaps the painter isn't needed at all.

By moving these considerations into the realm of the human being, we become aware of how natural science has sinned. Without the original (although unconscious) cooperation of *imagination*, *inspiration*, and *intuition*, we would not have arrived at any natural science at all; but, in fact, this has ignored the higher, moral soul attitude.

38. We have demonstrated how to view human beings in their *image* nature, and the human spirit that reveals itself in this way. Once we have developed this perception, we are also at the point of being able to see—in the

---

Hermann Poppelbaum, *A New Zoology* (Dornach, Switzerland: Philosophic-Anthroposphic Press, 1961), chapter 1; and Rudolf Steiner, *Between Death and Rebirth*, lecture 7.

1   See *Cosmic and Human Metamorphoses*, lecture 4; and *Building Stones for an Understanding of the Mystery of Golgotha*, lecture 3.

spiritual world, where we see human beings living and moving as beings of spirit—the reality of the soul's moral laws. Thus, the moral order of the world is realized as the earthly image of an order that belongs to spiritual realm. The physical and moral world orders are bound together now in undivided unity.

39. The human *will* acts out of the human being. This will encounters the natural laws we derive from the external world as something completely alien to their essence. The nature of the sense organs can still be understood scientifically because of their similarity to the objects of external nature. The will, however, cannot yet unfold itself in the activity of these organs. The nature of the human rhythmic system manifests in a way less similar to anything external. To a certain extent, the will can work into this system, but the rhythmic system is constantly becoming and passing away; thus, in these processes, the will is not yet free

40. The nature of the metabolic and limb system manifests in material substances and in their processes. Yet, these substances and processes are really no closer to this nature than the artist and materials are to the finished picture. Consequently, the will can enter and work directly. Behind the human organization, which lives in natural laws, we must be able to apprehend the human essence that lives and moves with its being in the spirit. This is the realm where we can become conscious of the true activity of the will. The human will remains a mere, insubstantial word for the sensory realm, and the scientist or thinker who claims to take hold of it within the realm of the senses leaves the true nature of the will behind and replaces it with theory.

CONCERNING THE WILL

Leading Thoughts 38 to 40, as well as those that follow, present the human spiritual essence as will. Therefore, we accomplish the great transition—described in previous studies as the threshold experience—in a new way. The difficulties in understanding these leading thoughts recall our experience of Leading Thoughts 11–16, where the "I"-being was presented. It is useful to look again at these leading thoughts on the "I" in this new context.

There the human being is presented beginning with known facts. Spiritual facts are added to the physical aspects, and spirit is shown to be reflected in the physical. The relationship between these two realms is indicated by showing how the spiritual facts may be discovered. We have treated this polarity as concept and reality and endeavored to gain some understanding of how, at a decisive transition (between the etheric and astral bodies), we can discover the threshold of the spiritual world in the human being.

These leading thoughts also speak of the evolutionary path of consciousness from physical to spiritual knowledge. For example, during meditation we permeate our experience in thinking with the will. The will appears as an aspect of meditation practice. It is left to the individual to decide how far one advances along the path of meditation. Nevertheless, our understanding of suprasensory facts does not depend on this. The facts themselves show us our true nature as physical and spiritual beings. In order to *understand* these matters, however, requires an understanding of how they can be found. Without some understanding of the path, we cannot walk it properly.

Now we find the will again, and we already know how human beings pass through the gate of death, set aside the physical body, and continue the life of spirit; thus, we come to understand pure spirit in humankind. Then came our studies of how spirit is revealed in the physical. As a result, we have returned to facts relating to the human being in earthly life. Our way of asking questions, however, is different; we begin to direct our inquiry toward the relationship between spirit and the earthly in humankind. The comparison with a painting in Study 21 brings us to a new kind of inquiry.

We can also describe the difference in this way: previously we had to proceed from the physical to find the spiritual; now we proceed from the spiritual to find the physical. We asked: How do we cross the threshold to the spirit? Now we ask: How did we cross the threshold into the physical world? In Studies 5 and 6, this reversal was dealt with more in terms of a *theory* of knowledge. Now a different perspective arises from *practical* knowledge (Study 19). This expresses, at the same time, the historic change in the moral foundation, from after death until a new birth (Study 21). Our task now is to understand the dominion within the physical realm of the will, whose principle is morality, and whose realization on Earth is destiny.

> 41. In the third of the previous leading thoughts, we indicated the nature of the human will. We penetrate with understanding this sphere of the world where destiny, or karma, works once the nature of will is recognized. As long as we perceive only the principles that rule the relationships of nature, we will have no understanding of the laws working in destiny,

> 42. Once the principle of destiny is discerned, we see that destiny cannot manifest during a single physical life on Earth. As long as we inhabit the same physical body, we can realize only the essential morality of the will as allowed by this particular physical body in the physical world. The spiritual nature of the will is fully realized only after we have passed through the gate of death into the realm of spirit. Then, good and evil is recognized in various ways—spiritually at first—according to their results.

> 43. Through this realization of spirit, we pattern and shape ourselves between death and a new birth. In being, we become an image of our actions during our earthly life. When we return to Earth, we form our physical life from this being. The spirit actively weaving in destiny is realized in the physical only if its corresponding cause has withdrawn into the spiritual realm before this realization. All that emerges in our life through destiny emanates from the spirit; it cannot otherwise take shape within the flow of physical phenomena.

The activity of the sense organs still belongs entirely to nature (Leading Thought 39). It shapes those organs and looks into them as if into a mirror. Our *being*, situated behind our sense organs, views this natural process between sense organs and outer effects on them (eye and light, for example).[1] In this process, however, nature draws toward herself the human spirit, who had separated from the spirit of nature. She lures the human spirit to herself along paths of sense perception. Sensual knowledge is gained through the object. Our being experiences itself surrendered to the object. *Human knowledge of nature is nature's self-knowledge*, which is, at the same time, an appeal to the human spirit; the selflessness of the sense organs is the precondition for nature's self-knowledge. *True knowledge of nature is a training in selflessness.* When we interfere with perception and the activity of the sensory organs through like and dislike or through the will, we are destroying them. "If your right eye causes you to stumble, gouge it out and throw it away" (Matt. 5:29).

---

1   *The Gospel of St. John in Relation to the other Gospels*, lecture 10; *Genesis: Secrets of Creation*, lecture 8.

The human cognitive nature is permeated by spirit. Selflessness expresses the moral aspect of perception. Spirit is active in the will. We could invent the word spirit-"I"-being (Geistselbstigkeit) to distinguish the spirit's moral activity, just as we designated its permeation of the human being as self-lessness. The will directly engages the system of the limbs and metabolism (Leading Thought 40). Its true being remains hidden, however, and weaves as the expression of independent spirit being out of the spiritual realm. There the will reveals its tendency to act in the same way as nature; just as natural science can become nature's self-knowledge, so Spiritual Science can be human self-knowledge. These thoughts need only to be followed through. The vehicle of such self-knowledge is the spirit self.

This term for our higher self was first offered by Rudolf Steiner in Theosophy.[1] The spirit self creates for itself an organ of spiritual perception through its work on the metabolic and limb system; the object of this perception is destiny.

Consequently, the will looks down from the spiritual realm into earthly life between birth and death. Although we are unaware of this, our actions in earthly life express the will's tendency to create a head from the limb system (Study 20). Thus, it is clear that the bearer of consciousness is not created by the will but originates in the life before birth. Nevertheless, there is a way to shape genuine revelation for the being of the will. That is art, which reveals spiritual self-knowledge. This is expressed most clearly in eurythmy. If we could see the movements and forms from the spiritual level, they would be revealed as human self-knowledge—reversed nature.

With Leading Thoughts 41–43, we begin exercises that lead to an understanding of destiny and karma. Much of what was new—what Steiner presented after Christmas of 1923—was described by him as karma exercises. These words were also meant to indicate a high moral standard, which is the only way we can speak definitively of karma. Any concept that can be applied to destiny belongs to a sphere that is inaccessible to ordinary consciousness as such. Such concepts are will transformed into knowledge, or will permeated with wisdom—in other words, morality. In order that Steiner's teachings about destiny become exercises, they must be preceded by preliminary exercises in morality.

---

1   "The 'I' dwells in the soul. Although the highest manifestation of the 'I' belongs to the consciousness soul, it is also true that the 'I' radiates outward from there, filling the entire soul and exerting its influence on the body through the soul. And within the 'I,' the spirit is alive and active. The spirit streams into the 'I,' taking it as its 'garment,' just as the 'I' itself lives in the body and soul. The spirit shapes the 'I' from the inside out, and the mineral world shapes it from the outside in. We will call the spirit that shapes an 'I,' that lives as an 'I,' the spirit self, since it appears as the human 'I,' or self." Theosophy, pp. 50–51.

STUDY 23

PRELIMINARY KARMA EXERCISES

Rudolf Steiner showed in his philosophical writings that a view of the world must begin with the human being—not a hypothetical beginning, such as a primeval mist or abstract principle, but the most newly manifested, which is the proper place to begin for knowing the universe. In *Intuitive Thinking as a Spiritual Path*, there is a line in chapter 3, where Steiner points out that starting at the beginning is a matter for the world creator. One who seeks knowledge, however, must begin with what was created most recently—in other words, *here and now*. Science must actually go the other way in time, however, which is backward. True knowledge begins with our own being, which we must understand from within. This occurs in contrast to the nature surrounding us.

Contemporary consciousness is based on the fact that human beings, in their essence, *confront* nature. This is the strength of modern natural science, but it also provides the essential amorality of science. The objectivity of natural investigation implicitly assumes the reality of the investigator. But this is a clumsy, erroneous attempt to explain the human being from the side of nature, since, at the same time, another process is occurring unconsciously; knowledge of nature arises only by presupposing one's own being. Steiner worked out this relationship with great precision. If we continue to *confront* nature, our comprehension of destiny is merely an empty illusion.

In our second study, we distinguished between a relationship to the world through nature, and a relationship through the "I." Through nature we experience the world though its opposition; through the "I" we experience it inwardly. In every introduction to Anthroposophy this opposition is shown to be only a necessary first step. A powerful decision in considering the world must follow, since the "I"-experience of nature does not happen according to natural laws but according to *moral laws*.

This means we experience our own being by confronting nature, and we find the essence of nature within ourselves. This constitutes the polarity between *cosmic-knowledge* and *self-knowledge*. Steiner once wrote, "On various occasion I have often given these words to friends who ask me for a formula:

> *If you would know your own being,*
> *Look all around in the world.*
> *If you would truly penetrate the world,*
> *Look into the depths of your own soul.*"[2]

---

2   *The Foundation Stone...*, "To All Members," Mar. 30, 1924.

If we take this as our attitude toward life, it becomes the means for a preliminary karmic exercise, since it embraces nature and morality as one. If we can objectively acquire the impression that, in the world around us, we encounter traces of our own being, and that, within the depths of our own soul, we carry the spiritual foundations for the world's evolution, we are approaching an understanding of destiny.

Initially, the path of thinking leads to sharp distinctions and analysis; the great world polarities reveal themselves as they did in Study 10, for example. If, however, the results of clear and truthful thinking are taken up into the whole human being—into our life of feeling and will—then we can reconcile extreme opposites. When we look into the surrounding kingdoms of nature, we need to consider the great diversity and sharp divisions; this is where human beings rise above the other kingdoms of nature.

If we examine our relationship to the world through feeling, a mood can arise, and Steiner evoked this by speaking of *The Washing of the Feet* in such a wonderful and impressive way as a deep mystery.[1] Christian Morgenstern, in his poem, devoted the whole wealth of his art to this mystery. Human beings have been indebted to nature since primeval times through the sacrifice on which we base our own being. Thus, we remain forever connected to her. It is really only one part of our being we carry within ourselves—the other part is nature herself. If this feeling is taken up into the will, it becomes the impulse for the future. From actions of the past (which become human feeling in the present) grows the impulse for future world development. By transforming the will, Christ's act of redemption becomes reality for humanity.[2]

Humankind has inherited a great cosmic past, but must also administer a great legacy for the future. Following the path of anthroposophic knowledge implies not only living in the cosmos after death (as discussed in relation to Leading Thoughts 23–28), but also during life. There are grand rhythms in the cosmos, and the sharp distinctions among the kingdoms of nature indicate the great world epochs. According to Steiner's cosmology, the kingdoms surrounding us as mineral, plant, and animal are in fact the beings of Saturn, Sun, and Moon, the cosmic planetary predecessors of the Earth.[3]

The great cosmic past surrounds us spatially; but through the inner coordination of our sentient, intellectual, and conscious aspects of soul, we have simultaneously—in a spiritual experience—joined these world epochs. When a soul experience passes from the sentient soul through the intellectual to the consciousness soul (though with only a twilight awareness), we actually

---

1   See *Rosicrucian Wisdom*, pp. 156ff; and *From Jesus to Christ*, lecture 10.

2   See *From Jesus to Christ*, lectures 9 and 10.

3   See *Founding a Science of the Spirit*, lecture 10; *Theosophy of the Rosicrucian*, lecture 10; and *The Gospel of St. John and Its Relationship to the Other Gospels*, lectures 3 and 4.

experience the course of Moon, Sun, and Saturn. Human freedom is shaped through this inner participation of cosmic experience from space, into time, and into causality (compare Study 18). As in previous studies, a rejuvenation of the Categories also can be experienced here: cosmic rule, which in space compels as natural law, becomes our own life and field of activity during earthly life. Thus, through exercises, we can enter the realm where we may discover the principle of destiny.

We begin a new journey through life when we mold the basic teachings of Anthroposophy into preliminary karma exercises. We shape the same king-doms of nature through scientific investigation, through our art, and as happy human beings. But now, in the midst of life, through research, creation, and enjoyment, we can continually meet ourselves. This can be made into a spe-cific exercise. We can cultivate the feeling that, with every step, we go to meet ourselves, especially also in our interrelationships with others. It is certainly not the small self that we go to meet with expectation, but the cosmic human being. In this way, we learn to act differently when our destiny comes to meet us from the same surroundings—it is a part of our own being.

Through this kind of preliminary exercise, the question arises: How did this destiny that meets us enter our surroundings? We can say with certainty that it is not within the laws of nature; within the processes of awareness that form the laws of nature, self-knowledge of nature arises (as we saw in Study 22). Human beings present nature with her own being. But how does nature, in the form of destiny, present us with what is still lacking in our being? Its origin is not the laws of nature nor the actions of our present life. If, for example, someone travels for the first time from Europe to America and encounters a stroke of destiny, that person certainly did not evoke the causes for this in this life in America; and only the disposition toward a cer-tain destiny was brought from Europe.

Only that can become destiny that previously has been carried through the spiritual world.[4] We can find evidence of this everywhere in Steiner's works, but also in the preceding study of the great cosmic rhythms—the kingdoms of nature differ from one another, because a new spiritual principle is added occasionally to the flow of world evolution. This is a new growth from the spiritual realm. Whenever a new principle is added, however, all that has existed until then will also be changed.[5] Within ourselves, we experience the stage of this evolution that is most recent. The kingdoms of nature surround us—we even belong to them in our natural being—but, at the same time, we carry them in soul form within us and permeate them with our "I"-being. We

---

4   See *Manifestations of Karma*, lectures 2 and 8.

5   See "*Mathematik als echte Symbolismus*" ("Mathematics as Genuine Symbolism"), *Die Drei*, Stuttgart, Sept. 1927.

could not rise above the kingdoms of nature if we did not permeate them in soul form.

Thus, human evolution on Earth must have been preceded by a spiritual state, which has forged this soul form from all that evolved on Saturn, Sun, and Moon. What Steiner described in *An Outline of Esoteric Science* and in many lecture cycles as "cosmic human evolution" is indeed present in our own soul. We repeat the great world rhythms in our small rhythms of repeated Earth lives, and they are repeated in the even smaller rhythms of waking and sleeping, and finally, in our breath and heartbeat.

Our ordinary soul capacities are a repetition of previous stages of world development—Saturn, Sun and, Moon.[1] What cycles as destiny through Earth lives is the seed for future cosmic development; the new principle that Steiner calls *spirit self* will accrue to the human being and will bear the future world of Jupiter.

---

1   See *The Mission of the Individual Folk Souls*, lecture 15.

THE HUMAN BEING AND DESTINY

Destiny is more than what we perceive as fortune or misfortune. It is our participation in world evolution and the cosmic judgment of our actions. Our knowledge is like the letters from which words are built by our actions, and destiny passes judgment. The *Logos* is the Being who harmonizes humanity with world evolution through the rule of destiny. At the same time, the great world polarities are also the polarities of destiny—each polar opposite is the destiny of the other. Where world polarities are repeated in human beings, destiny can become active—for example, in waking and sleeping, birth and death, body and spirit, man and woman, youth and old age, good and evil, past and future, head and limbs, joy and sorrows, health and illness, and so on.[2]

In *Manifestations of Karma*, Rudolf Steiner brings a wealth of detail from his spiritual research; he considered this sphere to be virtually unlimited. He pointed to important differentiations:

> We can best show how karma can have a meaningful effect in the world by considering an example in which karma works without moral overtones, where it works in the greater world without having anything to do with what people develop out of their own souls as moral impulses that then lead to moral or immoral actions.[3]

Now he shows how, in consecutive Earth lives, male and female incarnations are related. He points out "that a woman must, through the very fact that she is a woman, have very different experiences from those of a man. Thus, we may say that a woman is led to perform certain actions that are closely related to her life as a woman." Something else must also be considered, however:

> Our more strongly psychological and emotional aspect, which tends toward the inner part of the soul during life between birth and death, also has the tendency to intervene more deeply in our bodily organization, impregnating it much more intensely.... Because of this, her experiences tend to work into the organic structure of the body more deeply and embrace it more strongly in the future.... However, to work deeply into the body, to penetrate the body thoroughly, means to produce a male organism.... So,

---

2 See *Manifestations of Karma*, lecture 1; and *The Christ-Impulse and the Development of Ego-Consciousness*, lecture 2.

3 *Manifestations of Karma*, lecture 9.

you can see that experiences as a woman in one incarnation produce a male organism in the next incarnation. The very nature of esoteric work supplies you with a relationship that transcends morality. This is why esoteric teachings say that the man is the karma of the woman.[1]

This applies also to the opposite:

> A man's nature, therefore, is more condensed and contracted; it has been more compressed and made stiffer and harder by the inner human being. It is more materialized. Now, a less flexible brain is a suitable tool primarily for the intellect, but less so for the psyche, since the intellect is something that relates much more to the physical plane.... We will be reluctant to believe that intellectuality is something that runs its course in a fairly superficial way, does not penetrate deeply into our soul life, and does little to grasp the inner aspect of the human being. But a materialistic point of view in particular does not comprehend our soul life. As a result, however, men who do not work deeply into the soul during this incarnation acquire the tendency to penetrate less deeply into the bodily organization in the next incarnation.... This, however, brings about the tendency to build up a female body in the next incarnation. Once again, it is true when it is said in esoteric teachings that the woman is the man's karma. (Ibid., p. 46)

The karmic polarities of health and illness form a transition from the cosmic to the moral; these polarities are expressed most clearly by *good* and *evil*. One enters the domain of true freedom to the same degree that one practices the moral aspect of karma.

It is important to bring all of these considerations into relationship with the part of our work where the leading thoughts point in particular to our own activity (Leading Thoughts 41–43). Leading Thought 41 points out how human beings, in contrast to their way of considering nature, must rise to an entirely different level, which requires the practice of a special method of consideration. It requires looking at our life from a cosmic perspective. Leading Thought 42 shows that this is the same as the realm into which we enter after death.

To understand the reign of destiny, however, we must realize that after-death and pre-birth belong to the same realm, and we must focus our soul directly on the prenatal realm (Study 21, Leading Thought 43). Again, we encounter a change in perspective, undoubtedly related to the earlier passages where we were able to show the necessity for such a shift in our view (Studies 12 and 19). First, there are three viewpoints that justify such a change—three dimensions at right angles to one another. In all three, it is a matter of exchanging polar opposites. In the first direction, *inner* and *outer* are exchanged; in the second, *past* and *future*; and in the third, *cause* and *effect*. Coming to

---

1   *A Western Approach to Reincarnation and Karma*, pp. 44–45.

understand these opposing dimensions is a process of spiritual development, which can only be hinted at here.

In the leading thoughts that follow, Steiner points more specifically to our own activity in this effort. It should not be overlooked that the leading thoughts, when first published, were given to groups who were actually working with them. It is important that groups are addressed directly when questions of destiny are being dealt with, because karma points very strongly to human communities.

> 44. We should pass on to a spiritual, scientific treatment of the question of destiny by taking examples from the life experiences of individual men and women. Thus, we can show how the forces of destiny work themselves out and their significance for all of human life. We may show, for example. how a man's experience in his youth (which he certainly could not have brought upon himself entirely of his own free will) may greatly shape all of his later life.

> 45. We should describe the importance of the fact that, in the physical flow of life between birth and death, the good may become unhappy in their outer life, and the wicked (to appearances, at least) become happy. In explaining these things, pictures of individual cases have more weight than theories; they provide a much better preparation for a spiritual, scientific approach to the subject.

> 46. We should cite the events of destiny that enter human life in such a way that their causes cannot be found in our current life. Faced with such occurrences, a purely reasonable view of life already indicates former earthly lives. Our means of describing such things must not imply anything dogmatic or binding. The purpose of such examples is simply to direct one's thoughts toward a spiritual, scientific treatment of the question of destiny.

Such descriptions of individual destiny may be found in Steiner's lectures; they illustrate the general principles that always indicate the passage of human experience through the spiritual worlds.[2] Steiner gave the karma exercises themselves at the Goetheanum in his later life.[3] They describe the repeated earthly lives of important individuals and great leaders of humanity. It is possible to speak in general of how such descriptions of specific Earth lives can become exercises (we will do this in our next study). The considerations suggested in Leading Thoughts 44–46 are part of the preliminary karma exercises.

Examples of this can be found everywhere in history, poetry, and ordinary life. However, only in our time have such destinies assumed a completely enigmatic quality. A whole era of writers demonstrates the depth of the problems

2   See *Life between Death and Rebirth*.

3   See *Karmic Relationships: Esoteric Studies*, vols. 1–8.

related to being truly human. Look at dramatists such as Hebbel, Ibsen, Strindberg, not to mention epic poets, who present us with insoluble problems for our time. The point is that they cannot be solved by what is available to ordinary consciousness.

Therefore, three forms are presented in Leading Thoughts 44–46. First, an experience in youth greatly shapes all of a person's later life. Second, there could not be a greater dissonance between a person's moral standard and life's external circumstances. Third, there are instances of destiny for which we cannot find causes in the current earthly life. Here are three examples taken from life, corresponding approximately to these three forms:

1. A young man is mortally injured by a friend through an accident. He thinks he is dying, and that his life is ending. He realizes the meaning of this short life, however, by seeing repeated Earth lives as a way to understand serious life problems. Then, however, he sees himself recalled to life and feels overwhelmingly oppressed. It gradually becomes clear to him that, although his life had been lost, it is returned to him so that he could dedicate his life to a new way of thinking about continued life after death. This revelation leads him directly to Anthroposophy.

2. A woman grows up as the child of wealthy parents. Because of unjust treatment, she develops a tremendous urge for justice—so strong that this feeling later becomes a kind of faculty that foresees trouble. Her idealism always leads her to actions that have violent and evil consequences. The more she wants to turn toward truly good impulses, the more she encounters undeserved hardship. This leads to a break with her family and to disinheritance. When she encounters the anthroposophical movement, a change occurs in her life's circumstances. Her idealistic demands become even stronger but, without apparent cause, she loses her position and feels that all of her motives are misinterpreted. Everywhere she is compelled to experience with particular intensity how there are others who, with no real sense of justice, no idealism, and no impulse toward good, lead comfortable lives. By understanding how karma works, she is able to carry on her difficult and courageous battle.

3. A young man feels the irresistible desire to end his life. With great ingenuity, he proves to himself that this is completely justifiable, although no one else can understand it. No external reason in his present life can be found. He is well acquainted with Anthroposophy and takes his verifications from it. Finally, it becomes possible to convince him not to commit suicide. This is accomplished by showing him that a true knowledge of Anthroposophy makes it clear that, if it were his destiny to pass out of life as a young man, his own subconscious, superintelligent "I"-being could easily find a way to let him die through some accident. His later life became very difficult, but to this day has not led to the accident he expected.

Study 25

KARMA EXERCISES

Rudolf Steiner pointed out the relationship between destiny and repeated earth lives in Leading Thoughts 43 and 46. This theme is continued in these leading thoughts:

> 47. Of all that is latent in the formation of human destiny, only a very small portion enters ordinary awareness; it works primarily in the subconscious. Yet the unveiling of our destiny, most of all, teaches us how the subconscious can in fact be made conscious. In effect, it is incorrect to speak of what is provisionally unconscious as though it must remain completely in the realm of the unknown, thus barring knowledge. With every fragment of our destiny that is unveiled to us, we lift something that had been unconscious into the realm of consciousness.

> 48. In this way, we become aware that matters of destiny are not fabricated within the life between birth and death. Therefore, the question of destiny impels us most of all to contemplate the life between death and rebirth.

> 49. Conscious human experience is thus motivated by the question of destiny to look beyond itself. Further, as we contemplate this truth, we begin to develop a real feeling for the relationship between nature and spirit. Those who can see destiny being lived out in the human being, already live amid the spiritual, since the inner weaving of destiny is completely unlike that of outer nature.

Contemplating the activity of destiny, if practiced properly, confirms the notion of repeated earth lives. General references to this practice may be found in the central chapter of Steiner's book *Theosophy*. The following thoughts are intended as a help to us to find the inner structure of that chapter. The soul is a twofold being between body and spirit; its activity is accomplished by taking in and giving out relative to the direction of the soul's experience. The direction *body-soul-spirit* indicates taking in; the direction *spirit-soul-body* refers to giving out. These passive and active modes of soul activity—receiving and giving—cross one another and form the living cross of the human soul. Steiner erected this cross in the central chapter of *Theosophy*; it shows how body, soul, and spirit are connected; the world is related to human beings through knowing and activity.

As the body turns its sense organs toward the outer world, sensations, perceptions, and *impressions* arise. They are received by the soul and preserved as *re*-presentations in the *memory*. The spirit takes from it anything that has eternal value and incorporates it into its being as *capacities*. In the reversed direction, the human spirit—whose nature gives rise to *will impulses*—influences the soul. It forms the acts that, through the body, go out into the world and transform it.

Thus, the soul continually sacrifices itself during earthly life on both sides—one aspect of its being flows into the outer world and its social human relationships, and the other flows into the spirit and to the beings of the spiritual realm. This is expressed after death. The human spirit that carries the fruits of earthly life through eternity also preserves the connection with Earth, where the other aspect of the human being remains. Earth and the human spirit are of one nature, since they carry the imprint of the same soul being. Because of this connection, the human spirit returns to Earth, and the forces underlying this relationship form the new soul for a new life on Earth.

Again, during earthly life impressions come to the soul from the world of the senses. But the human soul that learns to see through such connections

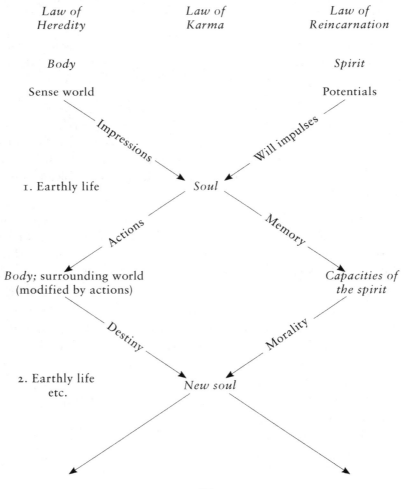

perceives these impressions as the bearer of destiny that has been preserved in the earth as the result of actions during the previous earth life. Moreover, the human soul that comes to know its spiritual relationship with the outer world again receives will impulses of a spiritual nature that can become the bearer of spiritual forces received by the soul as moral intuitions. What comes in this way to people as a task is the work of the consciousness soul. It takes shape in the exercises arising from the Leading Thoughts. The following illustration may be helpful in practicing these exercises.

It is the task of the consciousness soul to meet individual destiny—which comes to us from the outer world with the kind of selflessness we have learned only for meeting the *impressions* of the outer world—and to act in the world in a way that is sustained by morality.

What Steiner wrote in *Theosophy* about repeated Earth lives and destiny forms the basis for karma exercises, since it provides a firm foundation for a way of thinking that unites cosmic scope and natural-scientific precision. We then have the answer to the question (Study 23) of how destiny comes into our environment. A firm foundation is necessary in areas where thinking threatens to fly away; if the subconscious is awakened according to Leading Thought 47, powerful forces are invoked. Contemplation of destiny touches on spheres in which microcosmic resembles macrocosmic memory. Memories and representations can be brought into the spirit of the human being only when they are mastered morally; in other words, they must have been thoroughly immersed in the spiritual world. Only when feelings, sensations, and aspirations have been "baptized" in the spiritual world through the perception of repeated earth lives may they be considered in relation to macrocosmic memories of destiny.

In order to find the transition from preliminary karma exercises to the karma exercises themselves, we can turn to human connections, such those in the Anthroposophical Society; in which real, spiritually-based human connections are possible. From the realm of the spirit, they are seen as real; but, in our consciousness, such connections must be acquired despite considerable obstacles. It may be true that Anthroposophy individualizes human beings. The danger, however, is that the individual may be placed above the social. Rather, the questions of destiny must be lifted out of the individual into the social realm. Of course, it is also clear that an individual cannot have a destiny in isolation. The connection between members causes certain karmic relationships among them, since we all invoke our individual destiny through our activity in Anthroposophy. Indeed, the possibility of inner progress consists in this.

Anthroposophy causes future possibilities to manifest in the present and awakens the subconscious. Thus, destiny is drawn out of the particularly human environment as the primary point of experience. Consequently, one individual carries the destiny of another. This may happen as a conflict over earthly concerns (though, it need not). However, it then becomes like a dream of the true situation, and there is an adjustment in the spiritual realm, a *spirit conversation*.[1] It would be a true karma exercise if such spirit conversations could occur consciously; this would be an inspiration whereby one could awaken through the other.

One can work toward such a goal, and this is the great significance of the Anthroposophical Society. Human relationships can certainly lead to a revelation of the destinies of others. This cannot happen, however, through sensational inquiry that would dissect the soul or psychoanalyze. On the contrary—the point is to practice listening with love and patience; in this way we attain the moral overview of an assessment that can help. Then, when the being of another person has revealed itself, it is possible to place that image before the soul's eye and ponder it, seeing it surrounded by its destiny, enveloped in a spiritual being that begins to reveal itself; we see how the breath of life penetrates the gestures themselves. "Those who can see destiny being lived out in the human being, already live amid the spiritual" (Leading Thought 49).

At the end of his life, Steiner wished to place the karma lectures into such a moral human climate. These lectures are like an inspiration breathed out over the Anthroposophical Society. The facts of repeated Earth lives of great souls should be kept at a high level of spiritual morality; in this way they can act as a continual source of inspiration. There are great historical epochs that appeal to our cosmic memory and the question is often repeated: What has happened to the great initiates of ancient times; what became of their achievements in our age forsaken by the gods? Many have lived in our time who could not manifest their true being; they were confronted by the immense hindrances of civilization, education, and physical constitution. This fact elicits our innermost participation in the human tragedy. The powerful impulse of such human pictures—whose glowing colors appear on the golden background of Steiner's descriptions—is expressed in the words:

> *Change your viewpoint; change the entire form of your present life, so that the great souls can return and reveal their true being, so they may truly be recognized and received; otherwise, the inspirations of humanity will die. It must be possible to find them again when the great decisions of our time are made!*

---

1   Steiner illustrated this in his mystery dramas; *Four Mystery Dramas*; see also the fourth drama, *The Souls' Awakening*, published alone.

STUDY 26

KARMA AND HISTORY

Through earnest practice of the karma exercises, we become selfless in relation to personal destiny. To the degree that our efforts unfold a part of the
redemptive force of human karma as a whole, this also has value for spiritual
evolution. By inwardly understanding the karmic connection of the whole
evolution of humankind, we rid ourselves of any pretensions that might arise
as temptations due to knowledge of repeated Earth lives and of the law of
destiny. In this way, we prepare the path of knowledge for a new revelation of
the Christ, who will then be recognized as the *Lord of Karma*, since He has
taken on all of human destiny. This is a real transition that takes place in our
time, and it replaces that old picture of Moses pointing the dead toward the
strict law as shown in Study 14.[2] This leads us to one of the most important
chapters—"Karma and History."

> 50. It must be pointed out that the history of humankind is brought to life
> when we realize that it is human souls themselves, passing from age to age
> in their repeated lives on Earth, who carry the effects of one historic time
> into another.

> 51. It may be easy to argue that such a line of reasoning robs history of its
> innocent, elemental force. But this objection would be incorrect. Rather,
> our view of history is deepened by following it into the inmost being of
> humankind. History becomes richer and more substantial, not poorer and
> more abstract. When we describe such things, we must nevertheless unfold
> a real feeling of sympathy for the living human soul, which we contem-
> plate deeply through such thinking.

> 52. The periods of life between death and a new birth should be treated in
> relation to the formation of karma.

Additional leading thoughts will indicate how we may do this.

The consideration of history from the perspective of repeated earthly lives
is a task of Western people in sharp contrast to all the spiritual efforts of the
East. The views of the East have always contained the doctrine of repeated
earth lives, but without historical progress; rather, all events were seen in

---

2   See *From Jesus to Christ*, lecture 3.

recurring cycles.[1] Since the Old Testament was written, the West has tried to understand historical events in terms of definite goals: "Progress became an important element in the stories of the Old Testament. The Old Testament is the first great example of a historical method of observation. The historical method of observation was a legacy to the West."[2]

Until now, however, the truth of repeated earthly lives has not been included in this legacy. Rudolf Steiner's statement is a new interpretation of history that includes knowledge of reincarnation and karma. The Mystery of Golgotha is the distinguishing historical event and the central turning point of earthly evolution. At the same time, it is also a mystical fact through which individual human beings passing through earthly lives become spiritually conscious bearers of cosmic impulses.

In Leading Thoughts 50 to 52, the importance of history is brought home in two ways. Leading Thought 50 speaks of enlivening the study of human history; and Leading Thought 51 speaks of tracing history into individual living human souls. Thus, we must understand how history arises out of human development and out of history's influence on the contemporary human beings. We must therefore begin with the human being according to the previous leading thoughts.

From the perspective of nature's uninterrupted causality, there *is* no history. Any real understanding of the essence of history requires the flexible Categories and their interplay (Study 18). There are some signs of this in modern natural science, though ignored or unconscious. We must simply distinguish between *descriptive* and *explanatory* sciences; the difference has to do with the concept of evolution, which is so little understood today. The idea of evolution would never have come about in modern natural science if human powers of cognition did not have the capacity for real development. Thus, in Study 3, we stated: *All knowledge transforms the knower.*

We can consider mineralogy a descriptive science, and geology explanatory. If geology also considers time as a real factor, a history of the Earth according to the etheric formative forces may result. Physiology is the explanatory counterpart to botany, which is a descriptive science. In physiology, the etheric formative forces appear in service to a higher principle, which we have called (categorical) *causality*. Similarly, zoology leads to biology, which must understand the animal types through the higher category of *individualization*; this results in the biogenetic principle.

Thus, we need a principle for human beings (the *creative* principle) that surpasses the single individual being, just as the group-soul surpasses the single

---

1   When Unger wrote this, the "East" often implied the *ancient*, or traditional, religious doctrines of India. Westerners are more familiar today with the later developments of Mahayana and Vajrayana Buddhism as it moved east from India.

2   Rudolf Steiner, *The Gospel of St. Mark*, lecture 6.

animal. We find a real evolutionary aspect in genuine *biography*, as described
by Steiner in *Theosophy*. Biographies stretch beyond single incarnations; the
higher creative principle working in them from the spiritual world is *karma*.
Biographies form the higher explanatory science in contrast to anthropology.
This is history. Therefore, since biographies arise, we can understand history
in a historic sense.[3]

Rudolf Steiner calls ordinary history a *fable convenue*.[4] First, because the
real determining factors are not handed down at all, or they are passed on in
such a way that the modern historian cannot use them. Second, there is no
truth in the method used to connect traditional facts in contemporary consciousness. History is really made up of occurrences that, in earlier times, were
completely spiritual, but now are human and physical. Humanity in ancient
times lived without history. Because of this, the ancient East [India], which
always looked longingly toward the primeval spiritual state of humanity, has
no real history.[5] Indeed, they perceived themselves as entangled in the wheel
of reincarnation and, as individuals, tried to become free of it. Individual
experience was viewed as sin by Eastern consciousness; Earthly *maya*, or illusion, was viewed in contrast to the real events arising from spiritual beings,
who acted as inspirational forces behind human leaders.[6] These the ancient
initiates found their way back into the spiritual world, but they gradually saw
that this rise into the spiritual and their return as individuals to the primeval
human condition occurred increasingly at the expense of everyone else. That
is the real tragedy of the old initiates. Consequently, the activity of the old
consciousness forces had to be replaced with something else.

True history relates to human consciousness; it expresses the individualization of human beings. In keeping with the reality of repeated earth
lives, we can understand from the evolution of human consciousness that the
cyclic eras of history are progressive. Oswald Spengler sensed some truth in
his strange concept of historic simultaneity.[7] He noticed that the various cultural periods display an ascent and a descent; this represents their inner time,
and he calls the phases of different cultures that correspond to one another

---

3   See *Karmic Relationships: Esoteric Studies*, 8 vols.

4   Or "shared myth." See *The Gospel of St. John and Its Relation to the Other
    Gospels*, lecture 2; and *Earthly Death and Cosmic Life*, lecture 7.

5   This last statement should probably be understood in a relative sense, since every
    culture has some sense of history; but whereas some view history more in a cyclical
    sense, others are more linear in their approach. See *The East in the Light of the
    West*, lecture 4.

6   See *Occult History: Historical Personalities and Events in the Light of Spiritual
    Science*, lecture 1.

7   Oswald Spengler (1880–1936), German philosopher known for his theory of history.

"simultaneous." He finds a conforming principle and, from this, grandly attempts to predict history.

But Spengler knows nothing of the historic impulses that carry through the spiritual world, which alone gives rise to the historical epochs. From his perspective, Spengler cannot know anything of real biographies, which also develop only gradually. First, there are spiritual beings, who themselves work among humanity.[1] Then there are human leaders inspired by spiritual beings.[2] And finally, human leaders are left to act on their own. This brings with it real tragedy for the leading individuals, whose biographies shape history as they develop. We find of all these aspects—which we have only hinted at—fully described in some of Steiner's work.[3]

In this flow of history, everything that happens gradually leads toward a central point. In deeply concealed mystery centers, the old initiates experienced a tragedy related to the passing of the old spiritual bond; at the same time, however, they found comfort in looking forward to a cosmic mystery of the Sun Spirit, who would descend to Earth. This goal was placed before those initiates by suprahuman beings, and from this evolved the first truly historical document, the Old Testament.

As Steiner shows, the Old Testament not only describes history, but points to a future goal. Just as the descriptive sciences must be supplemented by the explanatory sciences, so descriptive history must be supplemented with an understanding of the goal of history. In this way, we can understand the immense significance of the Mystery of Golgotha, where the goal of the ancient Mysteries became historical fact. What we describe as the history of the ancient world must be understood in terms of this unique event; it alone gives history its correct context. Indeed, recent historical authorities and their methods cannot be concerned with this occurrence as a historical event. Since the Mystery of Golgotha, the nature of history must become *apocalyptic*. The Apocalypse—the reappearance of Christ—sets the new goal.

---

1   See *Egyptian Myths and Mysteries*, lecture 10; *The Spiritual Hierarchies and the Physical World: Reality and Illusion*, lectures 7 and 9; and *According to Matthew*, lecture 12.

2   See "The Guardian of the Threshold" in *Four Mystery Dramas*, scene 1, Hilary's speech "True to God."

3   *Occult History: Historical Personalities and Events in the Light of Spiritual Science*; *The Gospel of St. Mark*.

HISTORY, MORALITY, AND PREVISION

People today understand karma through individual experience, and a historical perspective arises from this understanding. Only selflessness in relation to our own destiny can lead to an investigation of real history. Aside from documents, Rudolf Steiner investigated broad areas of true historical facts and the earthly reflection of spiritual events, and he has illuminated our traditions. He saw how these are connected according to the principle active in them, which is *karma*. The spiritual investigation of history again shows the moral height of Steiner's investigative method; and his karma exercises, which present genuine biographies, must be maintained at that moral height.

There is another side to the twin task that arose in relation to Leading Thoughts 50 to 52 (Study 26). If we follow the historical element into the living human soul, we also find the path that leads to historical investigation. Steiner often pointed out that we can discover truths about the past by reading the so-called *akashic record*. Particularly in his earlier lectures, Steiner repeatedly spoke about the nature of the akashic record, of how it preserves traces of everything brought about at any time by conscious beings. We know, from the leading thoughts, that we can picture the way the akashic record manifests. We need only remind ourselves of how the etheric body—which also bears unconscious memory pictures—reveals itself after death in an objective panorama of life and then expands into the cosmos (Study 13).

We must look repeatedly at Steiner's method for introducing Spiritual Science to contemporary humanity. First, he appeals to ordinary consciousness and trains its capacity for understanding the truth. Then, out of a feeling for truth, he develops an understanding for suprasensory facts, after which he can go on to describe suprasensory facts themselves. Finally, he shows how knowledge of the spiritual world is attained. The best exercises for this path of knowledge arise from an understanding of spiritual facts and the path that leads to them.

For historical investigation, genuine *intuition* is necessary—uniting with spiritual beings—in true biographies. The akashic record is at the boundary between the spiritual and the supra-spiritual worlds in the realm where (in keeping with our studies of the Categories) the creative element passes over into the causal.[4] Steiner's own investigations thus become comprehensible to

---

4 *Founding a Science of the Spirit*, lecture 2; *Rosicrucian Wisdom*, lecture 4; and *According to Luke*, lecture 1.

ordinary consciousness. To transform them into exercises, however, it is necessary to begin with the fact that suprasensory worlds enter our ordinary consciousness.

Humankind is heir to an immense past (Study 23). This heritage comes from a twofold stream of evolution—successive *generations* and successive *incarnations*. The series of generations contains everything that comes to a person externally—in other words, what we are according to birth, family, nation, education, environment, and so on—our whole composition. In this way, we take our place in the continuing flow of history. In addition to this, there is also what a person brings from the series of incarnations, one's disposition and capacities. A person's great conflicts in the life arise from the meeting of these two streams; life's experiences are formed by their balancing. A part of our work on the consciousness soul is to evoke into awareness the traces of these two streams of evolution, which come together in our present Earth life. Thus, history can become real in human awareness, since we are connected through the sentient soul to the Egypto-Chaldean civilization, for example. Steiner explained how the human sentient soul was developed during that era, just as the intellectual (or mind) soul was developed during the Greco-Roman civilization.

Now, however, when we transport our current soul experience into the age of the intellectual soul, we must not work our way back by negating the consciousness soul, which arose in our time; in this way, we would find only the decadent remains of old experience. Certainly, the old Roman, for example, is somewhere within us, but in a rudimentary form. The ancient Roman brought a consciousness of justice into the world; the only relic of the Roman in ourselves is what we can perhaps call a dogmatist.[1] This old Roman, however, is our inner enemy; we must overcome these old forms within ourselves. Steiner once spoke of a hidden Pharisee within us, as well as a Sadducee and an Essene; and besides these, there are yet other enemies of Atlantean and Lemurian extraction. Only when these remnants are vanquished will they reveal to our consciousness soul their forces that are still useful for the future, when they will lead us to experience the Christ impulse. Only then will we gain the necessary selflessness in relation to our destiny that allows us to truly shape future history.

53. Our life between death and a new birth unfolds in successive stages. For a few days, immediately after passing through the gate of death, all of one's past earthly life is seen in living *pictures*. This experience also reveals the gradual severance of the vehicle of one's past life from the human soul and spirit.

---

1   *The Gospel of St. John*, lecture 8; and *Egyptian Myths and Mysteries*, lecture 9.

54. During a time equivalent to about a third of the past earthly life, the soul discovers through spiritual experiences the effects of that life according to an ethically just world order. During this experience, the soul gives birth to an intention to shape the next earthly life in a way that corresponds, and thus compensates, for the past.

55. A purely spiritual period of existence of long duration follows. During this epoch, the human soul fashions the next life on Earth in terms of karma, along with other, karmically connected human souls and with beings of the higher hierarchies.

In Leading Thoughts 53 to 55, it seems as though what was given earlier repeats Leading Thoughts 23 to 28. In reality, however, those earlier leading thoughts presented facts as such, with a view toward the cosmos; now the view has shifted toward the investigation of karma and history. A careful comparison of these two accounts can reveal much to us. The *life tableau* is described in Leading Thought 23 as the first experience in the spiritual world after death; it is a repetition of the daytime experiences of the past Earth life, from which we are gradually freed by death. In Leading Thought 53, however, we recognize from the whole context that, with the survey of the life tableau and "the gradual severance of the vehicle of one's past life"—or the severance of the *etheric body*—a prospect of the development of history opens out; in other words, the pictures vanishing into the distance insert themselves into the akashic record. Immediately after his entry into the spiritual world, the dead looks back and experiences a transformation of the human etheric into the cosmic akashic substance. But one knows that these vanishing pictures will be rediscovered.[2]

Here we have an objective memory that is experienced selflessly.[3] Our exercises in selfless memory, our looking back over the day and over life, are the exercises practiced during earthly life. Only when our memories have become selfless can they be controlled morally. In looking at the etheric body, which falls away from the human being (Leading Thought 53), we can say: *Thus history grows.*

Likewise, Leading Thought 24 may be compared to Leading Thought 54. In our experience of the astral body after death, the nighttime experiences of the past life are repeated in relation to the judgment of life. Nevertheless, the effect, compared to the experience of the etheric body, is completely different. Through objective remembering, the effects on the etheric body flow into the realms from which we receive the effects of the series of generations. This is the historical continuity that awakens a seemingly uninterrupted causality in

---

2   *The Inner Nature of Man and the Life Between Death and Rebirth*, lectures 5 and 6; and *The Being of Man and His Future Evolution*, lecture 4.

3   *Rosicrucian Wisdom*, lecture 3.

historical events. Our experiences of the judgment of life, which are connected with the astral body, are carried farther by the soul. They will reappear as a result of the series of incarnations as disposition and capacities in future earthly lives. We can add to the description in Leading Thought 54: *Thus morality enters into history.*

Leading Thought 55 is related to Leading Thought 26. We experience a "purely spiritual period of existence of long duration." The results of the repetition of past day and night experiences—the activities of the etheric and astral bodies—unite as a spiritual whole. This occurs in the realm of *intentions*, as the higher spiritual world is called by Steiner in *Theosophy* (pp. 129–130). What in later earthly lives reaches a person from two sides—from the two series of generations and incarnations—begins here, just as in the previous Earth life it arose from a unity. In this higher region of the spiritual realm, our true being, together with beings of the hierarchies, is entirely united with our own karma. There, we have completely drawn in our karma like a breath, and we breathe it out again when we descend to the next Earth life. We can add to this Leading Thought 55: *Thus prevision rules in history.*

If, in this way, we follow history into humankind's inmost being (Leading Thought 51), we become strongly convinced that "it is human souls themselves, passing from age to age in their repeated lives on Earth, who carry the effects of one historic time into another" (Leading Thought 50).

STUDY 28

A NEW SERVICE OF SACRIFICE

56. The period of existence between death and a new birth, when human karma is formed, can be described by means of spiritual research. We must always bear in mind that such descriptions appeal to our intelligence. We need only consider with open minds the realities of this world of the senses, and we become aware that it points to a spiritual reality—as the form of a corpse indicates the life previously lived within it.

57. The results of Spiritual Science show that, between death and rebirth, we belong to spirit kingdoms, just as, between birth and death, we belong to the three kingdoms of nature—mineral, plant, and animal.

58. The mineral kingdom can be seen in the human form at any time; the plant kingdom, as the etheric body, is the basis of our growth and becoming; the animal kingdom, as the astral body, is the impulse for our unfolding sensation and volition. Our conscious life of sensation and volition is crowned by a *self-aware* spiritual life, which makes our relationship to the spiritual world immediately apparent.

Leading Thoughts 56 to 58 in fact repeat what was given earlier in Leading Thoughts 27 and 28. Nevertheless, we can develop it further; since we considered those previous leading thoughts, with the help of Rudolf Steiner's descriptions, we have gone through a cycle from one incarnation to the next. Thus, we can try to let the facts presented in the these leading thoughts work in a prevision of the following Earth life. In Steiner's lectures we find clear indications that such a preview of the following incarnation in fact arises before a soul when descending from the spiritual realm. It follows, then, that the union between the descending human spirit and the astral and etheric bodies is accompanied by experiences that present us with the counterpart of the spirit's after-death experiences when leaving earthly life.

If we look from this life on Earth toward the next, it will appear to be thoroughly permeated by the spirit, since all that exists at that point has been carried through the spiritual world. After death, we meet all the beings who help us shape our karma, and when we descend we meet the spirit beings who represent the "I"-beings of the kingdoms of nature in their corresponding spiritual realms. Through them, when a human being sets foot on Earth, the kingdoms of nature become spirit-filled and interwoven with human acts. Thus, looking toward a future incarnation, we also see ourselves in a way that "makes our relationship to the spiritual world immediately apparent" (Leading Thought 58). We can also say: Because the spirit in nature and ourselves becomes perceptible in this earthly life, we contain the impulses that work toward the future.

Our attempt at such prevision can give us an idea of what Steiner said in the central chapter of the newer edition of *Theosophy* about a counterpart to the capacity of memory in relation to human acts.

> What is preserved in memory is waiting for a reason to reappear. Could it be the same with things in the outer world that have been made lasting by the character of the I? Are they waiting to approach the soul from the outside, just as a memory waits for a reason to approach from the inside? (*Theosophy*, p. 66)

The subject in question is a memory of past actions that works objectively. In karma exercises related to history, a person can successfully take part in this memory of acts. Karma exercises should not be practiced only in order to understand the past, but also to shape the future.

We saw in Study 21 that any expectation of a continued life after death, as taught in traditional religions, is always connected with egoism, and that it is more useful to consider the life before birth. When we look at repeated Earth lives, self-centeredness is primarily related to whom we might like to have been in earlier incarnations—regardless of how little it corresponds to facts—whereas selflessness is acquired more easily by looking forward to the activities of future earthly lives. In the current Earth life, it is always important to act through knowledge.

We can now proceed to statements in the leading thoughts, such as those that suggest our anthroposophic work should be lifted into the realm of the hierarchies of spiritual beings. This also implies an indication in relation to understanding what Steiner began in the final year of his life—placing the Anthroposophical Society on completely new foundations and becoming its president. This occurred on Christmas 1923. The original Anthroposophical Society of 1913 was established by human beings, and its purpose was to form a framework that would make it possible to receive the fruits of Steiner's investigations into the spiritual realm. The reorganization in 1923 was willed by the spiritual worlds and was a call to those who had already received gifts of infinite value to act for the spiritual world out of the depths of their own hearts. It is now like a new covenant in contrast to an old one.

If anthroposophic work is to be lifted into the realms of the hierarchies of spiritual beings, this can be seen as a *service of sacrifice*. This is earnestly related to karma exercises, which can form a foundation for new communities among men and women. Indeed, we can show how Steiner's works from the very beginning unites human beings with spiritual worlds on paths of knowledge. In 1926, a new edition of Steiner's introductions to Goethe's scientific writings was published as *Goethe the Scientist* at the Goetheanum in Dornach. In Chapter 6, "The Nature of Goethe's Knowledge," we read the wonderful statement: "Becoming aware of the Idea in reality is the true communion of humanity." It is not our particular task here to understand this sentence philosophically; many of its elements are already contained in the course of these studies. We can see, however, that these words express the lifting of a service of sacrifice into purely spiritual realms. If we pursue the original impulse of these words, we can refresh our understanding of all Steiner's work.

Until now, we have considered his Spiritual Science—especially its thought garment—as a language where it is possible to speak to people about the spiritual world. We have taken great care to understand its sounds. But there is another side to it. Whereas we can gradually learn to express the sounds of this language, this language of the consciousness soul should also enable us to speak of humankind to the beings of the spiritual hierarchies.

The religions of the great civilizations contain memories of the ancient divine being of a golden age; the gods created the world and humankind. Human beings were once placed in the world of God—with feelings of gratitude, they sacrificed the fruits of the earth, symbols of their own material existence that revealed the creative work of God. That is a picture of the cult of the past; what will the cult of the future look like? The purpose of the leading thoughts from now on is to answer this question.

If we recall the preliminary karma exercises in Study 23, we have the picture of the Washing of the Feet, which there arises according to natural scientific method. This constitutes reverence for what is beneath us. In Goethe's description of the pedagogical province in Wilhelm Neister's apprenticeship and wanderings, he refers to it as the *highest religion*. He refers to reverence for what is above as *ethnic religion*, the religion of peoples; reverence for what is equal with us, gives the foundation for the second, the *philosophic religion*; and Goethe refers to reverence for what is beneath us as the *Christian religion*. Steiner presents this religious element as *knowledge* and the path of knowledge as reverence for what is within us. *How to Know Higher Worlds* and many other places give devotional exercises; Steiner's whole work demonstrates that these in no way interfere with human freedom but, instead, enhance it.

Now, however, this kind of exercises also lead to definite understanding that can be represented by simple words. The being of the plant forms its body out of the mineral, above which it rises, and inhabits the mineral kingdom. Thus the plant (according to exercises given by Steiner) should bow in reverence to the mineral, since it owes its very existence to it. Likewise, the animal inhabits the plant kingdom and humankind the animal kingdom along with the other kingdoms of nature as well. But who inhabits the human being?

There is a passage where Steiner extends the mood expressed in the Washing of the Feet beyond the human being to the hierarchies of spiritual beings.[1] The beings of the third hierarchy inhabit humankind; they view humankind as the kingdom that provides them the foundations for their spiritual existence. Human thoughts are their primary dwelling place—not ordinary thoughts but, inasmuch as the human "I" has turned its astral body toward the eternal, pure thoughts become the sacrificial gift of human beings to the beings of the third hierarchy.[2] Steiner spoke in relation to this of how the modern human being allows these beings to suffer want and to hunger, and has allowed the sacrificial bread to spoil.[3] The thoughts of ordinary consciousness are corpses—they lived in the life before birth, where the spiritual beings had laid them in humankind as a seed. In ancient civilizations, what corresponds to thoughts today were still ripening as a harvest for the beings of the third hierarchy in the spiritual world; but it has now fallen to those beings who remained behind, who unlawfully inhabit human beings today and take possession of them. The essential task of Anthroposophy is to reconsecrate the sacrificial centers of our inner being.

---

1   *Gegenwaertiges und Vergangenes im Manschengeiste* ("Present and Past in the Human Spirit"), lecture 7 (CW 167); unavailable in English.

2   *Between Death and Rebirth*, lecture 1.

3   *Universe, Earth and Man*, lecture 9.

STUDY 29

ANALYSIS OF CONSCIOUSNESS

The previous study closed with a picture of the desecrated temple of the inner human being; it is inscribed in the history of human consciousness. We still find that three altars play a role in esoteric traditions, though today they are primarily connected only with the abstract ideals of *wisdom*, *beauty*, and *strength*. The fourth point of the compass in this kind of symbolic temple is like a door with two pillars through which human and spirit beings pass in and out.

Today, there are still battles around those sacrificial centers. This is presented in wonderful scenes in Rudolf Steiner's *Four Mystery Dramas*. We see there, in human destinies, how striving for knowledge is presented to us as the work of cosmic beings. Four temple scenes are described as well as a look back to an Egyptian site of initiation. They show how the reign of spirit beings is superseded by the decisions of human souls. Powers hostile to humankind try to capture the temple centers by creating confusion in human souls. In *The Souls' Probation*, Lucifer assumes the important position in the north of the temple (scene 13) after Johannes Thomasius handed himself over to his leadership (scene 12). Ahriman, however—the other cosmic enemy—must withdraw from the Sun Temple, since Maria (scene 11) eluded his attempted deception through her own strength of soul. We may ask: What position would Ahriman have gained in the temple had Maria succumbed to him? That question enters deeply into all that occurs in the inner temple of every human being. If Ahriman had been victorious, Benedictus, the leader of human and spiritual events, would have had to leave his position in the east, the region of wisdom.

The cosmic battle of our time is waged around human wisdom. Therefore, on the path of knowledge spelled out in Steiner's leading thoughts, all the spirit power of the higher worlds must be brought to the temple center of contemporary consciousness so that decisions may be reached. Such scenes touch on a mystery suggested by the leading thoughts, because, at this important juncture in our studies, these scenes present processes of the inner human being and the way the higher hierarchies are working. It is like the course of a drama that begins with the presentation, and, through the image and activity of Michael, shows the outcome in modern human consciousness—that is, how the radical change in his experience governed by destiny is brought about. In these leading thoughts, the presentation begins with an examination of the self.

59. Open-minded contemplation of thinking demonstrates that thoughts in ordinary consciousness have no independent existence, but arise only as reflected images. Nevertheless, we experience ourselves as *alive* in our thoughts. The *thoughts* are not active, but *we* ourselves are living *in* them. The source of this life is spirit beings, described (as in *An Outline of Esoteric Science*) as the beings of the Third Hierarchy—a kingdom of the spirit.

60. When extended to the feeling life, the same open-minded contemplation shows that feelings, although they arise from the body, could not have been created there. Their life is naturally independent of the physical body. Through the bodily nature, we can experience ourselves within the world of nature. Nevertheless, by realizing this with true self-understanding, we will experience, through the realm of feeling, ourselves within a spiritual kingdom. This is the kingdom of the Second Hierarchy.

61. As beings of will, our attention is directed not to our own physical nature but to the outer world. When we want to walk, we do not ask, "What do I feel in my feet?" but "Where do I want to go?" In willing, we forget the body; in our will, we belong not to our own nature, but to the spirit kingdom of the First hierarchy.

The previous study was entitled "A New Service of Sacrifice." That note sounds again here, and we must not take this too lightly. In terms of spirituality, much is said of sacrifice. It is often overlooked, however, that only those who have something to offer are able to sacrifice; and we must have acquired this ourselves, otherwise we have nothing to offer. If we wish to sacrifice ourselves, first we must have achieved something. If we give back to the gods only what we have received from them, it is as though we come to the sacrifice with empty hands.

A true path of devotion is shown by Steiner in *How to Know Higher Worlds*, and it can be followed only when people have become clear about what they have acquired in their own being that may be sacrificed. This refers to the self-examination that begins in Leading Thoughts 59 to 61, which speak of thinking, feeling, and willing. Many of our studies have discussed shaping the soul forces—especially thinking—that must provide the form for all our considerations. We have seen also how, through self-examination, we are placed before a void (Study 9), how our own being can disappear from us. That brings the fear of death before the soul, and this fear can be overcome only through the practice of standing before the abyss of existence in meditation, since, from the other side, Spiritual Science brings a new meaning to the desolate soul and courage to try. This question is completely renewed, however, if we consider genuine sacrifice when we have something to offer.

With regard to thinking in terms of self-examination, Leading Thought 59 says that "thoughts in ordinary consciousness have no independent

existence.... Nevertheless, we experience ourselves as *alive* in our thoughts."
This difference between ordinary thoughts that "arise only as reflected images"
and the experiencing oneself in thinking must be introduced into logic, so that
the logic can leave abstraction behind.

In logic, the thoughts are intended to illustrate, and they are primarily
taken from memory. The most important thing here is that the judgments and
even the conclusions of logic are not really thought, but felt. For example, we
form the conclusion found in any textbook on logic: All foxes have four legs;
Herod was a fox, therefore, he had four legs. There, we immediately have the
feeling experience that this is false, even without the laws of logic. The laws
of logic are really thought formulae that arise after spontaneous experience
through feeling. With this feeling we live in thinking; and, in contrast to this
process, thoughts are dead images of something related to the external world.
It is further said that "the source of this life is spirit beings, described as
the beings of the Third Hierarchy—a kingdom of the spirit." However, it is
returned to their sphere after death; this occurs in the reviewed life scene as it
leaves a human being. If, in such an experience, we free ourselves from ordinary thoughts, then it becomes an exercise, like anticipating an event of this
kind after death. However, if the life of thinking is to be associated in this way
with beings of the Third Hierarchy, the question arises: What then constitutes
our own being? And what does it mean to the spiritual world?

Essentially, this subject has to do with how a person must experience
one's whole unworthiness in relation to raising anthroposophic efforts into
the realms of the hierarchies. If we analyze the human *being*, we find that it
is created entirely by the activity of the hierarchies. This arises from analysis
as such, where you have "the parts in his hands" (*Faust*). This presents us
with the old problem—*what is a whole beyond the significance of its parts?*
Greek thinkers and Buddha's sermons dealt equally with this problem; and it
is found in another, completely abstract form in modern mathematics.

Analysis is not creative activity, and it considers the constructive capacities
of synthesis extremely insignificant in terms of human knowledge. The resolu-
tion of such problems is possible only in the spiritual world. Analysis draws
a whole out of its own sphere of existence into the one below. Consequently,
psychoanalysis, for example, shows the animal element, and, therefore, modern science pushes everything living down into the mineral world. On the
other hand, to work synthetically, we must climb to a higher level. As long
as we are satisfied with differentiating between thinking, feeling, and willing,
the complete soul will always be dissolved into its separate, interdependent
functions, which leads us back to their origin. When this occurs in ordinary
consciousness, it indicates schizophrenia. Thinking then has the value of the
mineral, feeling that of the plant, and willing that of the animal; nothing then
remains of the human being.

Now let us consider the other, spiritual side of this process insofar as it relates to thinking. Steiner spoke of after-death conditions:

> It becomes evident that, behind the thoughts, which were only shadow images while we were on the physical planes, there is something living, a living and weaving in the world of thoughts. We become aware that what we have as our thought representations in the physical body is only a shadow image, that in fact a vast host of elemental beings lives and expands there.[1]

We could say of these that we ourselves created them; later, however, they withdraw from the human being. In another reference, Steiner described elemental beings as the offspring of the beings of the Third Hierarchy.[2] Although it seems that we ourselves create elemental beings, in reality they are the result of the creative activity of the beings of the Third Hierarchy.

Beginning with this viewpoint, we can return to the facts of earthly consciousness and draw our conclusions. If our thoughts are to result in something of value to the spiritual world after our death, then even during earthly life, we must not live only in the thoughts of ordinary consciousness; rather, we must practice other higher, pure thinking. We may ask ourselves whether the thoughts in these studies are themselves of a higher order. Yes, if they are permeated by will (Leading Thought 12). Thus, after the analysis, we gain the synthesis. The best analysis is death. Only from the realms on the other side of death do we gain truly constructive forces. In these studies, we have drawn conclusions that will appear later only partially in the leading thoughts; we will then return to this subject.

---

1   *The Inner Nature of Man and the Life Between Death and Rebirth*, lecture 5.

2   *Spiritual Beings in the Heavenly Bodies and in the Kingdoms of Nature*, lecture 3.

STUDY 30

SOUNDS AND THE WORD

According to Leading Thought 59, any analysis of human consciousness begins with self-examination of thinking; this is extended to feeling in Leading Thought 60. Certain difficulties arise, however, with regard to the previous study; we must be aware that when we consider feeling we are really speaking of thinking applied to feeling. In the first place, self-observation applies only to thinking. Rudolf Steiner pointed to this in a unique way—he based his philosophy on it and, in this way, shaped a path of self-awareness that leads to the spiritual world.

In ordinary consciousness, we can think about thinking, but we cannot feel feeling—we can only think about feeling. Our previous study helps us here; feeling also brings life to thinking. Thus, in Leading Thought 60, the feeling of thinking changes into feeling itself. In this way, something like a feeling of feeling in fact arises. This, however, leads people away from ordinary consciousness, and they can only attempt this in deep meditation. This leads us to understand how the most important element in this case is connected with the spiritual realm of the beings of the Second Hierarchy, just as we may describe thinking of thinking as the substance of the beings of the Third Hierarchy. For the spiritual world, this appears in the conditions after death in this way: the beings of the Third Hierarchy lead us to those of the Second Hierarchy. It is even possible to see that the way beings of the Third Hierarchy perceive those of the Second Hierarchy is similar to the way we perceive the beings of the Third Hierarchy (Study 28).

In conclusion, therefore, we can shift our attention to willing (Leading Thought 61). But, for this, even deeper meditation is necessary, because willing itself remains hidden to ordinary consciousness, and only the manifestations of the will come to the surface. Of course, just as feeling emerges behind thinking, willing must be active behind both, just as it is in general behind the whole soul life. True willing, hidden from ordinary consciousness, now belongs to the beings of the First Hierarchy. Human participation in this hierarchy would have to be expressed by a formula that corresponds to the others—willing of willing. One can see that, through this whole treatment of the soul forces, we have a new introduction into the nature of *imagination*, *inspiration*, and *intuition*.

We find, therefore, how human soul nature is related to the hierarchies of higher beings in thinking, feeling, and willing. They have created these forces in humankind, and thus the question naturally arises: What belongs to human beings themselves? The new condition that should arise through humankind is this: The three principles of the human being mutually interpenetrate and become one. In Steiner's investigations, we can find such facts as the following: that beings out of their own forces have endowed other beings (for example, human beings) to experience something new themselves by this means. Thus, Steiner said:

> It is entirely possible that one being may give a gift to another and only come to know that gift through the other. Imagine a very rich man who has never known anything but riches and never experienced the deep satisfaction of soul that comes from doing good. Now picture this person doing something good; he gives to the poor. The gift evokes deep gratitude in the soul of the individual in need. That feeling of gratitude is simultaneously a gift; it would never have existed if the rich person had not first given. He originated that feeling of gratitude, although he himself does not feel it and is acquainted with it only through its reflection flowing back to him from the one in whom he kindled it. This is approximately how it is with the gift of love.[1]

For further work on Steiner's leading thoughts, it will be useful to review somewhat the path we have already traveled. This is in short aphoristic sentences that embrace whole series of thoughts and perceptions. In the introduction to these studies, we found this statement: "The leading thoughts are the words of a new spiritual language. If they resound in human souls, the sounds of the language of the consciousness soul may take shape in inner experience."

1. All knowledge transforms the one who knows (Study 3).
2. It is not due to us that we awake from sleep (Study 4).
3. Breathing in pure thinking is the first clairvoyance (Study 5).
4. In the etheric world, concept and seeing are equal (Study 5).
5. To differentiate the animal from humankind is a moral process (Study 6).
6. The reality of the "I" is the source of all knowledge (Study 8).
7. All knowledge is obtained from death (Study 9).
8. The soul dream of daytime consciousness is a mixture of sleeping and waking (Study 9).
9. Conscious forgetting leads to meditation (Study 11).
10. Conscious remembering leads to *imagination* (Study 11).
11. If memories are to be of value, they must be morally controlled (Study 11).
12. The investigation of freedom is a process of obtaining freedom (Study 12).

---

1   *Universe, Earth and Man*, lecture 9.

13. Nature is the other side of spirit (Study 12).
14. On the path of knowledge, thinking and willing cross one another (Study 12).
15. The strongest argument against freedom is death (Study 13).
16. The strongest argument against the necessity of nature is knowledge (Study 13).
17. The life scene after death is a cosmic dream (Study 13).
18. Morality is the necessity of the night retrospective (Study 14).
19. The initiate carries freedom into the moral world (Study 14).
20. Concepts constitute the conscious participation of spirit land in ordinary consciousness (Study 15).
21. The great turning point for causality is the midnight hour of existence (Study 15).
22. Knowledge, love, and sacrifice are the human path to freedom (Study 16).
23. *Imagination* transforms time into space (Study 17).
24. *Inspiration* transforms causality into time (Study 18).
25. *Intuition* transforms the permanence of being into causality (Study 18).
26. Work on the consciousness soul signifies redeeming the Idea from earthly death to cosmic life (Study 18).
27. The "I" experiences causality; its essence is permanence of being (Study 18).
28. The astral body experiences time; its essence is causality (Study 18).
29. The etheric body experiences space; its essence is time (Study 18).
30. The physical body suffers death; its essence is space (Study 17).
31. Anthroposophy as Spiritual Science teaches us to understand cosmic beings through earthly consciousness (Study 19).
32. Anthroposophy as a path of knowledge leads us to shape earthly lives out of the cosmos (Study 19).
33. The human physical organization as creation is half finished; the other half is passed on to human beings themselves (Study 19).
34. The law of the will is *morality*, its realization on Earth is *destiny* (Study 22).
35. Human knowledge of nature is nature's self-knowledge (Study 22).
36. Spiritual science is human self-knowledge (Study 22).
37. Spirit self sees destiny through the instrument of the human metabolism and limb system (Study 22).
38. Art reveals suprasensory self-knowledge (Study 22).
39. Every true introduction to Anthroposophy is a preliminary karma exercise (Study 22).
40. We experience our being in contrast to nature, and the being of nature within ourselves (Study 23).

41. We carry within ourselves only one part of our being; the other is nature, to which we are indebted from primeval times (Study 23).

42. Only what has already been carried through the spiritual world can become destiny (Study 23).

43. What pulses through earth life as destiny is seed for future cosmic development (Study 23).

44. Destiny is the cosmic judge of human actions (Study 24).

45. No one can have destiny only as a lone individual; destiny is the strongest social force (Study 25).

46. Questions of destiny must be lifted from the individual into the social realm (Study 25).

47. Historical standards arise through understanding karma (Study 27).

48. During the present Earth life it is important to act through knowledge (Study 28).

49. The language of the consciousness soul speaks not only to humankind about the spiritual realm, but should speak also to the spiritual realm about humankind (Study 28).

50. The cosmic battle of the present time is for human wisdom (Study 29).

51. Those who would offer sacrifice may not come empty handed (Study 29).

52. Those who would offer themselves must first have value (Study 29).

53. Through analyzing, a whole is drawn out of its own sphere into the next one below (Study 29).

54. To work synthetically, we must climb one level higher (Study 29).

55. The best analyst is death; we gain truly constructive forces only from realms on the other side of death (Study 29).

56. Thinking of thinking yields *imagination*; feeling of feeling, *inspiration*; willing of willing, *intuition* (Study 30).

The letters from the language of the consciousness soul can be experienced as the fruits of meditation. May these sounds be encompassed by the Word!

A NEW BEGINNING

To lift anthroposophic work into the realm of the hierarchies of higher beings, certain preliminary exercises are necessary. By means of an analogy, we were led to conclude that the beings of the third hierarchy inhabit humankind, as humankind in turn inhabits the animal kingdom, animals the plant kingdom, and plants the mineral kingdom (Study 28). This conclusion naturally implies more than a process of logic. Furthermore, it could not even exist as a conclusion if not for the activity of deeper realities. And the same must apply to this last statement as well.

Rudolf Steiner once said to this author many years ago that "a thought correctly thought is valid." It is essential, however, that we also acknowledge the difference between accepting as valid a thought that is correctly thought—that is, *universal*—and troubling ourselves to search the cosmic realm where it is in fact valid. Thus, thinking must become selfless and not its semblance; it must return to its spiritual reality that, although unconsciously, rules in feeling and willing (Studies 29 and 30).

Our analogical conclusion appeared in context with scientific method; it can act as an act of deliverance accomplished by independent thinking as opposed to the compulsions of the natural kingdoms; a barrier is thus broken. Now, however, a question certainly arises: How do the beings of the hierarchies live in human beings and the universe? To answer *how*—thinking alone can never provide an answer if it fails to consider its own thinking directly; an answer can arise only through facts. With regard to this question, however, these can be only spiritual facts, and they must be established through spiritual observation. In this way, a path is indicated that allows us to reach *Anthroposophy*, since it asks this very question of human beings and answers from the spiritual world. Human beings, however, must continually learn to ask questions and to understand the answers.

Thus, we can understand why Steiner repeatedly begins afresh, entering again and again into fundamental questions that can be asked by the ordinary, modern human consciousness. These numerous fresh beginnings cover everything given directly to contemporary consciousness; every individual today can thus enter Anthroposophy, regardless of one's position in life. But, for those who have already found Anthroposophy, the many faceted new beginnings are exercises that are effective because of their rhythmic repetition.

Thus, there really is no difference between beginners and advanced students in terms of the subject, to the *what*—only in terms of the *how*.[1]

Every fresh beginning to this inquiry has a quality that, for the last 150 years, has been called *epistemological*. The word, of course, sounds very abstract, but the process itself is repeated again and again, since every ascent into spiritual heights begins at the level of ordinary consciousness. As we learn to permeate ordinary consciousness with spirit, the path to the spirit becomes clearer. In the next leading thoughts (62–65), we begin again in this way. Steiner added a letter to these leading thoughts in which fundamental questions of human experience are discussed.[2] Such letters to the members of the Anthroposophical Society accompany a large number of the later leading thoughts and offer most significant explanations. These Letters will appear in print.[3] It will suffice in our studies to refer to them aphoristically.

Steiner points out two fundamental experiences in a new way that we can discover when we reflect. If someone has thoughts about the outer world, such a person may become aware of being in one's thoughts; the world is lost from one's consciousness and the "I" enters it. If, on the other hand, one's attention is directed inwardly, one's own existence will appear as the result of destiny experiences, upon which the world has encroached. In this way, one loses one's self from consciousness and the world enters into it. In perceiving these two experiences, we are faced with a question of world and humankind, and the answers provided by Anthroposophy can deeply affect the soul. Anthroposophy points to a deepened thinking, meditation that does not allow the sensory world to be lost, but reveals the spirit world. It further points to an experience of destiny that does not allow the self to be lost, but allows it an active experience of being active in the outer world. These leading thoughts refer to this.

62. In sense perception, the world of the senses affects only the surface of the being concealed in the depths beneath its waves. Penetrating spiritual observation reveals within these depths the aftereffects of what was done by human souls during ages long ago.

63. To ordinary self-observation, our inner world reveals only a part of what it exists within. Intensified conscious experience shows that it is contained within a living spiritual reality.

64. Human destiny reveals the activity of not just the external world, but that of the human "I"-being.

---

1   *Christ and the Spiritual world: The Search for the Holy Grail*, lecture 6.

2   Letter of July 13, 1924.

3   The letters that accompany the leading thoughts are contained in *Anthroposophical Leading Thoughts* (George and Mary Adams, trans.) and in *The Michael Mystery* (Marjorie Spock, trans.).

65. The experiences of the human soul reveal not only the "I," but a world of spirit, which the "I" can know through deeper spiritual knowledge as a world united with its own being.

The fundamental questions in these leading thoughts are not foreign to our studies. In Study 10 we find:

> The more we desire to remain a unity, the more our own being vanishes into the *other*, the world, until a mere point—as through nothing—is left. This is the tragedy of the "I." Any attempt to balance it with the world becomes dualistic in every way. The essential dualism is that of inner and outer worlds. We can try to grasp the outer world from the inner world, or the inner world from the outer world. *In either instance, the object being considered is withdrawn.*

Also, in connection with preliminary karma exercises we met the problem of the polarity of "I" and world (Study 23). And with regard to the experience of destiny, we found the sentence in Study 25: "*The world is related to human beings through knowing and activity.*" The point is to repeatedly experience the world in the "I" as an exercise in relation to the problem of experiencing the "I" in the world. Nevertheless, as we consider this dual problem in terms of a *new beginning*, we find that it forms the basis of what the soul needs today, just as it runs through all of philosophy when formulated scientifically. But neither the immediate experience of life nor philosophy has found the answer. Steiner, from the very beginning, through working out the clear definition—epistemologically, scientifically, philosophically, and ethically—answered these questions in all of these areas. He added them as fundamental questions of human soul life in a specific sense in his 1918 preface to *Intuitive Thinking as a Spiritual Path: A Philosophy of Freedom.*[4]

Anthroposophy's answers here indicate the entrance of new worlds in contrast to all other scientific formulae. But that must be the essential experience of everyone who is impelled today by the needs of the soul to seek out Anthroposophy. That can happen in the most varied ways and, consequently, there must be, as indicated, a variety of introductions to Anthroposophy. There may be external catastrophic conditions that tear a person away from former relationships—from family, nation, country, vocation, and society. Such sudden changes are related to destiny experiences.

Therefore, older people today who found themselves in the Anthroposophical Society are drawn from all over the globe through the activity of destiny, which can be traced in detail. As time moves on, we can see the entrance of a

---

4   "*First*, can we understand human nature in such a way that this understanding serves as the basis for everything else we may meet in the way of experience or science? ... *Second*, can we human beings, as willing entities, ascribe freedom to ourselves, or is this freedom a mere illusion that arises because we do not see the threads of necessity upon which our willing, like any other natural event, depends?" p. 1.

powerful inner experience of destiny. To young people (unless they are actually Waldorf students), this appears as a collapse of their previous image of the world—like standing before a void. It is like a death experience, related to inner destiny that wants to transform itself into the forces of knowledge. That is the experience of youth; it calls young people to become a part of Anthroposophy.

Steiner describes this kind of basic experience, which involves at the same time an encounter with the spirit of this world:

> The Mephistophelian spirits cast a veil over the spiritual foundation of the world and mocked humanity with an illusory world. Mephistopheles infused into human beings the belief that the world is only a material existence, that there is nothing spiritual in it and behind all matter. The scene Goethe depicts so wonderfully in his *Faust* is continually reenacted in humanity as a whole.

> On the one hand, we see Faust looking for the way into the spiritual world; on the other, Mephistopheles describes the spiritual world as "nothing," because it is in his interest to represent the sense world as everything. Faust responds with words that every spiritual investigator would have used in a similar situation: "In your 'Nothing' I intend to find my All!"[1]

This experience of the "nothing" comes spontaneously to many today. Anthroposophy makes possible the right answer. This, however, should not be done only once; rather, this experience should assume the form of an exercise—a preliminary exercise for raising the work into the realm of the hierarchies of higher beings.

---

1   *The Gospel of St. John in Relation to the Other Gospels*, lecture 5.

"EPISTEMOLOGIES" OF THE HIGHER HIERARCHIES

As we ponder the sensory world, it disappears; and, if thinking is strength-ened until it becomes meditation, the spiritual world replaces it through the experience of the "I." On the other hand, if the "I" considers itself in its destiny, it finds that it is connected with the events of the world, so that the "I" appears from the surrounding world (Study 31). In this way, an inter-change between the sensory and spiritual worlds arises. To what degree is this a preliminary exercise for raising anthroposophic work into the realms of the higher hierarchies? In different words, Rudolf Steiner presented a thought in verse form that emphasizes the polarity of self-knowledge and knowledge of the world. In Study 23, one rendering is presented; here is another:

> Search in your own being,
> And you find the world;
> Search in the realms of the world:
> And you find yourself;
> Mark the pendulum's swing
> Between self and the world;
> And revealed to you is
> Human-world-being,
> World-human-being.[2]

Here we are concerned with the swing of the pendulum. Two of Steiner's books are far too little known—*A Way of Self-Knowledge* and *The Threshold of the Spiritual World*. They begin with this swing of the pendulum. Even the words *swing of the pendulum* come in the first chapter of the second book in reference to the rhythms of waking and sleeping as well as life and death. These polarities bind human beings to the cosmos and its being, tear them away again into earthly aloneness. When we consciously raise ourselves into the sphere of cosmic beings, we realize, as spiritual experiences, the *episte-mologies* of those belonging to the higher hierarchies, a term once used by Steiner. He describes forms of consciousness pertaining to the hierarchies as *rhythms* and shows how we must practice placing these together with our own element of consciousness; in this way, we can rise to their realms. There, it is possible to understand how the human being has arisen from the activity of

---

2   *Truth-Wrought-Words.*

the hierarchies and how those hierarchies extend their rule into humankind. That is presented comprehensively in Leading Thoughts 66–68—that is, the role of the higher hierarchies on the stage of the human soul.

66. The beings of the Third Hierarchy reveal themselves in the life that is unfolded as a spiritual background in human thinking. This life is concealed in human thought activity. If it worked in its own essence in human thought, we could not attain freedom. Where cosmic thinking ends, human thinking begins.

67. The beings of the Second Hierarchy reveal themselves in a soul realm beyond humanity—a world of cosmic soul activity, hidden from human feeling. This cosmic soul world is always creative in the background of human feeling. From human beings, it first creates the organism of feeling; only then can it enliven feeling itself there.

68. The beings of the First Hierarchy reveal themselves in spiritual creation beyond humanity—a cosmic world of spiritual being that lives in human willing. This world of cosmic spirit experiences itself in creative activity when human beings will. It first creates the interrelationship between human beings and the universe beyond humanity; only then do the human beings become, through their organism of will, beings of free will.

Steiner describes the forms of consciousness belonging to the beings of the higher hierarchies as compared with the alteration of the human consciousness between outer life (perception) and inner life. There we find that the beings of the third Hierarchy are of such a nature that they "perceive whenever they reveal themselves; when they express what they themselves are; and they really perceive their own being only as long as they wish to reveal it, as long as they express it outwardly in any way."[1] Steiner calls this form of consciousness *revelation of being*. This revelation of their own being corresponds to human perception. In the beings of the third Hierarchy, another form of consciousness corresponds to human inner life: "When they enter their inner being, they do not enter an inner independent life as does man, but a life in common with other worlds. Instead of an inner life, they have the experience of higher spiritual worlds" (ibid., p. 98). Steiner calls this consciousness *spirit-filling*—being filled by beings of higher hierarchies.

In ordinary consciousness, human beings turn in perception to the kingdoms of nature below them; in their inner life, they turn to spirit and can attain the kingdoms above. Thus, the *spirit-filling* of the beings of the Third Hierarchy involves turning toward higher beings, and, similarly, we can understand *revelation of being* as a turning toward humankind below them. This is contained in Leading Thought 66. The revelation of being of the

---

1   *The Spiritual Beings in the Heavenly Bodies and in the Kingdoms of Nature*, pp. 52–53.

Third Hierarchy is the spiritual background of the human activity of thinking. The substance of this revelation is the essence of *truth*. Those of the Third Hierarchy can live only in the purest honesty and truth. From the previous quote, Steiner went on to say:

> Let us just suppose that these beings had a desire to be untrue to their own nature; what would result? Well, in the beings we have designated *angels*, *archangels*, and *spirits of the age*, or *Archai*, we find throughout that everything that reveals itself to them—everything they can perceive is, so to speak, their own being. If they wish to be untrue, they would be obliged to develop something in their inner being that would be inconsistent with their own nature. Every untruth would be a denial of their nature. That would mean nothing less than a deadening, a damping down of their own being. (ibid., p. 99)

Thus human thinking is based on truth, but people base their own lives on the fact that they have torn themselves away from the revelation of being of the Third Hierarchy. Here we encounter deeply moving knowledge—that, essentially, individual human existence is based on a spiritual lie, since now there are in fact beings of the Third Hierarchy who do not reveal their being but desire it for themselves. Consequently, they have fallen out of the community of the normal beings of their hierarchy; they are the beings who have remained behind, and thus they are forced into the realm of human evolution. They are the leaders, or misleaders, of human beings into individual existence. Rudolf Steiner calls them *luciferic* beings. We must conceive of these luciferic beings, however, from another viewpoint; they have sacrificed themselves in order to make freedom possible in the world, and we should develop this freedom.[2] If we accept this sacrifice in the right way, however, the human activity of thinking—which begins where the cosmic activity of thinking ceases—will eventually reveal our own being to the Earth and to the cosmos (Leading Thought 66).

Similarly, Leading Thought 67 tells us how, in the essential background of human feeling, the cosmic soul element of the beings of the Second Hierarchy is active. True, because of the nature of their consciousness, it is much more difficult to comprehend the participation of the Second Hierarchy in human feeling. Again it is a matter of their outer consciousness, through which they turn toward the beings below them. Continuing from the previous statement, Steiner refers to this as *self-creating*.

At this point, we will not consider the connection between the outer consciousness of these beings and *spirit-filling*, or the inner consciousness of the beings of the Third Hierarchy. But when we see Steiner's descriptions of the nature of the consciousness *self-creating*, we find that it deals with shaping

---

2 See *The Gospel of St. John in Relation to the Other Gospels*, lecture 5; and *Manifestations of Karma*, lecture 11.

forms as images of themselves. Such forms are permanently connected with the life of these beings. In human soul experience, we sense that this cosmic soul element in feeling suggests a susceptibility to art. The connection of these beings with their *self-creating* makes it possible to awaken the perception that human feeling is based on love through the dominion of beings of the Second Hierarchy, just as thinking is based on truth through the beings of the Third Hierarchy.

Finally, we can extend this method to Leading Thought 68, which shows how the cosmic spirit element of beings of the First Hierarchy experiences itself as *self-creating* when human beings will. Certainly, this activity is even farther from us than the relationships previously considered. We may ask again, however: What is the basis of the human will? When we follow the way Steiner describes the outer consciousness of the beings of the First Hierarchy, we find that their self-objectification remains in existence as cosmic activity, even when the creating beings separate themselves from the object of their creation. Steiner calls this form of consciousness *cosmic-creating*. By following his detailed description, we can perceive that the rule of the beings of the first Hierarchy bases human will on morality.

Leading Thoughts 66 to 68 make it obvious that human freedom begins with thinking, as Steiner showed in *Intuitive Thinking as a Spiritual Path*. In relation to this, where we study the human soul element from the perspective of the higher hierarchies, it should become apparent to us that we receive our impulse to freedom in thinking from the luciferic beings. Because of the activity of the higher hierarchies, humankind gains the power through thinking to take Lucifer's gift from him, thus redeeming the spiritual lie. By attaining freedom in thinking, however, we encounter the danger that this gift may become the prize of Ahriman. This will be dealt with in subsequent leading thoughts.

What later becomes the human soul element is first carried in the consciousness of the beings of the hierarchies. This process belongs to the outer consciousness of the hierarchical beings and corresponds to human perception. Such epistemologies are a creative act. Thus, human self-knowledge is lifted into the realm of the higher hierarchies. We attain what we find in Benedictus' book of life in Steiner's mystery play *The Soul's Probation*:

> *The plan divine then will you recognize*
> *When you have realized yourself within you.*

STUDY 33

COSMIC REALMS OF THE HIERARCHIES

The revelations of higher hierarchies in the realm of the human soul indicate one swing of the pendulum in the consciousness of those hierarchies to the side Rudolf Steiner compared to perception—the outer human being. Following Leading Thoughts 66–68, our previous study took up this point, since it concerns humanity. We must now add the other pendulum swing in the consciousness of higher hierarchies; it is related to the inner human being. The following diagram, which is merely a summary, complements a similar one by Steiner.[1]

HIERARCHIES:	Third	Second	First
OUTER BEING:	Revelation of being	Self-creating	World-creating
INNER BEING:	Spirit-filling	Stimulation of life	Creating of being
HUMAN SOUL:	Thinking	Feeling	Willing

The other side of the consciousness of higher hierarchies—their inner being—is described in the following leading thoughts as spiritual cosmic realms.

69. The Third Hierarchy reveals itself as pure soul and spirit. It lives and moves in all that human beings experience in the soul, or inner life. If this were the only active hierarchy, no processes could take place in the etheric or in the physical; only soul life could exist.

70. The Second Hierarchy reveals itself as soul and spirit active in the etheric. Everything etheric is a manifestation of the Second Hierarchy. This hierarchy, however, does not reveal itself directly in the physical; its power extends only to the etheric processes. If only the Third and Second hierarchies were active, only etheric and soul life would exist.

71. The First (and strongest) Hierarchy reveals itself as the spirit principle active within the physical. It renders the physical realm a cosmos.

---

1   *The Spiritual Beings in the Heavenly Bodies and in the Kingdoms of Nature,* lectures 4 and 5 (see p. 87).

The beings of the Third and Second hierarchies minister to it through this activity.

In relation to these leading thoughts, Steiner wrote a letter to the members about spiritual, cosmic realms and human self-knowledge. In it a path is shown that leads, through the practice of self-knowledge, to the cosmic realms of higher hierarchies.[1] Another aspect of such self-knowledge is that we do not avoid coming to terms with the difficulty of conceptualizing them; the *inner being* of those belonging to the higher hierarchies is described as their cosmic realm. Of course, *cosmic realm* has nothing to do with any spatial representation; rather, it has a cosmic quality. This might become less difficult if we first investigate the human cosmic realm. In terms of this view, we see that the subject of our consideration is concealed in the inner human being—not in ordinary consciousness but in the other swing of the pendulum provided by sleep. We find our own cosmic realm only when we embark on a path into the spiritual world and approach forms of consciousness belonging to the beings of the Third Hierarchy.

According to our earlier studies, the result of this is *pure thinking*; in other words, it is a form of thinking that does not depend on any sense perception—one that thinks about thinking. Consequently, even simple descriptions of the thought processes characteristically express its laws, or being. In considering itself, thinking has—as *percept*—only what reveals itself from its own being. Here, we clearly recognize an approach to the outer being of those belonging to the Third Hierarchy. If, however, it withdraws its being from self-revelation, it arrives at the boundary of consciousness as the sum of all potential thinking (Study 4)—as pure "I"-being—which is *spirit-filling*, through which we also approach in our inner being the form of consciousness belonging to beings of the Third Hierarchy. These words thus become inner experience: "In pure thought you will find the 'I' that sustains itself."[2] When we introduce this experience into our ordinary consciousness, we fill it with the substance of freedom as our cosmic realm. Freedom is the human cosmic realm.

In Leading Thought 69, the cosmic realm of the Third Hierarchy is said to be pure spirit and soul; this corresponds to the *spirit-filling* of its inner being. For the beings of the Second Hierarchy, Leading Thought 70 specifies a form of spiritual soul nature that works in the etheric; this points to a form of consciousness called *Stimulation of Life* in the diagram. The cosmic realm of the First Hierarchy is spiritually active in the physical (Leading Thought 71); this corresponds to a form of consciousness called *Creating of Being*. In Leading

---

1   *Anthroposophical Leading Thoughts*, pp. 42–45. Steiner describes a path of self-knowledge that investigates *memory*, *speech*, and *movement*, corresponding to the Third, Second, and First hierarchies.

2   Rosicrucian saying written on a pillar by Steiner in 1907.

Thoughts 66–68, we were shown that the outer being of the higher hierarchies is related to human soul life through thinking, feeling, and willing. Thus, in the letter just mentioned, this subject is continued by showing how the other side of the consciousness of higher hierarchies, or their inner being, is related to the higher principles of the human being—to the etheric body, astral body, and "I"-being. These relationships are extremely complicated and they cannot be understood unless our efforts toward knowledge are permeated with cosmic impulses.

The path specified in Steiner's letter again uses the pendulum's swing in human self-knowledge. To begin with, the phenomenon of memory is indicated; it has a shadow-like character in contrast to the living element of soul where memory has had its home. "Dead shadows have their being in memory; living reality has its being in the soul where memory is active." Out of *imagination* knowledge, Anthroposophy points from shadow being to shining being; from the physical body to the etheric. The spiritual environment of the etheric body is the realm of the Third Hierarchy. Likewise, a shadow being may be seen in speech; by contrast, the astral body is the shining element.

Inspiration reveals the spiritual environment of the astral body as the realm of the Second Hierarchy. Finally, movement, "I"-being, and *intuition* belong to the spiritual cosmic realm of the beings of the First Hierarchy. Out of memory, speech, and movement, the etheric body, the astral body, and the "I"-being meet through *imagination, inspiration,* and *intuition*.

From this, the "I" enkindles itself by contacting its environment—the cosmic realm of the First Hierarchy, or *Creating of Being*, the spiritually active element in the physical. The astral body enkindles itself by contacting the cosmic realm of the Second Hierarchy, or *Stimulator of Life*, which is active in the etheric as a spirit-soul element. The etheric body enkindles itself by contacting the cosmic realm of the Third Hierarchy, or *Spirit-filling*, a pure spiritual soul realm. Perhaps it will be less difficult to comprehend this if we investigate a counterpart that may be found in early childhood development.

Children develop out of the spiritual realm through their spiritual soul nature, which works from outside and enters the organization itself only gradually. This is really in the realm of education. First, however, through spiritual activity, it effects three tremendous achievements, which Steiner describes in his wonderful book *The Spiritual Guidance of the Individual and Humanity* (pp. 6–8):

> The first capacity we must learn is to *orient* our body in space. People today do not realize what this means and that it touches on the most essential differences between human beings and animals. Animals are destined from the beginning to achieve their equilibrium in a certain way ... human

beings are not given an innate way to achieve equilibrium in space but must develop it out of their total being.

The second capacity we learn out of ourselves from our essential being—which remains the same through successive incarnations—is *language*.... In a sense, we must sow the seed for the development of the larynx in the time before our earliest memory (before we attain full "I"-consciousness), so that the larynx can become an organ of speech.

There is still a third, even less well known, capacity that we learn on our own through what we bear within us through successive incarnations. I am referring here to our ability to live within the world of thoughts and ideas, the world of thought itself. Our brain is formed and worked on because it is the tool of *thinking*.... The brain at birth is the result of the work of forces inherited from our parents, grandparents, and so on. It is in our thinking that we bring to expression what we are as individuals in conformity with our former earthly lives. Therefore, after birth, when we have become physically independent of our parents and ancestors, we must transform the brain we have inherited.

We may now speak of this in terms of the rule of the hierarchies. With effort, children learn to move, speak, and think. In acquiring the power of movement, the "I" masters the physical body and the physical world where the beings of the First Hierarchy are leaders and guides. The acquisition of speech can be understood through the astral body's mastery of the life functions; to that end, the beings of the Second Hierarchy help the child. When children learn to think, a pure spiritual soul element assumes its etheric body; this is possible through the cooperation of the beings of the Third Hierarchy.

The effort toward genuine self-knowledge (which we studied earlier in relation to Steiner's letter) takes the reverse direction back to childhood and forward nevertheless into the spiritual cosmic realms of the higher hierarchies. With this, we encounter a saying of Christ—a saying Steiner explains most expressively from his spiritual investigation in order to show how the words of the Gospel may again be taken literally if only we arrive at their real meaning. The description of what happens to a child in the first three years of earthly life ends in this way:

This leads to a realization that is very significant if we understand it rightly. In the New Testament it is said this way: "Unless you turn and become like children, you will never enter the kingdom of heaven" (Matt. 18:3).[1] What then seems to be the highest ideal for a human being if this statement is correctly understood? Surely that our ideal must be to approach an ever closer, conscious relationship with the forces that

---

1   "Yes, I say to you, if you do not turn about inwardly and reawaken the pure forces of childhood within yourselves, you will not find access to the kingdom of the heavens" (*The New Testament*, Floris Books edition).

worked on us, without our awareness, in the first years of childhood. (Ibid., p. 12)

Steiner also refers to the manifold meanings of this saying in other places.[2] He speaks of becoming as little children and explains it; and he always points to the impulses that lead us into the spiritual world.

---

2   *Founding a Science of the Spirit*, lecture 3; *Background to the Gospel of St. Mark*, lecture 6.

THINKING, MEDITATING, SEEING

It is clear from the previous studies that, if we wish to consider it from a human perspective, the activity of the hierarchies is extraordinarily complicated. The following leading thoughts show even more relationships, and it is important to become familiar with the fact that the activities of the hierarchies interpenetrate. Indeed, the highest beings work down through all the other kingdoms as far as to the lowest kingdom of nature. For example, Rudolf Steiner says we need to become familiar with thoughts such as these—that very exalted and sublime beings may approach us in our immediate surroundings often regarded by us as very lowly.[1] Out of nature, the power of such beings enters us and the principles with which we participate in the life of nature.

The next three groups of leading thoughts belong together (72 to 75, 76 to 78, 79 to 81). In a certain sense, we can combine them. The outer expression of the group 72 to 75 is such that they have the effect of disclosing—through thinking—the activity of the higher hierarchies. Here, we can look back to the beginning of Study 31, where the significance of such a conclusion was evident. We come to the point where we try to rise above what is merely given; this is a first step toward overcoming the illusions of ordinary consciousness. The next step, however, must be the formation of true representations of the spiritual reality to which we wish to raise ourselves. In terms of the higher hierarchies, this second step is hinted at in Leading Thoughts 76 to 78. The third step is a spiritual approach, as mentioned in Leading Thoughts 79 to 81. These three steps may be expressed according to words emphasized by Steiner in *Riddles of the Soul* ("Thinking, Meditating, and Seeing").

> 72. As soon as we approach the higher members of the human being—the etheric and astral bodies and the "I"-being—we must look for the human relationship to beings of the spiritual kingdoms. It is only the physical body's organization that we can illumine by referring to the three physical kingdoms of nature.

> 73. In the etheric body, the intelligence of the cosmos becomes embodied in the human being. That this can happen requires the activity of cosmic beings who, in their combined activity, form the human etheric body, just as physical forces shape the physical.

---

1   *Genesis: Secrets of Creation*, lecture 7.

74. In the astral body, the spiritual world implants moral impulses into the human being. That these can show their life in the human organization requires the activity of beings who can not only think the spiritual, but also shape it in its reality.

75. In the "I"-organization, human beings experience themselves in the physical body as spirit. That this can happen requires the activity of beings who, as spiritual beings, live in the physical world themselves.

Thinking, as presented in these leading thoughts, could be considered yet another new beginning. The three physical kingdoms of nature can illumine the organization of the physical body. This is a starting point for science. By its very methods, it contains intelligence within itself. If we direct our attention toward intelligence when considering the human being scientifically, we turn our thinking toward the etheric body. A similar line of thinking arose in our first studies. With regard to the dominance of the intelligence, it *presupposes* the activity of cosmic beings in a purely spiritual world, whom we had come to know as those of the Third Hierarchy (Leading Thought 73). The nature of intelligence is still a mere abstraction to humankind. Moral impulses (Leading Thought 74) are nearer to our own being, though much more difficult to see through than are the impulses of intelligence. The astral body is the human principle where these impulses live (Study 13); they point to foundations built by beings of the Second Hierarchy in the etheric realm. Our own *being*—as spirit—is closest to the thinking human being; our own being is the most closely veiled of all. Its foundations in the physical world have been made by beings of the First Hierarchy (Leading Thought 75).

If we go from *thinking* to *meditation*, Leading Thoughts 76 to 78 tell us how we can imagine the higher hierarchies:

76. To evoke images of the First Hierarchy (Seraphim, Cherubim, Thrones), we try to create pictures in which the spiritual (what can be viewed only in the suprasensory) reveals its activity in forms that manifest in the sensory realm. Spirit being portrayed as sense-perceptible images must be the substance of our thinking about the First Hierarchy.

77. To evoke images of the Second Hierarchy (Kyriotetes, Dynamis, Exusiai), we try to create pictures in which spirit reveals itself—not in sense-perceptible forms, but in a purely spiritual way. Spirit being portrayed in purely spiritual images rather than in sense-perceptible ways must be the substance of our thinking about the Second Hierarchy.

78. To evoke images of the Third Hierarchy (Archai, Archangeloi, Angeloi), we try to create pictures in which spirit reveals itself, not in sense-perceptible forms, nor even in a purely spiritual way, but through the way thinking, feeling, and willing are expressed in the human soul. Spirit being

portrayed in the imagery of soul life must be the substance of our thinking about the Third Hierarchy.

Representations—thoughts on which we can reflect—are different from all that we have previously recognized as the remnants of sense perceptions. Furthermore, we are concerned here with how we can approach beings of the higher hierarchies through meditation. In Leading Thoughts 76 to 78, Steiner shows the kinds of meditation that can accomplish this. In Leading Thought 76, we proceed from the highest beings, those of the First Hierarchy, whereas previously and later the path leads from below upward. The way to meditate on the highest beings is to picture a spiritual reality in sensible imagery. If we look for this kind of imagery, the human countenance can rise before us with a sublime, cosmic expression lifted to the highest divinity. Such imagery can awaken the sensation of rising to the creative primal cause, the image in which humanity is created.

Leading Thought 77 points to the path of meditation leading to the beings of the Second Hierarchy—a spiritual reality not in sensible, but purely *spiritual* imagery. Here we can feel moved to dwell reflectively on the great ideals of humanity as the stream of life flowing through the worlds in truth, love, and goodness. The fundamental mood is indicated through the word.

According to Leading Thought 78, we are led to the beings of the Third Hierarchy on paths of meditation consisting of the soul's reflection on an imagery that manifests in the same way that thinking, feeling, and willing manifests in the human soul. Such meditation becomes a transformation of those soul activities; overcoming egoism in thinking, feeling, and willing leads to a spiritual reality in soul imagery and to a spiritual reverence that takes hold of the soul.

Further Leading Thoughts 79 to 81 show the results of *seeing* the spiritual approach to the hierarchies.

79. Spiritually, we can approach the Third Hierarchy—Archai, Archangeloi, Angeloi—by recognizing thinking, feeling and willing, so that we perceive in them the spirit active in the soul. First, thinking places only *pictures*— rather than an effective reality—into the world. Feeling lives and moves within this realm of images and bears witness to the presence of a reality in us, but it cannot live it or express it outwardly. Willing unfolds a reality, which presupposes the existence of the body but does not consciously help to form it. The spiritual reality that lives in our thinking establishes the body as the foundation for thinking; the spiritual reality that lives in our feeling causes the body to share the experience of a reality; and the spiritual reality that lives in our willing consciously assists in fashioning the body. All of this lives in the Third Hierarchy.

80. Spiritually, we can approach the Second Hierarchy—Exusiai, Dynamis, Kyriotetes—by awakening to see natural phenomena as manifestations of

spiritual being living in them. The Second Hierarchy thus has nature as its dwelling place where it works on souls.

81. Spiritually, we can approach the First Hierarchy—Seraphim, Cherubim, Thrones—by awakening to see the natural and human phenomena confronting us as the acts, or creations, of spirit being working in them. The First Hierarchy thus has the natural and human kingdoms as the effects of its efforts, where it unfolds its being.

Here we see the beings of the higher hierarchies at work. Living spirit works as our thinking, feeling, and willing, even giving these soul activities a basis in the body. Steiner's investigations are in accordance with this.[1] Angels work on the individual human being; they accompany us through our repeated Earth lives, rule specifically in our thinking, and help us to transform our astral body. Archangels rule in nations and races.[2] They largely determine the feeling we have in common and also give a higher tone to the thinking of individual human beings; this must be distinguished from the fact that feeling is the creation of the Second Hierarchy, who help us to transform our etheric body. The *Spirits of Personality* rule as spirits of the age within whole epochs.[3] They determine the particular way that human beings have a will in common and, at the same time, impress higher will impulses of an epoch on individual human thinking; they help in all that raises us—even in the physical body—above nation and race.

The beings of the Second Hierarchy penetrate even more deeply. In Leading Thought 80, we see how they shape natural phenomena in order to affect souls through nature; consider the way the human soul is planted into the threefold organism (Study 16). The soul supports itself in a threefold way on the body (the head, metabolic, and rhythmic systems) and is supported by the spirit in a threefold way. According to Leading Thought 81, however, when we see the creations of spirit in the human and natural realms, we may realize how nature and humankind are related to each other through their destiny. This is the work of the beings of the First Hierarchy—the *Lords of Karma*.

---

1 *Universe, Earth and Man*, lecture 3; *The Spiritual Hierarchies and the Physical World*, lecture 6; *Background to the Gospel of St. Mark*, lecture 6.

2 *Spiritual Beings in the Heavenly Bodies and in the Kingdoms of Nature*, lecture 3.

3 *Egyptian Myths and Mysteries*, lecture 2.

STUDY 35

UNDER MICHAEL'S BANNER

The following leading thoughts conclude our studies of the higher hierarchies in a way that has deep significance. The starry world and the Earth reveal the actions of spiritual beings to sense perception. The contemplative person stands on the Earth amid the three kingdoms of nature. Nevertheless, we need a spiritually oriented knowledge of the starry realms in order to understand these forces that play into human beings and into the kingdoms of nature from spiritual beings; but the beings of the higher hierarchies conceal themselves behind their deeds.

> 82. We look up to the worlds of stars; what is thus presented to our senses is merely the outer manifestation of those spirit beings—and their deeds—whom we have spoken of as beings of the spiritual kingdoms, or hierarchies.

> 83. The Earth is the scene of action for the three natural kingdoms and that of the human beings inasmuch as they manifest the outer, sensible glory of the activity of spiritual beings.

> 84. The forces working from spiritual beings into the earthly kingdoms of nature and the human kingdom are revealed to the human spirit through true—*spiritual*—knowledge of the starry worlds.

We can go a step farther. The whole Earth and its creations, including humankind, was formed from the cosmos; one part of the creative principle, however, was born in human beings. Therefore, it is not just the natural, sense-perceptible connection between Earth and cosmos that appears as given; the spiritual association between Earth and cosmos in the activity of the spiritual beings also makes itself felt on the stage of the inner human being. Here, a new light illumines one of our previous studies. In Study 22, we find:

> The activity of the sense organs still belongs entirely to nature. It shapes the sense organs and looks into them as though into a mirror. Our *being*, situated behind the sense organs, views this natural process between sense organs and external effects on them (eye and light, for example). In this process, however, nature draws toward herself the human spirit, who had separated from the spirit of nature. She lures the human spirit to herself along paths of sense perception. Sensual knowledge is gained through the object. Our being experiences itself surrendered to the object. *Human knowledge of nature is nature's self-knowledge.*

Since the power of the hierarchies has been shown to us in the activity of nature, we can, with some audacity, call the cooperation of these beings in the domain of the inner human being an aspect of self-knowledge for the hierarchies.

Thus, beings of the hierarchies live in humankind. The answer to the question in Study 31 concerning *how* beings of the hierarchies inhabit humankind and the world assumes an ever more intimate form. In proportion to our approach to true self-knowledge, we will find release from the creative activity of the higher hierarchies and begin to build a new hierarchy. Before true self-knowledge appears in human beings, the activity of the higher hierarchies is concealed behind their own being and inner self. Accordingly, it is shown in the following groups of leading thoughts how beings of the Third Hierarchy are concealed behind ordinary day consciousness, beings of the Second Hierarchy behind dream consciousness, and beings of the First Hierarchy behind dreamless sleep consciousness in human beings. This is also apparent in further groups of leading thoughts in terms of other human soul relationships—thinking, feeling, and willing. This is true, too, for relationships in the life between birth and death, between death and new birth, and for carrying earlier lives into later ones. In other words, all of our being—which, in our previous studies of leading thoughts, we recognized in its various forms as the phenomena of inner experience and actions—reveals itself here as veils of the hierarchies.

Expressed in this way, however, this applies only until the new age arrives. The mission of Michael will then appear in the relationship between humankind and the beings of the hierarchies; and, if we carefully consider Steiner's investigations in this regard, we immediately discover that *all our previous knowledge is connected with Michael's activity.* This is the correct approach to Michael—to walk the path of knowledge with courage and then, at decisive moments, be aware of his cooperation. This can be experienced as an assent of Michael. To acquire certain conviction with regard to this, it will be helpful to consider a whole series of letters Steiner dedicated to Michael's mission. In this way, the following groups of leading thoughts also receive their own special interpretation.

Steiner began only in his final years to disclose the activity of Michael more clearly, and we may recognize this as a sign that his work had taken root in human hearts to the degree that such knowledge could resound as though they themselves had expressed it in freedom. In this age, this must lead to true service of Michael, if we follow Steiner as he guides contemporary consciousness to independent experience of spirit. Indeed, when looking back we notice much that he mentioned in a more general way in regard to Michael, and today we can see clearly how he brought onto the path to Michael all that he himself first gained in freedom.

As an example, let's take the following summarization:[1] When the "Maid of Orleans," Jeanne d'Arc (ca. 1412–1431), rescued the mission of the West, it was Michael who, as Christ's messenger, brought about this impulse through the most gentle and subtle forces of the human soul—apart from any understanding of the learned. That was before Michael had again assumed leadership of our time since November 1879. In earlier times, impulses had been given through dreams in which the leading spirits concealed themselves.[2] But a great change occurred; thereafter, the guiding spirit would influence waking consciousness. Consequently, Michael works not only spiritually but also affects physical understanding through physical reason; because of this, Steiner (in the passage referred to) compares Michael with gold, which is the only metal that has a medicinal effect like the Sun—not just affecting the etheric but also the physical body.

Thus, Steiner speaks of spiritualizing the human conceptual faculty and of the power of ideation; he points repeatedly to the possibility of really comprehending entirely through understanding and reason all that Spiritual Science brings. Such understanding, or reason, has been given to humanity since the sixteenth century. It has become the task and duty of our age, since it is the way that our powers of understanding and comprehending become a higher faculty for knowledge. Michael also takes hold of the will where it is least inclined to unfold its forces—in the earthly forces of ideation. Hence, the statement in Steiner's letter for Leading Thoughts 82 to 84: "Very much depends on this: that the ideas of human beings do not remain mere 'thinking,' but, in thought, develop into *sight*."

Under Michael's banner, we are concerned with the effort to explain thinking. To this end, Steiner provided all the conditions and necessary tools. The point, however, is not merely to know these explanations but to genuinely practice and accomplish them. For this reason, the necessity of exercising thought is maintained in terms of all that Steiner tells us—even as he leads us into the highest realms of existence. This is the purpose of our work. Thus, in his letters he connects thought problems with Michael in a way that helps us to gain the strongest impulses for the history of humanity and the individual, the reality of which arises for us hourly and daily.

What follows attempts to summarize in brief outline some thoughts from the first two letters about Michael, supplemented by much that Steiner presents to us in detail in his lectures of the same period at the Goetheanum.

The thoughts to be experienced as cosmic, spiritual power were originally with the gods; they thought them into human beings. Michael was the regent of the cosmic intelligence. "From the ninth century on, human beings no

---

1   Summarized from *Menschenschicksale und Volkerschicksale*, Berlin, 1914–1915 (CW 157); unavailable in English), lecture 5.

2   Compare *Christ and the Spiritual World*, lecture 5.

longer had the sense that their thoughts were inspired by Michael. Thoughts had fallen from Michael's dominion, had sunk from the spiritual world into the individual human souls." In his *Riddles of Philosophy*, Steiner describes this fact through the experience of thought itself. If we can actually experience this description of the history of human consciousness as an inner recapitulation of that course of evolution, we will be more able to make our souls receptive on the paths of thought, so they may comprehend—from the forces of our time—the spiritually vital aspect of such a historical process. Thus, today we can become coworkers in the affairs of the higher hierarchies. In keeping with this, in his Dornach lectures Steiner revealed how Michael was deserted by his companions and servants in the spiritual world at the time of the Council of Constantinople (AD 869). The passing of the intelligence from Michael to individual human beings is the desertion of those angelic beings who, as the guides of individual human beings, turned from Michael, the ruler in the Sun, to Earth.

In the earthly history of the spirit, we then had a battle between the *Nominalists* and *Realists*. "The Realists wanted to remain loyal to Michael; even though thoughts had fallen from his domain into that of humankind, as thinkers they still wanted to continue to serve Michael, as the prince of the intelligence of the cosmos."[3] Thus, Michael himself remained loyal to the Sun, from which his companions among the archangels had turned away. Although the Sun, as cosmic being, was blemished by sun spots, he endeavored to enkindle an "inner sun" in human hearts. Here, the significance of Leading Thoughts 82 to 84 becomes intelligible—that spiritual knowledge of the starry worlds reveals earthly events. In contrast to this, thinking with the head developed from Nominalism over the course of centuries. Only Steiner's victory over materialism through thinking enables the human soul to push its way through to the new realism of spiritual experience.

---

3   *Anthroposophical Leading Thoughts*, p. 52.

WHAT IS CONCEALED AND REVEALED
IN WAKING, DREAMING, AND SLEEPING?

In the letters referred to in the previous study, we may be particularly struck by the way Michael frees thoughts from the realm of the head and prepares their path to the heart. This path is found when the thoughts glow with enthusiasm. In his books and through what he had to say, Rudolf Steiner often pointed toward the inner warmth that accompanies thinking experience; nevertheless, again and again, we meet with views that throw thoughts of the heart and the head into the same vessel. Historically, this is merely the confusing of *nominalism* with *realism*. But we must be deeply conscious that the passage through nominalism—the *fall* into materialism—nevertheless indicates progress. "While the perception and vision of this age had to be limited to the external physical world, unfolding within the soul, as actual experience, was *a purified self-sustaining spirituality* of the human being.... Thought formation lost itself for a while in the material of the cosmos; it must find itself again in cosmic spirit" (*Anthroposophical Leading Thoughts*, p. 57). That "cosmic spirit" is Michael himself; but, in order to accomplish this tremendous advance of free thought life through him, human cooperation is needed. "It is a fact that immeasurably much depends on human representations going beyond *thinking* only, and that thinking become *seeing*."[1]

Given these considerations, it follows that, of all the beings of the higher hierarchies who conceal themselves behind the human soul life, Michael is the first to reveal himself; and the path by which he may be reached is through training our thinking. He rules, as Steiner often said, in a sphere separated only by a thin wall from human consciousness. The door to him must be broken with thinking. Then other doors of the human soul will open as if on their own, if the work begun in thinking is continued according to its own force. In chapter 8 of *Intuitive Thinking as a Spiritual Path* (p. 133), we find:

> For whoever turns toward *essential* thinking finds within it both feeling and will, and both of these in the depths of their reality. Whoever turns aside from thinking toward "pure" feeling and willing loses the true reality of feeling and willing.

The following groups of leading thoughts show us how, as a soul exercise, we may take these paths relating to the higher hierarchies.

---

1   Ibid., p. 58.

We found in the previous study that the whole human being appears as a veil of spiritual beings; but because human beings permeate themselves with Michael's impulses, they can attain his cosmic goals. If we neglect this opportunity, the beings of the higher hierarchies work to reach their cosmic goals within the realm of human soul life; and all that is unworthy for this purpose falls to Lucifer and Ahriman. We can also point to related passages where Steiner speaks of the fact that human beings, in attaining their cosmic goals, perform at the same time an act toward redeeming Lucifer. He expressed this in very pregnant words: "Human beings will redeem Lucifer if they receive the Christ power in the appropriate way."[2]

Michael, however, is the messenger of Christ. He appeals to the forces of human consciousness that are fully awake. This Michael Age guides the drama of human evolution, in one way or another, toward its turning point (compare Study 24). Here we are reminded of the drawing suited to our time, made years ago by Rudolf Steiner:[3]

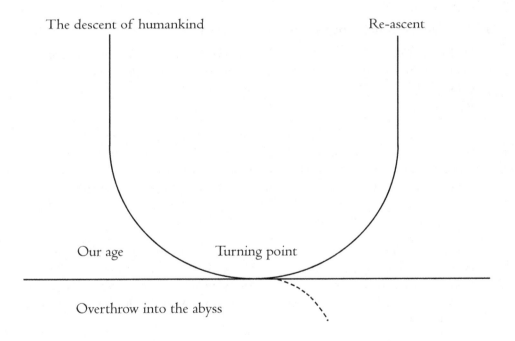

The descent of humankind

Re-ascent

Our age

Turning point

Overthrow into the abyss

---

2   *The Spiritual Hierarchies and the Physical World*, p. 162. Said another way: "If love is to enter the cosmos, it can do so only through freedom—that is, through Lucifer and the one who conquers Lucifer—the one who is also the redeemer of human beings—the Christ" (ibid., pp. 163–164). See also *The Manifestations of Karma*, lecture 11.

3   *The Apocalypse of St. John*, lecture 7.

Ours is the age of being awake. This is the starting point for the next groups of leading thoughts (85–90), which are closely related, as are those that follow them:

85. In waking day consciousness, human beings experience *themselves* first during the present cosmic age. This experience conceals from humankind the presence of the third Hierarchy in this waking state of human experience.

86. In dream consciousness, human beings experience, in a chaotic way, their own unharmonious unity with the world's spirit being. When *imaginative* consciousness is realized as the counterpart of dream consciousness, human beings become aware of the presence of the second Hierarchy in human experience.

87. In dreamless sleep consciousness, human beings unconsciously experience their own being united with the world's spirit being. When *inspired* consciousness is realized as the counterpart of sleep consciousness, human beings become aware of the presence of the first Hierarchy in their experience.

The following leading thoughts belong with these:

88. In the waking day consciousness during the present cosmic age, human beings experience themselves amid the physical world. This experience conceals from them the presence, within their being, of the effects of life between death and birth.

89. In dream consciousness, human beings experience, in a chaotic way, their own being inharmoniously united with the world's spiritual being. Waking consciousness cannot seize the true content of dream consciousness. It is revealed to the consciousness of *imagination* and *inspiration* how the spirit world—through which human beings live between death and birth—is helping to build up their inner being.

90. In dreamless sleep consciousness, human beings unconsciously experience their own being permeated with the results of past earthly lives. The Consciousness of inspiration and intuition penetrates to a clear view of these results and sees former earthly lives at work in the destined course, or karma, of the present.

The fact that these two groups of leading thoughts belong together is especially striking—the individual sentences begin with similar wording. We can understand the meaning of this important change best by focusing on the differences in these leading thoughts, which otherwise correspond. Leading Thoughts 85 to 88 deal with the waking, day consciousness. This follows the course of sense perception and thinking, a polarity that Steiner points to repeatedly, and that we have frequently brought into our studies. To ordinary consciousness, this signifies the contrast between inner and outer being. This is the difference between these two groups of leading thoughts; thinking itself draws the line.

In Leading Thought 85, we find, "In waking day consciousness, human beings experience *themselves* first during the present cosmic age." By emphasizing the word *themselves* somewhat, we have an inner experience that, in thinking, turns toward itself. Thus, in human experience, *it is really thinking that, in fact, veils the third Hierarchy from human beings.* If we go on to Leading Thought 88, we have the same wording at first, but then "amid the physical world." That is the other side of the polarity of the waking, day consciousness—the world of sense perceptions, the experience of which "conceals from them the presence, within their being, of the effects of life between death and birth."

The corresponding Leading Thoughts 86 and 89 are concerned with dream consciousness. The wording of the first part is again the same in both; in the following passage, they differ to begin with, since, in Leading Thought 86, *imagination* and, in 89, *imagination* and *inspiration* are added. *Imagination* is called the other pole of dream consciousness; imagery is common to both. But, in addition, it is said, in Leading Thought 86, that *imagination* consciousness can take place in *contrast* to dream consciousness. With this, a relationship is established for the dream, similar to that between the waking and ordinary consciousness. This therefore shows being awake in contrast to dreaming, and this is the consciousness of the second Hierarchy. Exactly the same may be said of Leading Thought 87. There, *inspiration* consciousness appears in contrast to sleep consciousness as its opposite pole. Here, we see waking contrasted to sleep consciousness, which is the consciousness of the first Hierarchy.

In Leading Thought 89, it is said that waking (our *usual*) consciousness cannot grasp the content of this dream consciousness. As we saw, *imagination* brings about waking in contrast to dreaming. According to Leading Thought 86, this new waking bears no content as yet; this is disclosed only when *inspiration* is added; indeed, this content, or object, is something that, to ordinary consciousness, is *inner life.* The life between death and birth is concerned with shaping this inner life as well as outer life, as shown in Leading Thought 88.

The same line of thought applies to Leading Thought 90: according to Leading Thought 87, waking in contrast to dreamless sleep is supplemented by *intuition,* which allows one to see the effects of earlier earthly lives on the present life in the course of destiny. In the words *see* and *effects,* there is again a corresponding polarity as a counterpart to the ordinary waking consciousness.

It is not easy to follow such complex relationships with our thinking. Thus, we will try to summarize them with a diagram; naturally, the same applies for this as for all previous diagrams—that they mean nothing as such, but are intended only as exercises.

	Inner being	Outer being
Waking	Leading Thought 85	Leading Thought 88
Dreaming	Leading Thought 86	Leading Thought 89
Sleeping	Leading Thought 87	Leading Thought 90

If, in the inner experience of thinking, new springs well up, then the Michael impulse is on the path of suprasensory knowledge.

STUDY 37

WHAT DOES THE WILL CONCEAL AND REVEAL?

The two groups of Leading Thoughts, 85 to 87 and 88 to 90, clearly originate from *waking day consciousness*. If we notice the emphasis placed on these words, two questions may merge: Is there also a *sleeping day consciousness*? And, is there a *waking night consciousness*? We can know that these do exist. Waking night consciousness can be recognized as the higher stages of knowledge—*imagination, inspiration*, and *intuition*. And sleeping day consciousness is the will. The two following groups of leading thoughts, like the preceding ones, are closely related; they deal with the will in terms of what it conceals and what it can reveal.

91. In the present cosmic age, the will comes into ordinary consciousness only through thought. Now, in this consciousness, we must always begin with something sense perceptible. Consequently, even through our own will, we apprehend only what passes from it into the world of sense perception. In ordinary consciousness, we become aware of our own will impulses only by observing ourselves in thought, just as we are aware of the outer world only through observation.

92. The karma that is active in the will is an attribute that belongs to it from previous lives on Earth. Consequently, this constituent of the will cannot be apprehended with the concepts of ordinary consciousness, which are directed only toward the current earthly life.

93. Since they are unable to comprehend karma, such concepts attribute what they cannot understand in human impulses of will to the mysterious darkness of the physical constitution, whereas it is in fact the working of past earthly lives.

94. In the ordinary life of concepts conveyed by the senses, a human being is in the physical world. In order for this world to enter consciousness, karma must be silent in one's thinking life. In the life of human ideation, we *forget* our karma, so to speak.

95. In the manifestations of the will, karma is active. But its activity remains in the unconscious. By lifting what works unconsciously in the will to conscious *imagination*, karma is apprehended. Thus we experience destiny within us.

96. When *inspiration* and *intuition* enter the *imagination*, the outcome of former earthly lives, along with impulses of the present, becomes perceptible in the activity of the will. The past life is revealed as an active force in the present.

In our previous study, the term *outer being* was used, which refers to our presence in the physical world. We will now consider that outer being in relation to its bearer. It is the will that upholds us in the physical world, but, to ordinary consciousness, our will makes its appearance only through representation (Leading Thought 91). Rudolf Steiner presented this immensely important knowledge to us in this way:

> I have often called your attention to the fact that, in terms of the limb organization, we are asleep, whereas in the head we are awake. And the will really works as if it were asleep. We have only the picture, or *representation*, of all that the will does. No one, while acting on a representation—*I move my hand*—is aware of how this is connected with all of one's organism. This is just as subconscious as the processes of sleep.[1]

Perception of such a movement belongs to the sense world, to the outer human being, and it is represented with the aid of the physical body. Our movement can be proved only by means of our ability to represent it after that act of will has induced the movement, which now belongs to the past. That past has permanence in the will; it is *capacity*, a quality that can never be comprehended in the representations of ordinary consciousness (Leading Thought 93). Furthermore, the ordinary life of representation must keep silent in relation to this. "In the life of human ideation, we *forget* our karma" (Leading Thought 94). Everything connected to the will from the past is karma for the present earthly life.

The fact that the word *forget* is italicized in Leading Thought 94 must be an important reminder for us. Steiner once gave an entire lecture on the subject of forgetting.[2] Through forgetting, everything belonging to the past becomes capacity. To forget means to carry through the spiritual world. We forget the separate experiences by means of which we learn to write in our childhood, but we *can* write.[3] Thus, what was before this earthly life must be forgotten so that the capacities arising then, having a purely spiritual nature, can affect our waking life. This happens on a large scale during the life after death, until the turning point Steiner so powerfully describes as the "midnight hour of existence," particularly in his mystery play "The Souls' Awakening."

---

1   *Gesunder Blick fuer Heute und wackere Hoffnung fuer Morgen* ("A Sound Perspective for Today and a Real Hope for the Future"), lecture 15 (CW 181); unavailable in English.

2   *The Being of Man and His Future Evolution*, lecture 4.

3   See *Theosophy*, chapter 2.

There, forgetting is a cosmic exercise that is a part of the transition from experiencing to creating;[4] and a second act of forgetting takes place before birth into a new earth life.

Through *imagination*, what was forgotten awakes to new consciousness. Steiner repeatedly compares the path of meditation, which leads to *imagination*, to remembering.[5] Thus, we find these two sentences in the summary contained in Study 30: "Conscious forgetting leads to meditation," and "Conscious remembering leads to *imagination*." Meditation imitates the passage through the spiritual world after death; *imagination* corresponds to awakening in a new world. Steiner once described it something like this: *imagination* arises like a memory, but whereas the memory presents consciousness with something that was once a direct experience, *imagination* is such that no prior experience corresponds to the emerging picture.

Here, we must clearly differentiate between Leading Thoughts 95 and 96. *Imagination* raises what really belongs to the past into our present experience, belonging not to the past of this earthly life—since then it would be memory—but belonging to past lives on Earth. Furthermore, it must also be said that neither does memory merely look back at something that has passed, as it seems to be; rather, it is a present act of perception—a new experience that perceives the changes that, through past experience, have occurred in the human organism, particularly in the etheric body.

The *imagination* of what acts unconsciously in the will presents us with the images of the karma at work. "Thus we experience destiny within us" (Leading Thought 95). In order to experience in our karma the results of previous earth lives as such, *inspiration* and *intuition* must enter *imagination* (Leading Thought 96), just as we saw previously in Leading Thoughts 89 and 90. This process remains hidden from the consciousness that can make only mental images, and it is concerned with the sleeping day consciousness, about which we inquired earlier. Consequently, it is also completely misinterpreted by the ordinary consciousness and contemporary science. Leading Thought 93 also refers to this. The faculty of representing is able to comprehend only the sense-perceptible effects of the will; those are the movements of the physical body.

Schopenhauer, not without justification, though in a one-sided way, linked these two together and thus framed his title *The World as Will and Representation*. Since contemporary science cannot see beyond this earthly life into pre-earthly life and earlier lives on Earth, it also looks for the causal element of the will in the current bodily life. Steiner points to psychoanalysis in Leading Thought 93, speaking, for example, of suppressed representations

---

4   See *Secrets of the Threshold*, lecture 8.

5   *The Inner Nature of Man and the Life between Death and Rebirth*, lecture 2.

that have a disturbing effect in the subconscious region of the physical constitution and act like will. Steiner often pointed to this in his lectures.

The way Steiner points to *imagination, inspiration* and *intuition* in these last groups of leading thoughts can illuminate in particular the relationship of these higher kinds of knowledge to one another and to the knowledge of ordinary consciousness. To begin with, we will express this only aphoristically:

> *Inspiration* is related to *imagination,*
>   as *imagination* is related to ordinary consciousness.
>
> *Intuition* is related to *inspiration,*
>   as *inspiration* is related to *imagination.*

The difference between these thoughts and those given previously about thinking, feeling and willing is that they are related to the activity of the higher hierarchies and with Michael's mission, which will continue to be defined more and more clearly. Indeed, it is the power of the beings of the higher hierarchies that is hidden behind these soul activities. But Michael is the first who is ready to reveal himself. Thus, when we view this as a whole, we will be able to understand that it is the beings of the higher hierarchies who lead us from one Earth life into another, who transform the acts of our earlier lives on Earth into karma, our experiences into capacities, and who, in a new earthly life, lead us to our karma. This is all effected in human life, whether or not we ourselves know anything of it. But the day has dawned when we should know something of these things. Anthroposophy is this knowledge. The forces that also carry waking into the night consciousness are developed from the waking day consciousness and, thus, it is within these activities of the higher hierarchies that we begin to become free.

Here is contained the responsibility of anthroposophic teaching. As we look farther back into the history of human consciousness, we can see that humanity was guided more by the influence of unconscious forces. In proportion to the knowledge obtained about the guidance of the human being and humanity by those who are being guided, such guidance can no longer continue. In ancient times, such knowledge was kept strictly secret. Now the time has come when humankind, through this knowledge, must withdraw from higher guidance. Knowing brings freedom and imposes responsibility. In this freedom, Michael is the leader, but he does not lead according to the old methods by working on the unconscious, but through knowledge arising from consciousness. That is the growing freedom of humankind.

STUDY 38

MORAL FANTASY

The distinction between thinking, feeling, and willing has illuminated many particulars. In the area of philosophy, this distinction is still new. Rudolf Steiner, in *Riddles of Philosophy*, ascribes this to Nicolaus Tetens, who first touched on it in a psychological sense around the turn of the eighteenth and nineteenth centuries. Since our Study 18, we have seen that thinking must permeate itself with willing in order to become reenlivened again; this claim appears as early as Leading Thought 12. Furthermore, we found that, by ascending into higher worlds, thinking is completely changed into willing and vice versa. Some details of this may be found in our Study 12. In another connection, in Study 29 the occasion arose to speak of feeling, insofar as it clarifies the logical distinctions in thinking. We also have an intimation that we should aim to restore life to concepts that have become rigid by again interrelating what has thus far been separated (Study 18).

Something else happens, however, in the following groups of leading thoughts. There, the human being is once again fundamentally integrated without the differentiations considered previously; in other words, the human being is restored to a unity, before the great cosmic and historic connections are carried farther.

> 97. For a less refined description, it is permissible to say: thinking, feeling, and willing live in the human soul. For greater refinement, we may add: Thinking always contains a substratum of feeling and willing; feeling a substratum of thinking and willing; willing a substratum of thinking and feeling. In the life of thought, however, thinking predominates; in the life of feeling, feeling predominates; and in the life of will, willing predominates over the other contents of the soul.

> 98. The feeling and willing of the life of thought contain the karmic results of past lives on Earth. The thinking and willing of the life of feeling karmically determine a person's character. The thinking and feeling of the life of will tear the present earthly life away from karmic connections.

> 99. In the feeling and willing of thinking, we live out our karma of the past; in the thinking and feeling of willing, we prepare our future karma.

Viewed in this way, we can see how all the activities of the human being, nature, and the hierarchies mutually interpenetrate, and, in terms of cosmic events, the human being is placed in the center. The significance of this process will be revealed more clearly as we go farther. First, we must see how the intimate interpenetration of thinking, feeling, and willing must bring about nine different combinations involved in the activity of karma.

By denoting thinking, feeling, and willing as a, b and c we can present the nine combinations as follows:

	Thinking	Feeling	Willing
Thinking	a in a	b in a	c in a
Feeling	a in b	b in b	c in b
Willing	a in c	b in c	c in c

Here "*a in a*" indicates thinking in thinking—that is, according to Study 30, the substance of the third Hierarchy and of *imagination*. Similarly, according to the same passage, "*b in b*" is feeling in feeling, the substance of the second Hierarchy and of *inspiration*; "*c in c*" is willing in willing, the substance of the first Hierarchy and of *intuition*. This is represented diagonally in our diagram. Thus, the hierarchies penetrate the human being, passing through the soul. The other combinations also show the harmonious activity of the hierarchies in the human soul, though here we must also look for forms that seem abstract and categorical. The same applies to them in relation to the special task presented to us in Study 18; this task was passed on to us by Rudolf Steiner; it is the freeing of ideas.

Feeling in thinking, "*b in a*," is the substance of logic, the inner connection between concept and idea, an area where nothing can remain permanently isolated. With the help of this substance—a kind of elective affinity—it is possible to arrive at any concept from any other; it is the "lifeblood" of thinking; we may also call it the inspiration for thinking. Willing in thinking, or "*c in a*," is the substance of conformity to law. Here is the active element we called the idea of causality; or, we may now say, the intuition of thinking. In this way, feeling and willing in thinking may be easily comprehended as the experience and activity of karma, but in retrospect, as it were, since they reveal themselves in thinking. Thinking is always directed toward the past (Leading Thoughts 98 and 99).

We can continue in the same direction and define thinking in the feeling life, "*a in b*." Ideas that live in feeling we call the ideals of the heart. Through the heart, ideas become ideals. In his book *How to Know Higher Worlds*, Steiner speaks of this, showing how it awakens the soul when ideas are transformed into ideals. Willing in the feeling life, "*c in b*," presents itself to us as the substance of the heart's morality. According to Leading Thought 98, this activity of the good heart and idealism karmically determine the character, but also in a negative way when they are not present.

Finally, in terms of thinking and feeling in willing, "*a* in *c*" and "*b* in *c*," we may look for something that corresponds to the foregoing. Let us think of the goals and purposes of action as Steiner presents them in his *Intuitive Thinking as a Spiritual Path: A Philosophy of Freedom.* Here, we are concerned with a kind of reversed causality where, in terms of time, the representation of the effect and the power of determining it precede the cause to be settled by the will (see Study 14).

Thus, according to *Intuitive Thinking as a Spiritual Path*, we can call thinking in willing, or "*a* in *c*," the substance of moral fantasy;[1] and we may call feeling in willing, "*b* in *c*," the substance of love for the action. Willing is always directed toward the future, as thinking is toward the past, and feeling toward the present. In moral fantasy, human freedom, or spiritual activity, begins to realize itself; human beings tear themselves from their karmic connection and determine their future karma (Leading Thoughts 98 and 99). The regular activity of karmic law will no more be broken in this way than will the activities of the hierarchies in human karma cease. Indeed, it is only through such activity that human freedom can become a reality.

Now it will not be difficult to apply the following leading thoughts to the foregoing discussion:

> 100. The true seat of human thoughts is in the etheric body. There, however, they are forces of real life and being. They imprint themselves into the physical body and, as *imprinted thoughts*, have the shadowy character by which ordinary consciousness knows them.

> 101. The feeling that lives in the thoughts comes from the astral body, and the willing from the "I"-being. In sleep the human etheric body certainly sends its rays into the world of human thoughts, but human beings themselves do not participate in it; for they have withdrawn from the etheric and the physical, with the astral body their feeling of thoughts, and with the "I" their willing.

> 102. As soon as the astral body and "I"-being loosen their connection with the thoughts of the etheric body during sleep, they become connected with *karma*, with a view of the events of repeated lives on Earth. This vision is denied ordinary consciousness, but suprasensory consciousness may enter it.

---

1   Rudolf Steiner stated, "I called one chapter of my *Philosophy of Freedom*... 'Moral Fantasy.' From the spiritual scientific viewpoint it could also be entitled 'Imaginative Moral Impulses.' I wanted to show that the realm otherwise dealt with only by the artist in imagination must now become the serious concern of the human race, because it represents the stage that humankind must reach to take hold of the suprasensory, which the brain is incapable of grasping" (Otto Palmer, *Rudolf Steiner on his book "The Philosophy of Freedom,"* [Great Barrington, MA: Steinerbooks, 2007], page 39).

Here is a significant, comprehensive view of the human being. With this, the diagram presented in this study can no longer be considered a mere abstraction. The activity of thinking, feeling, and willing—including the forces of the hierarchies they conceal—is related to the four principles of the human being, in which the hierarchies are also active in a special way. The connection of the four principles (the physical, etheric, and astral bodies and I) during waking life and their separation during sleep is made especially clear by the light shed on it here. We discovered how the threshold of the spiritual world passes through the human being (for example, Studies 6 and 21). Therefore, due to the fact that will and feeling penetrate thinking, the higher principles (the astral body and I) act as messengers between the spiritual and the physical worlds, and also between what is carried over to us through karma and previous earthly lives and the soul being of this present earthly life. This, too, is expressed in ordinary consciousness, and intimations of it may indeed be found in the *Intuitive Thinking as a Spiritual Path*. An illustration may interest those familiar with this work, which is of vital importance for our current era:

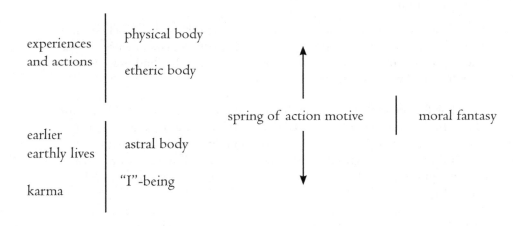

It would require a deeper search into *Intuitive Thinking as a Spiritual Path* in order to work this out in greater detail. But it shows without doubt how Anthroposophy, as a path of knowledge, leads us out of the shadowy quality of the thoughts of ordinary consciousness into the illumination of night consciousness, and that we may come to comprehend karma and see the events of repeated Earth lives. In taking this path of knowledge—with the shades of difference shown in previous studies—we sense that we are being led again to the unity of our being and to new tasks, to which we will be introduced in following groups of leading thoughts.

STUDY 39

RELIGION, ART, AND SCIENCE

The great successes of science are owed to the fact that humankind has learned to differentiate and analyze the phenomena of the world with ever increasing exactness. Continuing Study 29, we may repeat the statements made there as the sounds of the language of the consciousness soul (Study 30).

> Through analyzing, a whole is drawn out of its own sphere into the next one below.
> To work synthetically, we must climb one level higher.
> The best analyst is death; we gain truly constructive forces only from realms on the other side of death

When we apply differentiation and analysis to the human being from outside, according to scientific method, the only result can be to force the object of such treatment down. Humankind is degraded to the level of animals by such means, and it is no wonder that natural human feeling powerfully resists such treatment, especially when the methods seem to be of a soul quality—psychoanalysis is a kind of vivisection of the soul.[1]

Spiritual scientific analysis of the human being, on the other hand, may always be understood in this way: individuals themselves can perform such work and continue it within their own inner being. In no way can a degradation of soul life enter by such means; on the contrary, a practice of spiritual freedom can be attempted only in this way. We may assert that human beings have such power in their inner being by considering historically the evolution of human consciousness (Study 35). Over the course of human evolution through Saturn, Sun, Moon, and down to Earth, we must surely become familiar with the fact that the kingdoms of nature have been separated from what was originally a human wholeness. That is a cosmic analysis of the human being. Step-by-step, humankind has in this way driven aspects of its being into lower spheres.[2] Human beings bear within themselves the results of these events—sin, error, and death. Because of this, Spiritual Science leads instead into the kingdoms of the hierarchies, who are above human beings, who have step-by-step been separated from them (Study 32).

---

1   See the collection of lectures by Steiner, *Psychoanalysis & Spiritual Psychology*, particularly the introduction by Robert Sardello.

2   See *An Outline of Esoteric Science*.

Thus, humankind exists in soul between the kingdoms of nature and the kingdoms of the hierarchies. Through our own efforts, we should thus attain a unity of being amid the myriad facts of the various spheres that condition us. To this end, we must exercise our soul capacities in experiencing history. In keeping with the purpose of a sublime spiritual practice, this exercise is typified in Steiner's "Christmas Foundation Meditation" of 1923.[1] The *Anthroposophical Leading Thoughts* provide a concrete transcript of it; for this reason, it was placed at the beginning of the leading thoughts when first published as a book. The results of working on the leading thoughts can lead again and again to the practice of using these Christmas verses in meditation. Thus, all spiritual scientific knowledge gained in this way may strengthen the soul, for spiritual sight grows from such practice. The impulses from which the leading thoughts sprang have the unalterable goal of preparing a path to living spiritual activity. The diagrams in the previous study may also serve as subjects for meditation, although the soul must overcome a certain aversion to what appears diagrammatic; for this kind of illustration is intended only to present the inner harmony of the subject. Psychological considerations always contain something essentially difficult, and even painful, to the soul. Thus, they must take the form of exercises in inner experience.

The following reflections are intended to show another aspect of the same facts. They can, as they are developed, lead the psychological perspective into the realm of history. Within religion, art, and science, the human soul is seeking unity from the one-sidedness of the various activities that are possible. We are inclined to associate science with thinking, art with feeling, and religion with willing, in keeping with the old ideals of the soul—*truth, beauty,* and *goodness.*[2] Nevertheless, a contemporary person will in fact perceive the necessity of allowing each of these activities to include the work of the others. This may be clearly seen as follows:

> In religion, human beings are looking for standards of willing and acting. In doing this, however, something of a deep feeling quality lives in human consciousness. *The religious approach is a true soul process that comes about when feeling is active in willing.*

> Art is the revelation of feeling; but, in a similar way, the sum of all experiences, memories, and representations is behind it. As soul activity, this is related to thinking. At first, this may sound heretical to many. *The artistic approach is a true soul process that comes about when thinking is active in feeling.*

---

1   Contained in *The Foundation Stone / The Life, Nature, and Cultivation of Anthroposophy.*

2   *Aspects of Human Evolution,* lecture 6.

Science is the realm of thinking; but, again, it is not a matter of the absolutely one-sided soul activity of thinking. Behind the scientific impulse, there is meaning, striving, and purpose, though this is also not readily acknowledged by abstract scientists; therefore, behind the scientific impulse is something of the nature of will.

The scientific approach is a true soul process that comes about when willing is active in thinking.

With this, it is possible now to present the unity of soul in religion, art, and science as inner activity, at least as found in the longing of the modern soul.

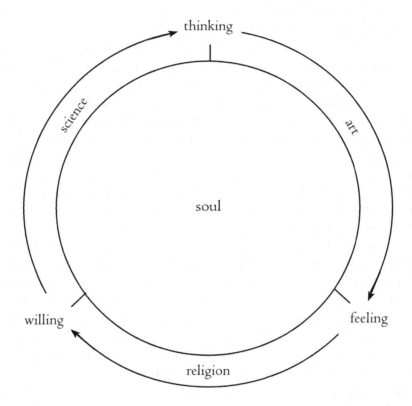

In contemplating this *circular process,* we will indeed grasp something of the soul's longing; yet, the crisis in modern spiritual life is revealed when we look at what that longing of the soul encounters in life today. It can truly be said that this crisis owes its origin to criticism—indeed, not just the effects of Kant's criticism, but the criticism that arises from the heart, from the soul itself, which cannot maintain itself as a being amid modern ways of life, but instead feels annihilated. In the lopsided course of scientific development in external, materialistic, technological forms of life, immeasurable soul substance has been poured out and now turns back, as though demonically on humanity itself, threatening the continuance of the human spiritual soul.

Let us look at the soul's three spheres of activity—religion, art, and science. What is their status in our time, and what is the particular crisis that surrounds each of these spheres? This will lead us back into the spiritual historical conditions from which the soul's present destiny arose. It will also help us to enter the next group of leading thoughts.

In the most ancient Mysteries, religion, art, and science were a unity.[1] That was when humankind, with a more dream-like consciousness, still participated in the divine spiritual world and was guided by higher beings. The impulse to act was the first to be released from this unity. To compensate for this, those souls were given the possibility of resuming their connection with the spiritual world and its beings; that *reunion* is religion. This led to the cultural conditions of the Middle East and North Africa, which Rudolf Steiner usually termed *Egypto-Chaldean*. Their character was essentially religious. The forms of Egypto-Chaldean cult have been transmitted through tradition until today. The expression for this is found in the old "thou shalt," which, for people of that time, still conformed to the innermost impulses of the soul itself. Today, however, this has been reduced to abstract categorical imperatives that in fact approach the soul only in an external way.[2] This applies also to traditional religious demands. When the soul seeks to unite itself today with religious traditions, it does so because it has remained, with this aspect of its being, two stages behind in the progress of human evolution.

The impulse of feeling was the next to be released from the Mysteries; this led to the cultural conditions of Greece, which were thoroughly artistic. Of course, there was a national religion, but this was represented through all the artistic forms of beauty, particularly in sculpture and drama. During that time, those who wished to turn to a primeval religious approach went to the Mystery centers, where they sought union with the ancient divine consciousness. Until today, the artistic impulse has been handed down by tradition. The soul crisis of our time in this sense is due to the fact that artistic practice has remained one stage behind the evolutionary progress of humanity and is unable to express the contemporary soul's longing.

We arrive completely in the present with the third impulse that left the ancient Mysteries. After the impulse of thinking, or science, was released, as institutions, the Mysteries had to disappear, concealing themselves to the degree that they could no longer be found on the physical plane. This impulse of science has now led to the present conditions, to a one-sidedness of science, together with the fact that *all* soul reality is in danger of dying. Since this is the impulse of the present time, however, it was necessary that science should become Rudolf Steiner's starting point in restoring unity to the human soul.

---

1   *Universe, Earth and Man*, lecture 11.

2   *Aspects of Human Evolution*, lecture 6.

THE CRISIS OF THE MODERN SOUL
AND HOW IT MAY BE HEALED

In continuing from the previous study, it will be useful to look back again to the primeval unity of the human soul life. Rudolf Steiner spoke of times when

> the various activities of the human mind and soul, which today we find separated as science, art, and religion, had not yet been separated from one another.... Religion was not viewed as something as a separate branch of their culture, but they still spoke of religion, even when their minds were directly concerned with the practical affairs of everyday life.... But this archetypal religion was inwardly very strong...its inspiration so strong that some of those particular workings took forms that were none other than those of art....
>
> But this archetypal religion and its daughter art were at the same time so purified, so lifted into the refining spheres of etheric spiritual life that their influence even brought out in human souls something of which today we have a faint reflection, however abstract, in our science and knowledge. When feeling became more intense and filled with enthusiasm for what overflowed as religion into artistic form, then *knowledge* of the gods and divine beings, knowledge of spirit land, was kindled in the soul.[3]

Of all this, longing alone has remained to contemporary humanity. If we now relate the particulars of the previous study to modern forms of religion, art, and science, it will become clear how, through a strange dislocation, such a constellation arose, how over the course of evolution, especially in the nineteenth century, all three soul impulses were inevitably paralyzed. We found that *"the religious approach is a true soul process that comes about when feeling is active in willing."* To a certain extent this is the concept of the religious approach. Now, however, after its separation from the original whole, modern consciousness finds, in the religious forms of worship coming indeed from the third post-Atlantean civilization, an experience where *feeling* has gained the upper hand. We can disregard the degeneration of the feeling element into sentimental extravagance, and look at the experience, which may in fact manifest today as a sense of esthetics. The most wonderful works of art in all spheres have originated in the religious traditions.

---

3   *Wonders of the World, Ordeals of the Soul, Revelations of the Spirit*, lecture 1, pp. 9–10.

We also found that *"The artistic approach is a true soul process that comes about when thinking is active in feeling."* What has become of art in our time? We find in this realm, as remnants of Greek culture, only science as it is practiced, for example, in art academies. It is the nineteenth century that has treated esthetics as though it were science.

Finally, also in relation to science, which is completely a part of our time, we may examine its current form in contrast to its concept: *"The scientific approach is a true soul process that comes about when willing is active in thinking."* Science is likewise no longer a pure revelation of its impulses; it has become dogmatic and authoritative; it is overpowered by an element that was originally religious, as is art by science, and religion by art.

Consequently, we see that the soul activities paralyze one another. In contrast to this paralysis, Steiner presents the transformation of thinking, feeling, and willing as *imagination, inspiration,* and *intuition.* Religion, art, and science will be redeemed in this way for the future. Abstract science, which has hardened into dogma, can allow an artistic element through *imagination.* This is also the way we acquire knowledge in the sense of Steiner's education. His scientific lecture cycles, presented to experts, show how this can occur without the slightest damage to proper scientific exactitude.

Steiner makes art into a language of spiritual experience—that is, *inspiration* as a religious force that redeems art. He confirmed this in all areas of art; we may refer in particular to architecture, sculpture, painting, and the Goetheanum stained glass windows. Steiner's works in verse—the greatest examples being his four mystery dramas—bear eloquent witness to this. The introduction of speech formation and drama is also related to this. He also created a new art of visible speech and song—*eurythmy.*

Finally, religion is rescued from paralysis by *intuition,* in place of original faith, creating a truly new spiritual meaning; and mediating this is knowledge of the spirit, or Spiritual Science. Steiner offered this as the authentic sacrament of the Christian Community. He also added a form of worship to the religious lessons in Waldorf schools that can be communicated through knowledge.

Such acts of redemption on behalf of religion, art, and science may be represented as a unity in a triangulation. The paralysis and the redemption of the three soul activities can be written one above the other (see opposite). The diagram is probably self-explanatory. The triangle pointing down represents the paralysis of the soul realms of religion, art, and science; the upward-pointing triangle represents their redemption through anthroposophic endeavor. In other words, the drawing indicates:

> Religion should operate in willing; it is paralyzed by art and is redeemed
> in knowing through *intuition.*
> Art should operate in feeling; it is paralyzed by science and is redeemed
> in a religious element through *inspiration.*

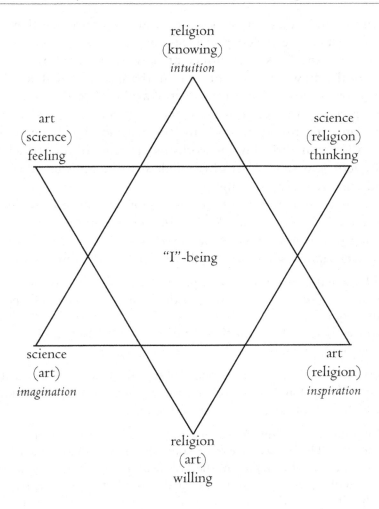

Science should operate in thinking; it is paralyzed by religion and is redeemed in an artistic element through *imagination*.

If the paradox of these sentences is disturbing, they should be penetrated with a living sense of culture.

We will be able to see that we are dealing with six combinations, each comprising two soul realms. In relation to the table in Study 38, we can present it this way:

	Religion	Art	Science
Religion		A in R	S in R
Art	R in A		S in A
Science	R in S	A in S	S in S

In contrast to the diagram in Study 38, you will notice first that the diagonal is missing. It is nevertheless possible to insert "s in s" ("science in science," or "science of science") as a seventh combination, indicated by "'I'-being" at the center of the drawing. Only this, within the sphere of soul activities, may be directed toward itself. There is no "art of art" or "religion of religion."

It was precisely this seventh possibility that Steiner seized upon in the 1980s in beginning his great work for the redemption of the soul's activities. This was accomplished in his works on epistemology, to which we must repeatedly return. It was an act of the highest freedom; it based thinking on itself, and thus created a "fulcrum."

This occurred at a moment of greatest importance in spiritual history. We read in the book Steiner left us, *Rudolf Steiner: An Autobiography*, that the decisive step in this matter was taken in 1879—that is, at the point in time when Michael again assumed spiritual leadership of the times.

> My efforts in this direction, in the sphere of scientific concepts, had finally brought me to see that the activity of the human "I" is the only possible starting point for true knowledge. I said to myself: When the "I" observes its own activity, it has something spiritual immediately present in consciousness. (pp. 53–54)

Because the leading thoughts that follow are based on them, it is most important to immediately comprehend the essence of those spiritual historic events, which took place at such a crucial moment.

> 103. In human evolution, consciousness descends on the ladder of unfolding thought. There was an earlier stage in consciousness when human beings experienced thoughts in the "I," experienced them as real beings, imbued with spirit, soul and life. At a second stage they experienced thoughts in the astral body; thereafter, thoughts appeared only as the images of spirit beings—images nevertheless still imbued with soul and life. At a third stage, they experienced thoughts in the etheric body, where they manifest only as inner liveliness, as an echo of a quality of soul. At the fourth stage—the present stage—human beings experience thoughts in the physical body, where they appear as the dead shadows of the spirit.

> 104. To the degree that the quality of spirit, soul, and life in human thought recedes, human will comes to life. Thus, true freedom becomes possible.

> 105. It is Michael's task to lead humanity back again, along paths of will, from which we came down when, with earthly consciousness, we descended on paths of thought from a living experience of the suprasensory to an experience of the world of the senses.

THE SIN AGAINST THE SPIRIT

In referring to Leading Thoughts 103 to 105, Rudolf Steiner continues his letters on Michael's mission, mentioned in Study 35. The events that have engaged our attention since that chapter—events that lead to the grand cosmic developments that now follow—are expressed in the letter:

> It is not possible to perceive in the right light how the Michael impulse breaks into human evolution if one shares the conception that is universally accepted today regarding the relationship between the new world of ideas and nature.[1]

Again and again, we found such indications, which, in contrast to the present scientific attitude, demand a moral element. In Leading Thought 7 Steiner pointed to the lopsided nature of scientific thinking; in Leading Thought 20 we read that modern science *sins*; and in the letter that accompanies Leading Thoughts 35 to 37 Steiner says:

> It is most important that it should be understood through Anthroposophy that the ideas that a person gains by viewing outer nature also be adequate for observing humankind. The ideas that have taken possession of human minds during the spiritual development of the last few centuries fail to realize this fact. (ibid., p. 27)

Our earlier studies were concerned with matters of karma; now we are concerned with the reign of Michael, and before it is possible to enter such spheres, it is apparent that something of a moral nature must be placed in opposition to the sinning mentioned. This is also true for this study of Leading Thoughts 103 to 105, which concerns the descent of consciousness on the "ladder of unfolding thought." Steiner's purpose in writing this letter on these leading thoughts is to provide a specific answer to the question: What does the human being experience in modern scientific ideas? If we want to enter this whole subject with sufficient depth, we must first ask a preliminary question: What makes the attitude of modern science a sin?

Through "the ideas that have taken hold of human minds during the spiritual development of the last few centuries [referring to Leading Thoughts 35 to 37]...people have gotten used to thinking through natural laws and using them to explain natural phenomena perceived by the senses."[2] This clearly

---

1   *Anthroposophical Leading Thoughts*, p. 66.

2   Ibid., p. 27.

shows that human beings themselves are the creators of their thoughts and think independently, according to the laws they present as the standard for understanding natural phenomena. Of course, "contemporary thinkers are concerned primarily with showing how to form ideas that will have a true relationship to nature or contain true natural laws. In other words, in human beings there is a spiritual aspect that rules independently, from which those who know modern science begin their work. In our present time, people feel that ideas are formed within them through their own soul activity, whereas only sensory perceptions come from without."[1]

Endless examples could be cited,[2] but given this premise, most significant are the consequences revealed when those who—provided with the results of ideas applied to natural phenomena—turn around and consider human beings themselves in terms of *natural phenomena*. Here, for example, it is obvious that the thinking employed by the more modern consciousness will produce ideas that can deal only with the inherent laws in mineral phenomena. If, however, *these* laws are now taken as fundamental to studying human beings, this is not only a logical impossibility, but a genuine denial of the true principles behind science—that is, the ideas produced by independent thinking. It denies the spirit, which is truly active in humankind. Consequently, such consideration must end before it reaches the human being, and, for this method of study, the human aspect presented as a natural phenomenon to the senses must appear as *image* (Leading Thought 16).

It would be good to examine these conclusions again and again; Steiner presented this in his epistemological works, in *Intuitive Thinking as a Spiritual Path*, and in many other places. This is indeed where the real task of modern consciousness lies. Scientific habits of thinking are far too short-sighted; the path leading to the application of such ideas to the human being is far too short. When scientific thinking is truly developed—as Rudolf Steiner worked it out, in relation to Goethe's theory of metamorphosis first, and then in detail through courses, lectures, and books—the result for scientific investigators will be the true spiritual faculty of comprehending images. Indeed, they could arrive at self-knowledge through their investigations, to the degree that they may find themselves on the path to seeing spiritual reality, or *imagination*. Neglecting this task is the sin against the spirit that is active in modern humankind.

The transition from the epistemological to the moral aspect, which indeed is accomplished in the *Intuitive Thinking as a Spiritual Path*, has also occupied us before (Leading Thought 12). It is again presented to us in Leading

---

1   Ibid., p. 66; the letter referring to Leading Thoughts 103–105.

2   For example, in terms of mechanics, see my book *Die Autonomie des philosophischen Bewusstseins* ("The Autonomy of Philosophical Consciousness" [Stuttgart: Verlag Freies Geistesleben, 1964]); unavailable in English.

Thoughts 103–105 as the transition from thinking to willing, but now from the perspective of the spiritual history of human consciousness. In relation to our studies of religion, art, and science, by returning to the origin of the sin against the spirit that is characteristic of our modern consciousness, we find our way into the aspect of this evolution that is essentially spiritual. This may be traced to earlier stages of civilization of a very different nature.

In terms of soul activities between the physical and spiritual worlds, people easily deceive themselves about the position of modern thinking, feeling, and willing. For example, people today attempt to be free in willing and try to conform to law in thinking. In relation to the way people inquire about freedom today, Steiner specifically stated, and in *Intuitive Thinking as a Spiritual Path* showed that we must begin with thinking in coming to terms with this question. Previous studies showed clearly that freedom begins in thinking (behind which willing is of course active), because human beings can be awake in thinking; human willing is asleep and thus bound by spirit (Study 10). In the sense of the alphabet contained in the language of the consciousness soul, we find a comprehensive axiom: *the spiritual compulsion of karma prevails in the will; the seeds of future destiny are contained in thinking.*

The objection will perhaps be raised that, in earlier Studies, it was said that thinking is directed to the past, willing to the future. But we must distinguish between the two aspects; previously the object of thinking and willing was meant, now the soul activities of thinking and willing are meant. In addition to this, we can remember that, in the course of evolution, thinking and willing exchange places (Study 12).

Let us begin again with the fact that thinking about the laws of nature is an independent human act, and that, on the other hand, we find karma to be active in manifestations of the will (Leading Thought 95). Spiritual compulsion in willing directs us back to the third post-Atlantean civilization when all that had been prepared during the great ages of the past and by planetary evolution was recapitulated for our whole post-Atlantean epoch. Then, as we saw, human willing was released from the Mysteries and entered the religious forms of culture (Study 39).[3] Human beings then began to emerge as individuals in accordance with the physical plane. The divine could no longer work directly within individual human beings; nevertheless, they recognized themselves as children of the Father through their religious experience. The *child of God* constitutes the pure substance of all the ancient forms of religion, which still have their effect today. At that time, solemn images arose, depicting the separation of humanity from the Father God. They are pictures of the *Fall*— but a fall into *knowledge* of good and evil.[4] The will element, or the moral aspect of this event, should be attributed not to humankind, but to the tempta-

3   *Man in the Light of Occultism, Theosophy, and Philosophy,* lecture 1.

4   *The World of the Senses and the World of the Spirit,* lecture 1.

tion by spirit beings. "Child of God" is the religious attitude that prevails in human willing. The sin against the Father arises from Lucifer, and from there it affects all of humanity.[1]

The next step is the release of human feeling from the spiritual realm. It is true that, because of this, the culture of art arose; but it was of the human being and no longer of divine law. Human self-awareness began then, accompanied by a sense of being isolated from God. Humankind could no longer maintain an attitude of "child of God." Rather, human beings became, as Steiner strikingly described, "children of Lucifer."[2]

Then Christ, as the Son of God, came with the fullness of this divine relationship into an individual human body. In this way, Christ became the great brother of humankind, inasmuch as he revealed complete divinity in a single human body. This revelation as historical event must be decided by human feeling. The decision falls on each individual as *yes* or *no*, the effects of which may be felt during many earthly lives. Christ's act of love leaves the individual free; but the individual's sin affects all of humanity. The soul seeks Christ's brotherhood in the feeling life; this is the religious attitude that prevails in human feeling.

The third step is human thinking, also released from the spirit's guidance. This has a particular effect in our epoch. Now a divine principle wills to become active in each human being. Consequently, we may describe the paths of thinking during the time since the Mystery of Golgotha as a search for the Holy Spirit. But these are the paths of individuals to the spirit, who wills to redeem human thinking; the human action in this matter is our own responsibility as individuals. The decision is made within Ahriman's kingdom, where one can remain only with the results of an absolutely clear judgment. Individual denial of spirit—the sin of modern scientific method and habits of thinking, materialism as a worldview as well as a soul attitude—is the sin against the Holy Spirit. It is unforgivable because human individuals commit it against *themselves*; but it also works back against the spiritual world and its beings in a destructive way.

Rudolf Steiner shows the path of true self-knowledge as a way to counter the sin against the Spirit. He leads humankind to the ruling spirit of our time by way of a kind of thinking that apprehends and understands itself. That is *Michael Community*, and it is the religious attitude that prevails in human thinking.

---

1   *From Jesus to Christ*, lecture 3.

2   *The East in The Light of the West*, lecture 8; included with this lecture cycle is Edouard Schuré's play, "Children of Lucifer and the Brothers of Christ."

STUDY 42

SPIRITUAL HISTORY

Spiritual history is the result of the reign of spiritual beings during successive eras and throughout human history; human evolution is merely the way it manifests outwardly. History, like human sense perception, may assume the form of an image for us as we view it. We saw our previous study as a preliminary exercise for Rudolf Steiner's investigations into spiritual history, which are presented with continually increasing force. As long as we generate within ourselves a true reverence in the presence of these revelations, they may lead us to feel drawn into the process of this spiritual history. Arising from this is the duty to follow the call of the spiritual world for participation in the process of spiritual history, giving form to these investigations within our own being.

Thinking, feeling, and willing have gradually been released from spiritual guidance into activity within the physical world. During the post-Atlantean era, human consciousness has been related to thinking, which separated itself from servitude to the spirit—the separation that was the last and most radical. We have dealt with the descent of consciousness "on the ladder of unfolding thought" (Leading Thoughts 103 to 105). Now we must similarly imagine how, as we go farther back through the ancient civilizations, we must look for thinking in increasingly higher worlds.

If we apply the descriptions of the higher worlds impressed on us by Rudolf Steiner, we may say that, during the ancient Persian civilization, thinking reached into the supra-spiritual realm; during the Egypto-Chaldean civilization thinking reached into the spiritual world; during the Greco-Roman time, it was revealed in the elemental world; and, in our time, it reaches into the physical world. But that was, simultaneously, the path and destiny of spiritual beings. This is difficult for contemporary humankind to comprehend, because we are at the end of this evolution and live in a twilight kind of thinking, which we experience as our own product. Within this realm of twilight, human beings are excluded from the community of spiritual beings, since only the human "I" can experience itself in a physical body.

In listening to reports from ancient times, we can learn many things; but we must take them seriously, not merely assuming that those ancient chroniclers made up stories as do those who recount events today. Out of primeval times, the longing for the supra-spiritual world and for the being *Sophia* still

159

reaches us.[1] Out of such lofty regions, this being was revealed until the times of the ancient Gnostics as the source of the light of all wisdom. That can give us a certain picture of how thought was still in the supra-spiritual world. If we pass on to a later time, we find, for example, the work *Consolation of Philosophy* by Boethius (AD 480–525), a noble man unjustly thrown into prison by Theodoric the Great. There, the prisoner describes how Philosophia came to him as a being to comfort him in his need. This conversation is a real spirit conversation, a true Inspiration. Thus, we are referred to the spiritual world, to which this being Philosophia belonged.

The phenomenon of the being Natura with her companions, the seven liberal arts, points more to the elemental world. It is in this revelation that the picture world, the imaginations of a Dante, have their origin. Of this, Steiner, during the last year of his life, gave wonderful descriptions which contain a wealth of revelation. Thus, we come to see the descent of thought more clearly as a real occurrence, especially when we remember that human thinking originates in the beings of the third Hierarchy (Leading Thought 66). Steiner spoke fully of the connections between spiritual beings, so that it is possible to speak without hesitation of the relationship of their descendant.[2] Thus, for example, there are the offspring of the beings of the third Hierarchy; they are the elemental beings that visited serious alchemists. Those ancient people had a living, realistic attitude toward thought. Steiner also speaks of elemental beings that originate from human beings.[3] It would not be very difficult to sense the reality of this in relation to the thinking life; thus, in Study 11, we spoke of beings that become increasingly demonic in the course of associating representations.

Human beings carry within them the rudimentary remains of this very real process, and we can consciously connect ourselves with these if we wish to share in spiritual history. Now, we can proceed from Study 18, where we were shown the need and possibility of resuscitating the *Categories* of Aristotle through Anthroposophy. Steiner's investigations showed us that Aristotle lived during a very important turning point in the history of human consciousness. He discerned the threshold over which humankind, in the thinking life, was passing from the previous state of being bound to spirit to a state of being forsaken by the gods, which belongs to our time. In his logic, Aristotle created the forms through which the essentials of disappearing thinking may be mirrored like a cosmic memory. He sealed the old experience of spiritual thinking within his forms of logic, and now the time has come to break those seals. Within the individual forms of Aristotelian logic,

---

1   *Christ and the Spiritual World: And the Search for the Holy Grail*, lecture 1; also *Ancient Myths and the New Isis Mystery*, lecture of Dec. 24, 1920.

2   *Spiritual Beings in the Heavenly Bodies and in the Kingdoms of Nature.*

3   *The Inner Nature of Man and the Life between Death and Rebirth*, lecture 5.

we will try to recognize the stages of thinking as it descended; in this way, we may be able to maintain a connection with our own rudimentary residue of ancient spiritual events.

In the letter that accompanied Leading Thoughts 103–105, Steiner describes the descent of thought in greater detail:

> In ancient times, people did not realize the meaning of their ideas as some-thing created by themselves.... There were various stages to this feeling; those stages were determined by which aspect of the human being within which they experienced what we today call *ideas*.... Now one may return to the times when thoughts were experienced directly in the "I." In those times, however, thoughts were not shadowy as they are today, nor were they simply alive; they were *endowed with soul and permeated with spirit.* This means that they did not merely think their thoughts but experienced a perception of actual spiritual beings.... It is different for the second stage of consciousness, where those real spiritual beings are hidden; their reflec-tion appears in the form of an ensouled life.... The element of thought was no longer experienced by the "I" but by the astral body.... A third epoch in the development of consciousness brings thought to awareness in the etheric body, now as living thought. The Greeks lived in this conscious-ness when their civilization was in its prime. Ancient Greeks did not form the thoughts with which they viewed the world, believing them to be their own creations; when they thought, they felt as though a life were being enkindled within them—a life that also pulsated within the objects and events around them.... When thoughts took hold of the physical, only the abstract shadow attached to the physical body remained, with spirit, soul, and life eliminated from the immediate content of thinking.[4]

Aristotelian logic, virtually unaltered, still applies today; it distinguishes among the principles of *concepts, judgments,* and *conclusions.* To these are added various principles, or maxims, such as *identity, contradiction,* and so on. The elements of logical thinking are concepts; several concepts are com-bined to form judgments. Thus, the uniting element again consists of definite concepts, also described as *Categories.* Again, conclusions are comprised of judgments, and the way these are united—also forming very different con-cepts—determine the various forms of conclusion. *Conformity to law,* which is presented to us in logic, is simply a description of the processes in thinking, which are present as facts of consciousness. Such evidence points to the pro-cesses in the evolution of human consciousness.

First, let us consider *concepts.* They have definite forms, which contem-porary logicians, and scientists in particular, wish to define with the greatest precision possible; they attempt to delineate individual concepts with great clarity. Whereas the *ideas* of Plato still display a "hovering," mobile quality, the concepts of Aristotle give us thought as *form.* By separating such forms,

---

4   *Anthroposophical Leading Thoughts,* pp. 66–68.

one from another, concepts are given an "I"-quality—clearly recognizable, though, in a sense, very abstract. We are given something that has been frozen into abstract form, which we can imagine was still a concrete, living experience in the consciousness of ancient times.

The first stage of consciousness, when thinking was still in the "I," was therefore represented by what logic termed *concept*. Concept still contains "I"-quality. This is proved when we enter the being of a concept through meditation. We can look for the final, highest, most comprehensive concept beyond every sequence and class of concepts; we then find—in the totality of all conceptual possibilities, in the concept of the concept—a *being*, the absolute or pure "I"-being. This has been shown repeatedly in other contexts.[1]

Next we turn to the *judgments*; in them is contained an abstract form that constitutes the soul element. We react in a naive way to the attractions of the world through sensation, feeling, impulse, and passion.[2] This field of activity belongs to the astral body. The way the consciousness of the astral body is related to judgments was shown in Studies 13 and 14, especially in terms of conditions after death. We saw how the astral body's consciousness runs its course in judging, and how it learns, after death, what it is to be judged. Thus, in the activity of judging, the second stage of the evolution of consciousness is represented when a person experiences thoughts in the astral body. Here, of course, such things can merely be indicated; but perhaps we can nevertheless come to see the possibility, through Anthroposophy, of having a logic that conforms to spirit.

"A third epoch in the development of consciousness brings thought to awareness in the etheric body." It is not difficult now to comprehend that the logical conclusion is the thought *form* that represents this stage in Aristotle's logic. It presents us with the images of progressive thinking; it is like a living process, even though a third emerges in an abstract semblance, as out of two judgments. We can summarize this in yet another way. Within the conclusion, the shadow of an *imaginative* process appears (etheric body); in the judgment appears the shadow of an *inspirational* process (astral body); and in the concept the shadow of an *intuitive* process appears ("I"-being).

There still remains, for the fourth stage only, the so-called principles of logic—particularly, the principle of *identity*, which is spatial.[3] Through this principle, thinking is fettered to the physical body.

Such considerations may be of value as we examine the mission of Michael.

---

1   See my *Die Autonomie des philosophischen Bewuaetseins* and Studies 7 and 9

2   *A Psychology of Body, Soul, and Spirit* and *Anthroposophy (A Fragment)*, chapter 7.

3   See my *Die Autonomie des philosophischen Bewuaetseins.*

THE FREE AND THE FETTERED THOUGHT:
NOT ONLY AN INTERLUDE

Anthroposophy is a path of knowledge that leads from fettered thinking to free thinking. At first, the thinking active in human beings is completely constrained—indeed, it is bound physiologically to the brain.[4] Even superficial observation demonstrates that thinking is not produced by the brain but reflected in it.[5] We must only learn to distinguish between the content of a thought and how it appears. This is subjective in a dual sense: once in terms of the human organization and then in relation to the soul's activity. The effort I must make in order to comprehend a thought is *my own*; the substance, on the other hand, is of the spirit—beyond subject and object (Study 10). Now, however, the content of thinking is also restrained—fettered to the history of thought's descent and, according to the spiritual history of humanity, the content is given by spiritual beings whose acts are concealed behind the *forms* of concept, judging, and conclusion (Study 42).

Now the question repeatedly arises as to whether or not human beings are correct in assuming they create their own thoughts, or if such an assumption is merely an illusion. This question has great cognitive value; indeed, to those working anthroposophically, it is the *most* important question, since its answer depends on whether or not free thought exists and, with it, freedom in general.

In relation to this question, Steiner wrote *Intuitive Thinking as a Spiritual Path: A Philosophy of Freedom*. In the first part, he treats thought more in terms of phenomena. In the second part, however, he shows how to attain the creative activity of thinking, which is a moral activity. A path of this kind constitutes a test of the soul. Steiner shows this in his *Autobiography*, which we may consider in particular from this perspective—that is, the way he plants free thinking within humanity and, in fact, within every sphere of thought activity. His reward was the deepest loneliness. Such loneliness appears as

---

4   *Universe, Earth and Man*, lecture 11.

5   *Wonders of the World, Ordeals of the Soul, Revelations of the Spirit*, lecture 17; *Initiation, Eternity and the Passing Moment*, lecture 7.

a test of the soul on the path of knowledge, and it truly shows that human beings fashion their own thoughts.[1]

Let us consider for once how thinking, according to its content, is connected to the stage of evolution, nation, language, tradition, associations (habits of thinking), and even to the personal memories of an individual. Essentially, our life depends on such ties, especially in terms of social matters. Those who truly seek freedom in thinking, however, liberate themselves step-by-step from this dependence; indeed, the tragedy of humanity's separation from the divine repeats itself in the individual. It is not accidental that the path of initiation is symbolically related to what we have termed "spiritual history."

If, by means of exercises, we want to approach free thinking, we must gradually remove from our consciousness the fetters that bind thinking. This leads to a state of meditation (Study 4). But this is also the point where thinking stops. It is easier to think than to stop thinking. *Thinking becomes free when it stands still.* We can indeed take this with unqualified seriousness—that our power of understanding comes to a halt. At this point, thinking is changed to willing; and the thought that is becoming free reveals itself as morality.

When we free thought from bondage, all our previous supports fail to act—especially those of the moral life, which rest on tradition, education, and so on, and to which our ordinary experience of truth belongs.[2] At this threshold of life, many turn back to the fettered thought, even though they may be familiar with Anthroposophy. Contemporary human beings are riddled with fear before free thinking. They are afraid not only of seeing their old supports giving way, but also fear seeing free thinking in others. Steiner often spoke of materialism as a manifestation of fear.[3]

Out of the current stage of evolution, modern science has, in fact, grasped free thinking somewhat. Science can be a great training for free thought; Steiner therefore stressed the value of its methods. In keeping with the nature of science, it removed the traditions of an older spiritual life. Of course, its freedom—the absence of any presupposition—is often merely an illusion. Steiner frequently pointed to the bondage of scientists—the Council of Constantinople, for example (Study 11). Exactly where scientists are materialists, they show fear before the free thought that prevails in scientific method. Traditional consciousness of God dwindles away; in its place, science places

1   *Initiation, Eternity and the Passing Moment*, lecture 4; *The Effects of Esoteric Development*, lecture 8; *The Bhagavad Gita and the West*, lecture 2; *Building Stones for an Understanding of the Mystery of Golgotha*, lecture 8.

2   *The Effects of Esoteric Development*, lecture 7; *Background to the Gospel of St. Mark*, lecture 1.

3   *Initiation, Eternity and the Passing Moment*, lecture 7; *The Bhagavad Gita and the West*, lecture 9; *The Karma of Materialism*, lecture 1.

a fetish, an idol; those are the atoms, electrons or the *thing-in-itself*, matter, energy, and so on—the creations of abstract thought.[4]

The approach to free thought is full of dangers. Steiner always noted this when speaking of the path of knowledge. Fear in face of such dangers—fear that often prevails quite unconsciously—leads many sincere anthroposophists either to compromise with the bondage of thought related to ancient times, or they misconstrue Anthroposophy itself as a way to constrict their own thinking and that of others. An unjustifiable demand for authority arises within Anthroposophy, and Steiner always warned against this with the greatest insistence; he often expressed this very clearly by saying that we should not *believe* his words, but *think* them—that is, make them the object of our *own* thinking!

In *Riddles of Philosophy*, Steiner shows the path from fettered to free thinking as the path of evolution for humanity. This, however, cannot be gathered from the thought content of philosophy's history, because, in terms of those contents, almost all of the philosophical problems and their possible solutions had already appeared in ancient Greece. Nevertheless, the thinking of that time must be described as fettered, since it was *seen*. Thought thus fell within the realm of percepts, or observations, which are transferable; and it is justifiable to accept the authority of those who have seen thoughts themselves.

When humankind lost sight of what had been seen during ancient times, it was appropriated by tradition and handed over to *faith*. The substance of faith was originally visions; and this not only refers to Greek thought, but even more to the essence of religion, belonging to still more ancient times. Each genuine revelation is communicated so that the one who receives it begins with the formula, "Thus I have seen," though perhaps expressed in different words. Thus, in *Intuitive Thinking as a Spiritual Path*, the problem of *faith and knowledge* is reduced to the relationship between observation and thinking. For modern consciousness, faith, along with authority, rightly exists within the sphere of observation and, indeed, within the realm of the sensible as well as suprasensory investigation. Nevertheless, our own inner activity—the particular work of the individual—is the decisive factor within the sphere of thinking, or one's interpretation and explanation of observed facts.

Rudolf Steiner brought Anthroposophy into the world, because it was needed for human progress; it works among us as an impulse that arises from free thought, even though such an impulse can be received in only a limited sense. For many, this is an experience of destiny, especially among the young; for them, the traditional view of the universe breaks down, and they are often overtaken by a tragic sense of loneliness. This leads to an urge to look for a new community for the quest of knowledge, which Steiner showed in his

---

4   *Wonders of the World...*, lectures 10 and 11.

lectures of 1923. When we strive for knowledge in community with others, not only can we overcome our fear of loneliness but also the danger of compromise with fettered thinking.

Steiner spoke to such a community of what he had presented as a result of his suprasensory investigation of the spiritual side of this cosmic event. Lucifer had the cosmic mission of bringing human freedom.[1] That is his lawful work, but he brought this impulse to humanity too soon by promising the *knowledge* of good and evil.[2] Now it is also our task to demand this knowledge; this takes place when free thought is transformed into morality. Humankind should not flee from Lucifer, but should withstand him. The means that Steiner gives for this is strong and free, moral conduct; otherwise, there remains only the ruins of a morality given by the gods.[3] But when free thinking is received only instinctively—as in contemporary science—its fruit falls to Ahriman.

Again, Steiner gives us the means to hold our own against Ahriman; it is sharp, clear, pure thinking—for example, when we think through scientific thought to the end and do not succumb to the sin against the spirit (Study 41).[4] This constitutes a universal battle that is waged between free thinking and fettered thinking; the battle is waged around the human soul, and it lurks behind every possible situation, where it is often difficult to recognize. Therefore, it is most valuable to be aware of this battle—not only where our human interactions come into play, but where spiritual concerns are equally manifest.

Steiner expressed this in a revealing way in his Mystery Plays. (We have space here for only a few indications.) At a decisive moment, Johannes Thomasius follows the leadership of Lucifer. Consequently, he is able to write a scientific work, but he is obliged to recognize that its fruits would necessarily fall to Ahriman. Johannes is unable, on his own, to produce the moral force needed to tear himself from Lucifer's seductions. Maria, on the other hand, did not succumb to Ahriman, who, with a truly devilish intellect, tries to attribute the experience of previous earthly lives to the trickery of Benedictus. Maria, through the strength of her thinking, is able to fend off Ahriman's assault by using his own weapons. Then, however, she changes the free thinking thus gained into a valiant act of sacrifice—a moral force that enables her to vanquish Lucifer on behalf of Johannes.

Anthroposophy is in the world, and it is active among humankind. Whether this activity is for good or for evil depends on human beings

---

1   *The Spiritual Hierarchies and the Physical World*, lecture 10; *The Gospel of St. John and Its Relation to the Other Gospels*, lecture 14; *According to Luke*, lecture 3.

2   *Universe, Earth and Man*, lecture 6; *The Gospel of St. John and Its Relation to the Other Gospels*, lecture 5.

3   *Manifestations of Karma*, lecture 7.

4   Ibid.

themselves. Once before, we had to note the fact that Steiner's work can also be turned to evil if we are not watchful (Study 16). If Anthroposophy itself is misused to bind thinking, Michael's mission will fail. The tenor of expression in Leading Thought 105 points to the path where the moral approach arises from free thinking. If Michael's mission in relation to free thought is accepted, "then the souls and spirits in the suprasensory worlds will incline toward the enlivened thoughts."[5]

---

5   *Anthroposophical Leading Thoughts*, p. 69.

STUDY 44

A NEW FORM OF MYTH

If, while fully awake, we repeatedly enter Rudolf Steiner's intimate modes of expression—the leading thoughts, for example—we become aware of a steadily increasing sense of wonder. Often, our thoughts cling to a word or a certain phrase, and an endless series of images from the wisdom of Anthroposophy can arise from it. These may be revealed in different ways for various people; consequently, in these discussions only individual examples can be chosen from the inexhaustible store to stimulate us.

Perhaps it will be helpful to say something about the letters that accompany the leading thoughts. Steiner himself constructed them in such a way that they would present the meaning of the leading thoughts in greater detail. The wording of these letters has not been published yet and, therefore, it cannot be assumed in these studies.[1] Neither could specific explanations of the letters be given much consideration, since they cannot be related to the leading thoughts themselves. It is indeed preferable to allow the wording, when accessible, to speak for itself. Nevertheless, it seemed necessary and justifiable to quote some sentences (as has been done already) and to interpret their meaning in abridged form. First, some characteristics of the letters on Michael's mission will be stressed; they may also be found later with various groups of leading thoughts.

When humankind looks back over its own evolution, reviewing in spirit the unique character that human spiritual life has assumed during the last five centuries, human beings cannot help but recognize, though dimly through ordinary consciousness, that during these five centuries, humanity has come to a critical turning point in the whole of earthly human evolution.[2]

Human progress may be traced from the stage of consciousness when human beings experienced themselves as part of a divine spiritual order up to the present, when we learn to experience ourselves as individuals, detached from divine, spiritual being and able to think for ourselves. One may trace this from the human perspective. It is also possible, however, through suprasensory vision, to sketch a picture of the experiences of

---

1   Since Carl Unger wrote this, the letters were published in *Anthroposophical Leading Thoughts: The Michael Mystery* (which includes the letters on Michael).

2   *Anthroposophical Leading Thoughts*, p. 71.

Michael and his hosts during this same evolutionary process—that is, to describe the same series of facts as they appear to Michael. (ibid., p. 76)

If we grasp the significance of these matters, it again appears that human-kind is drawn into spiritual history, as described in Study 42. This, however, implies participation in what may be considered a myth in a genuinely new sense—the interaction of the affairs of gods and human beings. But now we are concerned with something essentially different from the myths of ancient times. That difference is due to the crisis of our time, from which we must wrest it; for the new myth is manifested through free thinking.

The images of old visions will be repeated and perhaps reinterpreted (against which, of course, nothing may be said); but Steiner, who creates this myth, is himself a seer and investigator into the affairs of gods and human beings, both present and future. His is not the work of ancient times; instead of the god's activities on Earth, divine wisdom pours out and approaches human beings as revelation; then out of loneliness, we worked our way up from Earth into the realms of the hierarchies by way of unfettered thinking. Related to this is the initiation we should strive toward in our present era; such effort must arise from earthly forces as an extension of scientific method. Today, we call this methodical process "human intellect"; the following leading thoughts are concerned with this:

106. Michael returns upward along the paths on which, stage by stage, humankind descended in the evolution of the spirit, down to the use of the intellect. Michael will lead the will upward, however, retracing the paths by the wisdom descended to the final stage of intelligence.

107. From now on in world evolution, Michael merely *shows* his way, so that humankind may follow in perfect freedom. This distinguishes the present guidance by Michael from all previous guidance of the archangels, even those of Michael himself; those previous forms of guidance not only revealed their activity, but also worked themselves out in humanity. Thus, freedom was unavailable to human beings in the activity of their own lives.

108. To *see and understand* the truth of this is the current task of human beings, which will enable them to find, with all their soul forces, the spiritual path within the age of Michael.

Intelligence is the final stage of wisdom on its downward path. If it attains spiritual reality, it walks the paths of the will; this is the path of Michael. In order that human beings, with their whole soul, can find their own spiritual path during the age of Michael, they must have *insight*. Indeed, it is necessary to have insight into the significance of the turning point of time; true insight allows the will to shoot up into an individual's intelligence. Blind will and abstract intelligence are the opposite elements of our time, which appear to clear-sighted spiritual vision as beings. Steiner describes those beings as

Lucifer and Ahriman. *Insight* provides the balance for the activity of these two forces and, from them, produces a new element that can involve the whole human being. Again, this is *free thought*; this is expressed in Leading Thought 107. Again and again, Steiner appeals to this kind of insight. We can compare, for example, this passage from the letter accompanying Leading Thoughts 109 to 111.

> Those who look into the suprasensory world that borders the visible one, perceive Michael and his hosts...engaged in what they would like to do for humanity. Such people see how—through the picture of Michael in Ahriman's sphere—humankind is to be led in freedom away from Ahriman to Christ. When, through their vision, such people also succeed in opening the hearts and minds of others, *so that there is a circle of people who know* how Michael is now living among human beings, humankind will begin to celebrate festivals of Michael, which will then have the proper meaning.[1]

Here also it is insight that opens the heart and stimulates meditation (Study 34); for this meditation can lead to free participation in the great new myth.

Let us consider what is implied when Steiner entitles a Letter: "The Experiences of Michael in Fulfilling his Cosmic Mission." In such communications, one can ponder Steiner's path into the sphere of Michael and picture in a new way what it means, in the sense of ancient myth, when a person is received into the "Council of the Gods." Indeed, this is not only seeing the affairs of the gods, but participating in them. Here we are reminded of a pregnant saying from Steiner's mystery plays. In the wonderful myth in which Benedictus discloses her own being to Maria, he begins *The Portal of Initiation* (scene 3):

> When in life's pilgrimage I had attained
> The rank that granted me the dignity
> To serve with counsel in the spirit spheres...

He continues by expressing not an old vision, but active cooperation at a turning point in time; he points out the "links in chains, forged by the hand of destiny, whereby the acts of gods unite with human lives." On reflection, we recognize two perspectives. When we look at the individual Maria, through an example that affects us deeply, we are shown in the true myth how the human being participates in spiritual history through the true union of a spiritual being with individual human destiny. Furthermore, everything depends on the fact that Johannes Thomasius, who was present during this scene, understood all that happened with a deeper experience of wisdom than that of his ordinary consciousness; his manner of receiving it gradually developed

---

1   *Anthroposophical Leading Thoughts*, p. 79; Carl Unger's emphasis added.

true *insight*. Here the word *insight* must be taken much more literally than is typical in ordinary language.

If, on the other hand, we look more closely at Benedictus in this passage, we see before us the activity of an initiate raised far above the human sphere where he appears to the ordinary consciousness. From this *insight* can develop as well; for example, research in the higher spiritual spheres—in the realms of the beings of the higher hierarchies—does not involve a passive acceptance of truths, but an active cooperation in spiritual affairs.

It is possible that we will be granted new insight into the mission of Michael through our reflection on the work of such an initiate. We may experience how he has accompanied and protected the growth of humanity through eons of activity, until the all-important development of freedom; in this way, we can then understand the thought that among spiritual beings there are also *initiates*—that is, beings who not only have the rank of their hierarchies, but rise through all the hierarchies to participate in the administration of specific missions and as councilors. Steiner remarked that we will

> remind ourselves that, at that [Atlantean] time, human beings, based on direct experience, were convinced that there were other kingdoms above the human kingdom, to which they themselves belonged—to those of angels and archangels.... We must conceive of everything in the universe in terms of ranks; just as there are all possible ranks of beings in the animal and human kingdoms, there are also many different ranks among the beings above humankind. Some beings within the kingdom of the angels are very close to human beings, while others exist at a higher, more exalted stage.[2]

Something more may still be added; "Since the Atlantean catastrophe, ever since the post-Atlantean development began, we are living in an age when certain archangels, certain beings of the hierarchy of the Archangeloi, are ascending into the hierarchy of the Archai, or *Spirits of Time*."[3] In other contexts we are told that beings belonging to certain hierarchies rise to higher grades.[4] Furthermore, whole epochs of human events are connected with this.

A major question now arises: What is the situation for individual human beings today, given the fact that they know of these occurrences? Beyond the participation of the heart in all that is described here by Steiner, an individual *path of knowledge* opens up, which leads to personal insight into the spiritual worlds and to seeing what takes place there. Before each step on this path, however, the tremendous problem of the human individuality towers above us and demands a solution.

---

2   *Universe, Earth and Man*, lecture 9.

3   *The Mission of the Folk-Souls*, lecture 7.

4   *Earthly and Cosmic Man*, lecture 8.

STUDY 45

THE ENIGMA OF HUMAN INDIVIDUALITY

The final stage of wisdom on the downward path is human intellectuality. This statement corresponds to Leading Thought 106 and brings to mind one of the greatest of human mysteries. We might be tempted at first to proceed eruditely when approaching such difficult concepts. Rudolf Steiner uses such concepts again and again in relation to his leading thoughts and letters—that is, wisdom, knowing, insight, free thought, order of ideas, intelligence, intellect, intellectuality, and so on. Such concepts, however, are forms of understanding that are applied to very important events; direct human experience is summoned in order to make vital decisions in all our considerations relating to Michael and his mission. The question connected with the significance of the human individuality (with which the previous study ended) is as pressing as the most serious experience of destiny. Therefore, in order to gain a broader perspective with regard to these fundamental enigmas, we shall attempt to keep such concepts suspended axiomatically.

As an introduction into this whole sphere, Steiner speaks very generally of *ideas* by referring to the viewpoints held during these times of change. Here the word *idea* is used particularly with a view toward scientific goals. In relation to more ancient times, the term *content of ideas* is used as a provisional term. Later, this content is called *thought*—but, again, as applied to the present time. With regard to earlier times, it is otherwise called the *thought-like element*; only since the ancient Greeks is it again called *thought. Thought* always refers to something of the nature of "content." Thus, in Leading Thoughts 103 to 105, the word *thought* is used throughout to indicate its *content* at the various stages.

At a later stage, a soul force is indicated that is active today as the force of *intelligence.* This refers to something of the nature of *being*; forms of intelligence are beings; today, this element of being dwells in human beings themselves. During earlier epochs, however, what higher ranking intelligences created in humankind succumbs to death. "But this means that humanity is at the same time brought into the sphere of the ahrimanic spirit."[1] Divine spirituality, as far as it is concerned, thus dies away within the abstract *being of intelligence* of humankind—and when used in the wrong way, it becomes *intellectualism*!

---

1   *Anthroposophical Leading Thoughts,* p. 72.

Intelligence being of humankind is the expression Steiner used in connection with Leading Thoughts 106–108; Ahriman is this being's representative in those spheres where divine spirituality has died; there, human beings belong to their hosts. This is made clear in the letter that accompanies these leading thoughts. Thus, we have come closer to the question of the meaning of human individuality; for the dying out of the divine being in human beings is their destined condition; this applies also to freedom. As long as divine being works in human beings, they are not individuals as such, nor does freedom exist. To this, these leading thoughts are added:

> 109. To solve the mystery of human *freedom* in relation to the cosmos—insofar as the solution is necessary for earthly humanity—is to become truly conscious of Michael's activity in the spiritual order of the world.[2]

> 110. *Freedom*, as a fact, is given directly in the current period of human evolution to all human beings who have self-knowledge. People cannot say *freedom does not exist*, unless they wish to deny the obvious. We can, however, find a certain contradiction between this aspect of our experience and cosmic process. Contemplation of Michael's mission in the cosmos dissolves this contradiction (see Leading Thought 20).

> 111. *Intuitive Thinking as Spiritual Activity: A Philosophy of Freedom* proves the existence of individual human *freedom* as an essential component of consciousness in the present world epoch. Descriptions of Michael's mission presented here disclose the cosmic foundations of this *freedom* as it manifests.

Humankind finds Christ in the ahrimanic sphere. Michael shows the possibility of a choice between Christ and Ahriman—through his *example*, not through compulsion. Such choice can arise only through insight, since Michael offers free thought to humanity; it is the first truly free human decision in relation to cosmic activity. Anthroposophy is the herald of this insight.

In the letter related to Leading Thoughts 109 to 111, human individuality is characterized as the ability "to think for ourselves." The expression *order of ideas* appears strikingly often in this letter. Michael works within the force that originally flows through the cosmos as an ordering stream of ideas. This force is then termed "cosmic intellectuality." True human intellectuality now arises through the concentration in humankind of the intelligence working through the cosmos. The universal becomes individual, but this occurs in contradiction to its original nature. There, ahrimanic beings exert their power; they do not desire individuality, but only their own universal intelligence. Michael battles Ahriman on behalf of humanity.

---

2   The word *freedom* appears here in italics, because it is used in a sense that has a much deeper spiritual meaning than is usually assigned this word. See *Intuitive Thinking as a Spiritual Path*.

As we now consider the appearance of the Christ in an individual human body, we find in the following letter that "Christ came into the world with an intellectuality in every way identical to what it was as it had lived in the divine spiritual, when *divine spirit*, in its being, still informing the cosmos."[1] Here something immensely important is expressed; in this context, we will look at it only in relation to the question of human individuality.

Human individuality has arisen from a death process of divine spirit, and because of this humanity was made the prey of Ahriman. Now, however, human individuality is confirmed through Christ, and life is once again brought within the sphere of death—a new aspect of the conquest of death. This becomes increasingly true of each person's consciousness and leads to the possibility of understanding the Mystery of Golgotha with free thinking. This is the process through which the human individual can feel justified before the divine; it is the *path of knowledge* of Anthroposophy and leads to validation through knowing, no longer merely through belief. The great work of attaining free thinking is not only of significance for the individual but decisive as well for humanity. And, beyond that, it becomes active within the spheres of spiritual life itself; for humanity is sent forth to acquire new territory for life in the kingdoms of death. This is the significance of human individuality.

The question of human individuality is as old as the first dawning of individuality in human beings. The answer can grow only on the basis of the individuals themselves, not someone else. This is the very meaning of the individual—that individuals stand on their own feet. Those who seek outside themselves for an answer to the question of human individuality deny the essential existence of the individual—despite the fact that this is in fact impossible, since actual denial would also annihilate the individual.

Throughout the history of human consciousness, the conflict has centered around the question of continued individual life after death. This battle over human individuality has been waged in three stages; its leaders are Aristotle, Thomas Aquinas, and Rudolf Steiner. Aristotle terminated the clairvoyant retrospect in primeval times, with its longing to conceal the individual within the bosom of the divine. With great force, he points the growing human individuality toward Earth and nature. Thomas Aquinas led the battle against Averroes, who taught the dissolution of the individuality after death. With a truly intelligent belief in the tradition of the Mystery of Golgotha, he directed the human individuality toward Christ and His appearance in an individual human body. Rudolf Steiner understands this question through the forces of our time; he relates it to human beings themselves, just as they are. He shows the individual how to find the answer through free thinking.

The essential question in this matter can appear in myriad forms. Steiner asks it in new ways again and again. In what follows, the question is necessarily

---

1   *Anthroposophical Leading Thoughts*, p. 83.

closely related to our studies. Are human beings correct in considering themselves to be the makers of their thoughts, or is this an illusion (Study 43)? *Intuitive Thinking as a Spiritual Path* begins with the question: "Can we human beings, as willing entities, ascribe freedom to ourselves?" (p. xxiii). The answer depends on the answer to another question: Is there a view of the human being that supports the all of knowledge? In the introductions to *Goethe's Scientific Writings*, this question takes an even more general direction: What is knowing? Here the emphasis contrasts with Kant's question: How is knowledge possible? We may also ask about the meaning of life or the goal of humanity. The point of such questions always relates to how much value they have for our experience. They are questions that arise from human loneliness, questions filled with the strongest, most concentrated activity. But this is not true of the subtle reasoning of abstract answers. Today's consciousness will not be satisfied by any philosophy that is alienated from the world and spun from such questions, but only by the real spiritual process that springs from deep individual distress, from loneliness itself.

This is the decisive experience that, only in our age, can give rise to spirit birth. We can see how this has gradually come about since the time of the Scholastics, for example, through Steiner's statements in *Christianity as Mystical Fact* and *Mysticism at the Dawn of the Modern Age*, where he shows how current scientific methods follow this line of evolution. Without this decisive experience, Averroes would still be correct Yes, contemporary human beings must still consciously go through Averroes' basic phenomenon in some form before they can attain the new spirit birth of free thinking. The well-known, historic battle between Thomas Aquinas and Averroes is recapitulated today in the soul of every individual.

Now we must go on to the question: What is the basic phenomenon of Averroes?

THE VICTORY OVER AVERROES IN OUR TIME

The basic phenomenon of Averroes has already been mentioned. Indeed, to gauge its enormous significance for the most vigorous philosophical battles of the Middle Ages, we must consider the great distinction observed in those times between the actual facts of human consciousness and the awareness of them. Such distinctions went deeply into the soul's life and became decisive for life's greatest questions—for example, the matter of survival after death, but also in relation to one's approach to the Mystery of Golgotha. Even today, it may still be important to discuss such questions, because our modern consciousness has evolved from such conflicts; thus, they continue in the depths of our souls (Study 45). Of course, these battles have also assumed other forms, so that their origin can no longer be recognized at first glance.

A philosophical problem that has become popular goes: If I were a king and did not know it, of what use would it be to me? This question can be interpreted in various ways: If I am immortal, and know nothing of it, what good does it do me? What does it mean to me if past lives are behind me, and I do not remember them?

It is clear that a person's attention can indeed be drawn to the phenomena of human consciousness but, to verify them inwardly, individual consciousness must itself be active. Now, however, the facts of logic are among the most significant in conscious experience. They demand absolute truth, and the basic phenomenon of Averroes rests in this implicitness, or absoluteness. It is based on the fact that thinking has universal nature, and thus the truth of its content is independent of how they are revealed in the field of consciousness.

We are concerned here with the first spiritual experience of ordinary consciousness, which, in the subjective life of the soul, is clearly emphasized as being beyond subjective and objective (as absolute). We have often encountered this form of the basic phenomenon of Averroes in our work (Study 10, for example, and the beginning of Study 43). Again and again, we find this phenomenon presented in a most impressive way in Rudolf Steiner's work, especially in *Intuitive Thinking as a Spiritual Activity*: "Our thinking, unlike our sensing and feeling, is not individual. It is universal.... There is only one concept 'triangle.' It makes no difference to the content of this concept whether it is grasped by A or B—by this or that carrier of consciousness" (p. 83). There are many such passages. The point, however, is the kind of conclusions that are deduced; if they are simply the conclusions of thinking, then their content is universal—independent of the consciousness of "A or B." And if, from this phenomenon alone, we reach a conclusion about the continuation of life after death, nothing more may transpire than what Averroes concluded from Aristotle—that is, a doctrine of universal, rather than individual, survival. Thus, he considered the human spiritual being to be a drop in the universal, spiritual ocean, united at birth with the earthly body, and, after death, once more becoming one with the spiritual ocean.

If we now wish to understand the conflict concerning Averroes, we must bear in mind that, in keeping with the frame of mind at that time, the point was not to refute the original phenomenon of Averroes—that would be impossible—but to understand that this phenomenon as such is not the only authoritative one. Averroes' view is still based completely on the ancient thought process, as Steiner showed in *Riddles of Philosophy* and elsewhere. It was a process of perception, where the soul's own activity had no particular part.[1] At that time, it was simply a matter of showing the thought phenomena as such. The transition to the Middle Ages occurred because the soul's own activity came increasingly to prominence; thoughts could no longer be perceived, but seemed to be produced by the soul's effort. In other words, there had to be soul effort before cosmic thoughts were surrendered to human beings. Here, we have before us one of the great discoveries recorded by Steiner in *Riddles of Philosophy*. In recent times there has been an awakening of interest in the Middle Ages, which were so thoroughly maligned; but it will not really be possible to understand that period unless we take this discovery seriously in terms of its far-reaching importance.

The transition from antiquity to the Middle Ages has historic significance for the whole world, because the Mystery of Golgotha lies between the two ways of approaching thought—that of the ancients and that of the Middle Ages. This unique historical event—the appearance of highest Divine Being in an individual human body—presents us with the task of attaining a spiritual experience inspired through soul warmth. This goes beyond the Averroes phenomenon, since it strives for something that cannot be given through perception—that is, the after-experience of the Mystery of Golgotha within individual human souls. The historic event itself, however, could be comprehended as a percept and handed down through tradition. It was in this sense that the Roman Church was formed; it made use of the ancient way of apprehending thoughts in making the Mystery of Golgotha known. Thomas Aquinas, on the other hand, appealed for the greatest effort, as in ancient times, to acquire knowledge as a basis for this new experience. To this end, he had to purify the deepest feeling and power of perception, that humankind might attain the experience of universal thinking, thus justifying human individuality. What

---

1   See the "Psychosophy" lectures in *A Psychology of Body, Soul & Spirit: Anthroposophy, Psychosophy, Pneumatosophy*.

Thomas Aquinas found in this way through the highest spiritual effort was continued in German Mysticism through warmth of heart and mind.

There is another significant turning point in our time; the old conflict adopts new forms. In the realm of worldviews, there is a new spirituality arising in opposition to materialism, which is a continuation of Averroes' view. In the new spiritual striving, genuine Thomism must expand anew, no longer only in feeling, but also in the will. The phenomenon of Averroes must be recognized if we wish to understand Thomism; likewise, we must recognize the essential methods of science without surrendering to materialism. Then, we realize that it is in fact German Mysticism that provides the basis that leads to a contemplative method, which is fulfilled in Spiritual Science. Indeed, it was Steiner's goal in *Mysticism at the Dawn of the Modern Age* to show this. He repeatedly affirmed that, if Spiritual Science is to manifest, the will must come into thinking.

If we look at *Intuitive Thinking as a Spiritual Path* from this perspective, we may clearly realize that it is not simply concerned with thinking, and thus distinguished from every other philosophy or system; it is definitely *not* a system. Systematic philosophy is only an introduction to it. Of course, the initial part, which may be referred to as *epistemological*, begins with thinking; but the important thing is that it begins with *thinking*, not with the thought—the concept, or ideas. And in this way, it reaches its source on the path of thinking. The final paragraph of the first chapter, for example, is characteristic: "It only grows clearer that the question regarding the nature of human actions presupposes another, that of the origin of thinking" (p. 17). Only when we arrive at the origin of thinking does willing also become accessible to us in our studies. In an addendum to chapter 3, we find:

> It may be that the essence of thinking requires that it always be *willed*. But the point is that in this case nothing is willed that, in its execution, does not appear to the "I" as wholly its own, self-supervised activity. We must even acknowledge that it is precisely *because* of the essential nature of thinking put forward here that thinking appears to be completely willed. (p. 46)

Here, thinking is conscious of its origin, and thereafter ordinary consciousness—which can fall recklessly into materialism at any moment—is lifted above itself. This is the beginning of a path followed in the second half of *Intuitive Thinking as a Spiritual Path*. This path leads to new forms of human consciousness that are not simply phenomena, but must be created from our inmost being.

The realm of willing belongs completely to the individual. By purifying the will, individuality is raised; thus, without losing itself as such, it gains the value of universal thinking. In this way, the ideal element in our activity attains something of a truly spiritual occurrence. This is, in fact, described as the task of *Intuitive Thinking as a Spiritual Path* in the "Preface to the Revised Edition, 1918": "To demonstrate how an unprejudiced consideration of simply the two questions characterized above, which are fundamental for *all* cognition, leads to the view that human beings live within an actual spiritual world" (p. 3).

We see that it is not a question of proving Averroes wrong, but of overcoming him. This is the meaning of the familiar representations of the Middle Ages in pictures that made people aware of a victory. In our time, this occurs in a different way; but the problem has lost none of its significance. Today, by fighting Averroes, we must achieve a transfiguration of the individual arising from the universality of thinking. Individuals themselves should be raised to spiritual existence, so they may be received as spirit beings among spirit beings.

STUDY 47

WRESTLING WITH THE ANGEL

In accordance with the previous study, one who struggles against the Averroes temptation in order to attain a transfiguration of the individual out of the universality of thinking approaches the true being of love.[1] Love can spring only from the transfiguration of individuality, so that human beings may bring it to the spiritual world as a prize won by life from the kingdom of death. Today, Spiritual Science, the spiritual accomplishment of Rudolf Steiner, is confronted by the universality of thinking. The figure of light connected with spirit-filled thinking is Michael; the figure of love among humankind and spirits is the Christ. The leading thoughts direct our striving to high goals, but, again and again, we must turn our attention toward the way Steiner had to struggle against the strongest opposition for his Spiritual Science. We can see this clearly through the way he conquered Averroes in modern times.

Modern human beings are waging a titanic struggle to place themselves as free beings in opposition to the whole world, challenging it to fight for knowledge; the beginning of this struggle appears to those guided by such fettered thoughts as arrogance and presumption. Yet, it is, in truth, wrestling with the angel: "I will not let you go unless you bless me." One who wrestles in this way does not avoid the wounds from which the blood of old spiritual bondage must flow. Goethe preserved the expression of *piety* as a deep longing of the human soul, and yet he came to establish a new science based on pure human experience; and he met with the blessing of a new piety: "Whoever aspires unwearied...." Nevertheless, he had to clothe it in the imagery of old spirituality. Steiner repeatedly pointed to this.

Let us look at Steiner's *Autobiography,* which appeared as a legacy.[2] We have, on various occasions (for example, Study 43), had to consider Steiner's loneliness, caused by the inability of others to understand his spiritual sight. At the close of the chapters where he expresses this most forcefully, he speaks of the change in his soul that confronted him after his thirty-fifth year. In chapter 51, for example: "Knowledge and experience of the spiritual world had always been self-evident to me, whereas to comprehend the sensory world through physical perception caused me tremendous difficulty.... This changed entirely from the beginning of my thirty-sixth year" (p. 163). Rudolf Steiner had to struggle against his own spiritual vision, as it were, in order to attain

1   *Universe, Earth and Man,* lecture 8.
2   *Rudolf Steiner, Autobiography.*

what otherwise comes much earlier to contemporary human beings—that is, the soul's transition from "involvement in the spirit world to experiencing the physical world" (p. 163).

Perhaps it is not too much to say that this was the fruit of his *Intuitive Thinking as a Spiritual Path*—that he was able to struggle to Earth and exact sense perception. In this battle, he gained his Spiritual *Science*: in other words, from his experience of the spiritual world, it was possible to attain an exact investigation of it. Chapter 51 of Steiner's *Autobiography* can be vitally important for readers who truly penetrate it. "I also thought: The whole world, except for the human being, is a mystery—the actual 'world mystery.' *And human beings themselves are the solution*" (p. 164). This wrestling at the end of the 1890s faced Steiner's soul when he composed Leading Thoughts 109–111 and the letter that accompanies them; at the same time, he came to a description of that period of his life in the periodical *Das Goetheanum*.[3]

Thus, this may be to us the clearest reminder that these very leading thoughts are directly related to *Intuitive Thinking as a Spiritual Path*. The accompanying letter is entitled "Michael's Experiences in the Fulfillment of His Cosmic Mission." We have become familiar with parts of it in Study 45. There, related to human freedom, our vision is lifted to events in the spiritual world. At the same time, we must see it as a warning against losing the sensible world; on the contrary, through this very experience of freedom within the physical world, we should come to understand the development of freedom within the spiritual world. Only on such paths—*Intuitive Thinking as a Spiritual Path* also points to this—can we approach Michael, but no longer through the mood of an earlier kind of piety. This new piety, which arises from free thinking, is certainly no less inward. Steiner himself anticipated objections that might be presented on this matter. For example, against the outlook of *Intuitive Thinking as a Spiritual Path*, the following passage is given in the "Addendum to the new edition (1918)" (chapter 8):

> It is precisely the richness, the inner fullness of experience, that makes its reflection in normal consciousness seem dead and abstract. No other activity of the human soul is so easily misunderstood as thinking. Feeling and willing warm the human soul, even when we look back and recollect their original state, whereas thinking all too easily leaves us cold. It seems to dry out the life of the soul. Yet, this is only the sharply contoured shadow of the reality of thinking—a reality interwoven with light, dipping down warmly into the phenomena of the world. (p. 133)

If we wish to describe the difference clearly between the old and new piety, we can say that, instead of *not being allowed to know*, now there comes a reverence of conscious participation. Thus, it is clear that we must not take the leading thoughts as a devotional book. In the same sense, Steiner

---

3   The weekly newsletter from the Anthroposophical Society in Dornach, Switzerland.

protested that we should not listen to his lectures as we might to a Sunday afternoon sermon.

In the same chapter of his *Autobiography,* Rudolf Steiner states that "one's ability to stand fully in this contrast with the soul means that one understands life. The experience of such contrasts, when balanced out, dies and becomes lifeless" (p. 164). Opposition, contradiction, and conflict arise and create life. Let us consider the rousing contradiction in Leading Thought 110, which says that freedom as a fact of direct experience is given to everyone who has self-knowledge in this present period of human evolution. Leading Thought 111 states that "*Intuitive Thinking as Spiritual Activity: A Philosophy of Freedom* proves the existence of individual human *freedom* as an essential component of consciousness in the present world epoch." Does this mean that freedom is a given fact? If it is given, is it still freedom? When it is stated elsewhere that something is "given," or a fact, we think of it in relation to law, or necessity. Thus, there must be a different kind of "given" in this matter.

The stage on which *Intuitive Thinking as a Spiritual Path* is played is in the human individuality. The experience of "freedom" indicated in *Intuitive Thinking as a Spiritual Path: A Philosophy of Freedom* is something that ordinary consciousness, with its various givens, must—or rather *can*—work its way toward. But now a new question can arise: from what source is human freedom given or granted? This question can function only between being and being.

Certainly, we can say of an earthly event that one person gives to another—to a slave, for example—freedom. But, in this way, we in no way experience the reality of the freedom of the human being. This can, therefore, occur only in the spiritual world; not until a human individual is admitted into the spiritual world can the other side of freedom be experienced. Thus, there is a problem of freedom that may be solved in the context of its cosmic background (Leading Thought 109). But "to become truly conscious of Michael's activity in the spiritual order of the world," a victory must be won in *wrestling with the angel.*

The blessing of wrestling with the angel is the new call addressed to human beings from the spiritual world. This means that human beings, as individuals, are allowed to enter the spiritual world. One who experiences this as an individual on the path of initiation becomes *one's own nation,* as it is expressed in the language of the Old Testament, the origin of this image of wrestling with the angel. To become a "nation" means to be freed from the blood relationships of Earth and received into the realm of the folk spirits.[1] One who attains this stage has, as an individual, the stature of a whole nation.

When we thus reach a solution to the problem of human individuality in the spiritual world, we can also better understand the empirical individuality of the ordinary consciousness. If we look at the central chapter of Steiner's

---

1   See *Theosophy,* chapter 3, especially p. 157.

Theosophy, we find a kind of preliminary stop to this rise of the individual. Our attention is drawn to the individual biography in order that we are able to follow the human being on the other side of birth and death. The result for a truly scientific view is that an individual human being cannot be compared to a single animal, but rather to an entire animal species; one human being is equal in stature to a whole animal species. "If we think about the nature of biography we will realize that, with regard to the spirit, each human being is his or her individual genus."[2]

An intermediate stage is established through revelations concerning the mission of Michael. They apply to all who wish to understand them—those who can awake "to become truly conscious of Michael's activity in the spiritual order of the world" (Leading Thought 109). They are thus received into a community lifted above all earthly communities, as typified by nations, languages, and so on. This community is recognized in the spiritual world nearest earthly consciousness—the Michael fellowship to which Anthroposophy calls us, toward which individuals can work through the forces of ordinary consciousness. Michael, through his role as Time spirit, overcomes all varieties of human associations and, in the spiritual world, forms a people not rooted in blood ties, but a community of our own time, a people of a new fellowship.

---

2   *Theosophy*, p. 73

MACROCOSM AND MICROCOSM

Much is contained in the letter Rudolf Steiner wrote in connection with Leading Thoughts 109 to 111; this may be added to what is presented in Study 45 about the acts of the gods, which led to the origin of humankind. It is indicated there that during the very earliest eras, only in one corner of the gods' realm of activity, was there anything resembling humankind that is perceptible to spiritual investigation. All that was said in the last study—which could imply a self-conceit—loses all meaning in view of such spiritual fact; for human existence is shown to be only a modest aspect of cosmic events.

Current views are very willing to give up modesty concerning the cosmos, but in studies such as we have here, there is absolutely no need for a lack of modesty. Thus, at that time, humankind had arisen as having secondary importance. In that corner of activity, Michael cared for humanity. Modern knowledge views humanity at the beginning of all that has occurred because of the cosmic limitation of our sight; from the cosmic perspective, this is willed by the gods. The gods certainly see humankind, though perhaps in the same way that human beings look at an ant hill that is interesting because of its *social arrangements*. Ants and bees seem to have solved a problem that human beings have not yet been able to settle; for humanity, of course, it is a completely different problem. Thus, human beings are engaged in solving the question of freedom, and the gods watch these human activities; but, for them, *freedom* means something different.

Now the course of cosmic events is presented so that we can sense, through the fulfillment of Michael's mission, the events that were initially of a purely cosmic nature, find their counterpart in human evolution. This is reflected again in the individual human life, and finally, repeated in the everyday flow of an individual human life through waking and sleeping. Humankind as microcosm therefore carries the whole of past cosmic events within.

Steiner covered these parallels in detail; for example, in *Cosmic and Human Metamorphoses* (lecture 2) he deals with the rhythm of number; he ends his descriptions with this:

> It is a great and wonderful thing, and its significance must cut deeply into our very hearts—that number and measure regulate the great cosmos, the macrocosm, exactly as they regulate us, the microcosm. This is not merely a figure of speech, and not merely felt mystically; the wisdom-filled con-

templation of the world teaches us that we, as microcosms, exist within the macrocosm. (p. 18)[1]

The whole affects the small, humble part. This principle of repetition in circles, or spirals growing ever smaller—as detailed in Steiner's *Outline of Esoteric Science*—also leads finally to the individualization of humankind. For a person, as one who knows, this cosmic occurrence (described in the letter accompanying the previous leading thoughts from the perspective of Michael) becomes understandable through the term *sequence of ideas*, which is especially emphasized here; thus, the line that leads to humanity is indicated.

It is inseparably connected with the nature of human knowledge that we should pay attention to the sequence of ideas. Sequence of ideas is the categorical relationship that humankind seeks, as opposed to the chaos of what is immediately given. We have already considered this in itself, but also in relation to the stages of higher knowledge (Studies 17–18). Now this categorical relationship has also developed. The various suprasensory spheres, or worlds, are characterized by its stages of development. Only the principle of the sequence of ideas remains for us in our modern consciousness forsaken by the gods—that is, unless the power to free this *sequence* arises from the activity of individual consciousness itself (Study 18).

Here it is worthwhile to refer to our brief remarks about Thomas Aquinas in Study 46. In Steiner's book *The Redemption of Thinking: A Study in the Philosophy of Thomas Aquinas*, there are three lectures concerning Aquinas' philosophy. Those lectures have an enormous meaning, not only historically, but indeed for the development of consciousness in our time. Near the end of the second lecture, we find: "*How can thought be made Christlike?* This question confronted world history at the death in 1274 of Thomas Aquinas, who, right to the end, had never been able to answer it" (p. 83).

For us, this very significant question must be connected with another one that has remained dormant since Study 41: Do human beings really produce their own thoughts or is this an illusion? From the perspective of ordinary consciousness, people must recognize that thoughts are produced by them, though this is an illusion according to a deeper knowledge. Nevertheless, through this illusion, human beings experience their "*I*" as a being of spirit. A real process is behind the experience of human thought, but it is not exactly what it appears to be. The sequence of ideas comes to a person as reality and dies away. It can, however, rise again if one's thinking can be made Christian. Let us try to give an account of how this question—so tragic and absorbing in the year of Thomas Aquinas' death—received an answer through Rudolf Steiner.

The *sequence of ideas* so strongly emphasized, now appears in a new form in the leading thoughts that follow:

---

1   See also *The Karma of Materialism*, lecture 2.

112. Divine Spirit is expressed in the cosmos in various ways and in successive stages: first, through its own inmost *being*; second, through *manifestation* of that being; third, through *activity* when its being withdraws from manifestation; and fourth, through the *finished work*, when the Divine is no longer present in the outwardly visible universe, but only Divine forms.

113. In the contemporary concept of nature, humankind has no relation to the Divine, but only to the finished work. With all that is imparted to the human soul by natural science, humankind can unite either with the forces of Christ or with the dominions of Ahriman.

114. Working through his example in perfect *freedom*, Michael is filled with the endeavor of embodying within human cosmic evolution a relationship to the cosmos, still preserved in human beings themselves from the ages when the Divine Being and the Divine Manifestation held authority. In this way, all that is said from the modern perspective of nature—which relates purely to the image, or *form*, of the Divine—will merge with a higher, spiritual view of nature. This view will indeed exist in humankind, but will echo in human experience the relationship between the Divine and the cosmos that prevailed during the first two stages of cosmic evolution. In this way, Anthroposophy confirms the views of nature evolved by the age of the spiritual soul, while supplementing it with what is revealed to spiritual vision.

Steiner's descriptions of the world's evolution—through the cosmic stages of Saturn, Sun, Moon, and down to Earth—form a cosmic background for his very significant investigations. As the fourth stage of evolution, Earth itself carries within itself and all its phenomena the effect of these three preceding stages in increasingly smaller circles or spirals.[1] We see this in Leading Thoughts 112–114 and in more than one earlier context (Study 14). In one way or another, every occurrence connected with it has an influence that reaches as far as our ordinary human consciousness. Out of this relationship, these events can also be understood by humankind. With such knowledge, human beings can proceed from concepts and ideas as the ordering principles, bound up with their own being; they consider them to be an expression of their being or to be self-created. Certain philosophies consider them as given a priori; a deeper knowledge, however, can penetrate them and show that they originated from spiritual cosmic evolution.

Now we find a series of concepts indicated in Leading Thoughts 112 to 114 and in the accompanying letter; in their sequence, they represent for human consciousness the ancient stages of evolution: *being, manifestation, activity,* and *finished work.* This sequence of the order of ideas is the cosmic order of chronology, so to speak; the sequence of ideas, according to human knowledge,

---

1   *The East in the Light of the West,* lecture 4.

takes the reverse direction. In effect, human thinking and the search for knowledge flow backward—for example, in the direction that is opposite the course of time known to ordinary consciousness. As human beings consider objects of the sense world, they appear in space side by side. If they look for the relationship between phenomena, their activity in time is considered; this is the second step. The third occurs to the degree that process as an effect can be comprehended, and thus the cause is sought. This must exist farther back in time than the effect and, when found, that cause may be understood as the effect of a cause even more remote in time, and so on.

Through this means of seeking knowledge, which is methodically employed by modern science, we may also, however, stumble on complexities where the relationship between cause and effect reveals something of the nature of *being*; we then feel the need to find the beings themselves, from whose will those revelations have flowed. Naturally, for ordinary consciousness, they must be *human* beings. But, since we and those who know are beings ourselves, our efforts toward knowledge in the highest sense will be fully satisfied only when we reach beings within the phenomenal world or nature, not just within human affairs. Thus, in the course of knowing, we find in the *sequence of ideas* a direction opposite to that of cosmic chronology.

HOW IS THINKING MADE CHRISTIAN?

At the close of the previous study, we saw that our modern search for knowledge is accomplished in stages, which may be expressed as the "sequence of ideas": *finished work, activity, revelation,* and *being.* According to the stages presented in Leading Thought 112, this sequence of ideas appears in the direction opposite to that of Divine Spirit's expression in the cosmos—*being, revelation, activity,* and the *finished work.* Today, in the realm of philosophy, such a sequence of ideas is allowed only because of its systematic value for purposes of classification. They are, it is true, also grouped in tables of categories and so on; but today, nothing of their cosmic, spiritual significance is experienced within the realm of philosophy.

This has not always been true; rather, during the time of early Scholasticism and even earlier, there was a living sense that this sequence of ideas reflects cosmic, spiritual truths. This is also expressed as early as the time of Dionysius the Areopagite in the terminology that refers to spiritual beings of the hierarchies. This connects him, in particular, with the older Eastern Mysteries; essentially, this older terminology is based completely on spiritual reality.

Rudolf Steiner also presents the names of the successive hierarchies, which may be reflected in human consciousness as sequences of ideas. He speaks of the *Spirits of Will,* the *Spirits of Wisdom,* the *Spirits of Movement,* and the *Spirits of Form*; in these names we clearly find the cosmic sequence of ideas mentioned in Leading Thought 112. We need to add only that, according to Steiner's *Outline of Esoteric Science,* these very beings—during the cosmic evolution in Saturn, Sun, Moon, and Earth—were actively creating the human being and the four principles: the physical, etheric, and astral bodies and the "I"-being.

It is clear, however, from Steiner's whole work that sequences of ideas such as those in Leading Thought 112 only gain their meaning for human consciousness when taken as subjects for meditation. In the short statement at the close of our previous study, we had in mind the attitude of natural science when we mentioned the sequence of ideas in the contemporary search for knowledge. "Anthroposophy confirms the views of nature evolved by the age of the spiritual soul" (Leading Thought 114). This view, however, is such that, through a momentary one-sidedness, it can deviate into the Ahrimanic sphere (Leading Thought 113) if not supplemented "with what is revealed to spiritual vision." This supplement is brought about for ordinary consciousness only when cosmic, spiritual truths are taken into the life of meditation. This means that human beings begin to raise themselves out of ordinary consciousness through exercises.

It is easy to see that the sequence of ideas, from finished work to being, corresponds approximately to the Categories, which, in Study 18, were related to the steps toward higher knowledge:

> *Finished work* corresponds to space.
> *Activity* corresponds to time.
> *Revelation*, or manifestation, corresponds to causality.
> *Being* corresponds to permanence.

If our search for knowledge is applied to such an inner development of the Categories, then another sequence of ideas arising through "what is revealed to spiritual vision"—*being, revelation, activity*, and *finished work*—begins to act as a key to knowledge. Through this, we may understand certain spiritual truths already discussed here from other perspectives.

Now, let us consider the experience on the other side of death from this viewpoint (Studies 13 and 14). The true path of knowledge is an anticipation of after-death experiences. In Study 9, we were able to say that "*all knowledge is taken from death.*" And in Study 13, there followed the statement: "The anthroposophic path of knowledge leads to an understanding of what happens in terms of everything relating to the soul after death." Thus, we can say that experiences on the other side of death proceed in the same direction as the path of knowledge in our consciousness on this side between birth and death. This moves, and we saw above, in the direction opposite to that of the chronological flow of events—out of space backward in time, in reversed causality; thus, after-death experiences are lived in reverse.

Some of Steiner's investigations show that the dead initially pass into the cosmos.[1] In the final year of his life, Steiner described this transition in great detail, especially into the so-called *planetary spheres*—the stages of evolution by which one finds a way into the spheres of the spiritual worlds. Since this path is, at the same time, like a return to the original divine forces of humankind, we can understand that, in this case also, the direction is opposite to that of the chronological flow of the spiritual creation of humanity. In reality, it is the same direction as that taken by human knowledge between birth and death.

Steiner portrayed this reversed living toward the midnight hour of existence through wonderful scenes in his mystery drama *The Souls' Awakening.* The midnight hour of existence is the soul's turning point. How far into the cosmos this turning point reaches depends on a person's own spiritual forces acquired

---

1   *The Inner Nature of Man and the Life between Death and Rebirth*, lecture 5; *The Being of Man and His Future Evolution*, lecture 4.

during earthly life.[1] Then, the will for a new earthly life awakens. In the subsequent journey into a new Earth life, the flow is again reversed and follows the direction of cosmic events. In experiencing this flow, human beings repeat in a shortened form the cosmic course from *being* to *finished work*.

In other contexts, the descent of human beings from the cosmos to new Earth life occupied our attention in Studies 17 and 18. Now, however, beyond what we have already considered, powerful impulses follow for these very stages in the rhythm of consecutive earthly lives. We must imagine to ourselves that, before human beings set foot on Earth to unite with a physical body, they are still able to connect with Divine Spirit in ways that, in terms of their earthly life, may be recognized only as finished work. In relation to this, the letter accompanying Leading Thoughts 112–114 contains exceptionally important knowledge:

> When human beings have fulfilled their life between death and a new birth, they begin their way toward a new earthly life. In their descent, they attempt to establish a harmony between the course of the stars and their own coming life on Earth. In ancient times, such harmony existed as a matter of course, since Divine Spirit was active in the stars, which was also the source of human life. Today, however, when the course of the stars is merely a continuation of the way Divine Spirit worked in the past, such harmony could not exist unless humankind looked for it. Human beings bring their divine, spiritual nature within as an after-effect of an earlier era.
>
> In this way, something of the Divine enters humanity's relationship to the world, which corresponds to former ages, yet appears in these later times. *This is so because of Michael's activity.* (p. 82)

Michael does not work directly in the realm of finished works, to which humankind belongs while incarnated; he stands at the threshold of birth and, from him, humankind is able to receive enlightenment again during earthly life. The human quest for knowledge is a search back toward those prenatal experiences. But this sphere of the spiritual world, through which human beings pass shortly before incarnation, is also the realm where Ahriman awaits descending human souls so that, toward his cosmic goals, he can enlist their help during earthly life, to which he has access.

We can also find clear indications of this in the letter relating to Leading Thoughts 112–114. Michael's battle with the dragon follows humankind as an image into earthly life. All such activities have heavenly prototypes in the starry worlds. According to Steiner, the realm of comets is that of Ahriman, and when we see the meteors caused by comet activity, it is the sword of Michael that shields human beings prior to birth from the overpowering

---

1   *The Inner Nature of Man and the Life between Death and Rebirth*, lecture 6.

influence of Ahriman.[2] A picture from ancient folklore may occur to us—that of children's souls coming to birth, announced by shooting stars.

In earthly life, humankind belongs to a world of *finished work*, from which divine spirit has completely withdrawn. The consciousness soul fashions itself there by gaining knowledge of natural laws—those of finished work. Out of their prenatal experiences, human beings retain only the *sequence of ideas*. When Michael's mission shines through this, the language of the consciousness soul is changed into the language of Christ.

> Christ came into the world with an intellectuality that is, in every sense, of the same essence as once it lived in the divine spiritual.... If today, however, we speak in such a way that our thoughts can also be the thoughts of Christ, then we place something in opposition to Ahrimanic forces, and this will save us from falling prey to them. To understand the meaning of Michael's mission in the cosmos means to be able to speak in this way.... To understand Michael today means to find our way to the *Logos* as lived by Christ among humankind here on Earth.[3]

Thus, thinking is made Christian along anthroposophic paths.

---

2   *The Spiritual Beings in the Heavenly Bodies and in the Kingdoms of Nature*, lecture 10.

3   *Anthroposophical Leading Thoughts*, pp. 83–83

STUDY 50

CONCERNING MIRACLE

The immense, incomprehensible nature of the Mystery of Golgotha has always been perceived as a miracle. What is a miracle? It is anything that, at a given time, cannot be understood through the customary means of knowing.[1] However, since the human capacity for knowledge has changed radically over the course of time, there have repeatedly been changes in what humankind considers to be a miracle; even when similar events occur, miracles are interpreted from various viewpoints. Since ancient times, when human consciousness began to separate from the world of Divine Spirit, a miracle has always been understood as proof of the direct intervention of the Divine. Although the concept of miracle is now connected with faith, we can no longer believe in it, since we are confronted by our modern consciousness of knowledge, which can no longer believe as the ancients did; such consciousness wants to approach miracle through knowing. It is just to those who *have knowledge that many things must seem to be miracles, but which to the naive consciousness are natural and comprehensible without further consideration.*

The greatest miracle of all time is human freedom; this is the reason it is so controversial. To the degree that natural science acknowledges only the concept of uninterrupted causality, it must also deny the miracle of human freedom, as well as any other encroachment of a spiritual element into physical events. If, on the other hand, the feeling of freedom is a direct experience of human consciousness (Leading Thoughts 20 and 110), then we must also look for the living spiritual foundation for ordinary physical events. Human freedom, however, is not simply an empirical fact; it is continuously active, occurring always afresh in individual human beings. It does not occur in the empirical human being, who would then be an object of knowledge like any other, but in human activity. Thus, the simplest movement truly contains a miracle—a spiritual element affecting physical matters. The role of the will in this kind of process, however, will go unnoticed (Study 22). Since consciousness is gained through the activity of the will, the miracle of freedom can directly manifest its convincing power. One who consciously participates in this miracle through great effort also begins to apprehend the miracle taking place in all of humanity. We are concerned here with decisive events that raise humankind above ordinary consciousness into spiritual realms.

---

1   *Wonders of the World, Ordeals of the Soul, Revelations of the Spirit*, lecture 3.

We can prove again and again that, in *Intuitive Thinking as a Spiritual Path*, Rudolf Steiner had provided all the necessary elements for such an evolution of consciousness. One of the important considerations in terms of human freedom is expressed in this question: How can individual freedom be compatible with that of everyone else? We find the following passage on this subject in chapter 9:

> The difference between me and my neighbor is not that we live in two completely distinct spiritual worlds, but that my neighbor receives intuitions other than my own from the world of ideas common to both of us. My neighbors want to live out *their* intuitions, I *mine*. If we all in fact draw from the Idea and follow no external (physical or spiritual) impulses, then we can only meet in the same striving, or intentions. An ethical misunderstanding or clash is impossible among ethically *free* human beings. . . .
>
> A free person lives in trust that the other free individuals belong to the same spiritual world, and that they will concur with one another in their intentions. Those who are free do not demand agreement from others but expect it, since it is inherent in human nature. (pp. 155–156)

Expressions such as this in *Intuitive Thinking as a Spiritual Path* show us the higher stage of a spiritual world, to which the consciousness of a free individual is raised.

Let us now continue with the leading thoughts and letters. Steiner repeatedly connects the mission of Michael with *Intuitive Thinking as a Spiritual Path*. Nevertheless, the invaluable contents of the letters (to which we referred in our last studies) show new miracles connect the path of humanity with freedom. In continuation of what was pointed out in the letter concerning Michael's work on human beings before birth, the following relates to the life of human beings between birth and death:

> In this world of Sun-like divine glory—though no longer the divinely alive—humankind lives. Yet, as a result of Michael's work on them, human beings have maintained their connection with the essence of Divine Spirit. They live as beings permeated by God in a world no longer permeated by God. Human beings will carry what is within them—what the modern human being has become—into this world emptied of God. Humanity will unfold toward a new world evolution. Divine Spirit, from which humankind originates, can become the cosmically expanding human being, radiating with a new light through the cosmos, which exists now only as an image of Divine Spirit. The Divine Being, thus radiating through humanity, will no longer be the same Divine Being that once constituted the cosmos. In its passage through humanity, Divine Spirit will realize Being never before possible. (*Anthroposophical Leading Thoughts*, p. 83)

In these words, the individual stages of the *sequence of ideas* from Leading Thought 112 again ring out. Now, however, all that is found in this sequence will in the future no longer be merely an aspect of knowledge, but something that actively arises from humankind. Here in fact lies the path of human freedom—that ideas, or intuitions, are drawn from the spiritual world, in order to become, at the same time, motives and impulses to action. This is expressed in the second part of *Intuitive Thinking as a Spiritual Path*: "The Reality of Freedom." Into the world of *finished work*—a world now void of God—humankind will carry within its own *being*, all that, through the *activity* of Michael, has been preserved in him as *revelations* of God. When *being* flows from humankind into the dead *finished work*, miracles will take place through humanity. This process, which will unfold more and more in the future, corresponds completely to every conceivable definition of what may be termed *miracle*.

By seeing into the nature of this miracle-working, we can open our eyes to the miracle of the Mystery of Golgotha—to truths that, only now in our present age of consciousness, can be received into human thinking; thus, our thinking may become Christian. The miracles of Christ's life are not so much the signs He worked, but the truths of His life itself—the appearance of primordial Divine Being in a human body. This occurred at the beginning of a stage, when only *finished work* was still in the world, no longer *activity*, *revelation* and *being*: The light shone in the darkness.

Steiner directed the most important of his spiritual investigations toward enabling humanity to participate consciously in this miracle, now that the age of darkness has run its course—an age when human souls could approach this miracle only through faith. This is not the place to go into such research in detail, but we may refer in particular to his lecture cycle *According to Luke* (lecture 4). There, Steiner shows how even the body of Christ was a miracle, since it was formed from a primeval human element that had not participated in the Fall. By using that body as a medium, Christ as a human being with primordial *Divine intelligence—Logos*—was able to restore the originally implanted forces to a sick humanity. This is Christ the Healer.

Before the Christ miracle may reach individuals, human beings must first understand the mission of Michael. Understanding and speech belong together. Understanding Michael leads to the *language of the consciousness soul*, which flows from the impulses of a knowledge of nature.

> At the present time, we must be able to speak of nature in the way demanded by the evolutionary stage of the *consciousness soul*, or spiritual soul. We must be able to receive into ourselves the purely natural scientific way of thinking. But we should also learn to feel and speak about nature in a way that accords with the Christ. We should learn the *Christ language*—not only of redemption from nature and of the soul and the Divine—but about the cosmos. (Ibid., p. 84)

This, however, is a process that occurs through inner development and not merely a matter of knowledge. The miracles of the future take place within a sphere to which humanity will pave the way only through freedom.

This Michaelic and Christic impulse is pursued in the following leading thoughts:

115. Humankind passes through the cosmos in such a way that, one's gaze into past ages can be falsified by the impulses of Lucifer; and thinking into the future can be deceived by the temptations of Ahriman.

116. The appropriate relationship to the falsifying influences of Lucifer may be found by permeating one's attitude toward life and knowledge with Michael's being and mission.

117. Furthermore, by doing this, one stays the temptations of Ahriman; for the path of spirit into outer nature—which Michael inspires—leads to an appropriate relationship to the domain of Ahriman, inasmuch as a true and living experience of Christ is also found in this way.

How is thinking made Christian? This necessary question arose from humankind's past and cosmic source (Studies 48 and 49). Another question comes to us more from the future of humanity and its future cosmic workings: *How can life be filled with Christ?* First, however, we must penetrate even more deeply the relationship between *Intuitive Thinking as a Spiritual Path* and everything Steiner speaks of in his continued leading thoughts and in his letter, "The Human Experience of Michael–Christ."

GRACE

Intuitive Thinking as a Spiritual Path: A Philosophy of Freedom contains a wonderful exercise related to the possibility of developing the human individuality. It might be important to note this exercise in relation to our prior studies, which should help us to penetrate those spiritual truths more deeply—that is, the spiritual guidance of world events connected with the present and future of humanity. It is certainly not difficult to find places in *Intuitive Thinking as a Spiritual Path* (especially in the addendums of 1918) to which the results of Rudolf Steiner's later investigations may be added without alteration. In practicing *Intuitive Thinking as a Spiritual Path*, however, it is very important that we refrain completely from curiosity in regard to the truths provided by Spiritual Science.

Many passages in *Intuitive Thinking as a Spiritual Path*, especially chapter 12, "Moral Imagination (Darwinism and Ethics)," address the idea of evolution. It is impossible to succeed with this idea if we are looking for an analogy in the moral sphere; we must be absolutely clear about the theory of knowledge concerning the relationship between the earlier and the later in an evolutionary sequence. In contrast to the typical and thoroughly misleading ideas on this subject, Steiner says this:

> People understand *evolution* to mean the *real* development, according to natural laws, of what is later from what was earlier. People understand evolution in the organic world to mean that later (more perfect) organic forms are real descendants of earlier (more imperfect) forms and developed from them according to natural laws. Adherents of the theory of organic evolution must actually imagine that there was once a time on Earth when a being—if it were present as an observer endowed with a sufficiently long lifespan—could have followed with its own eyes the gradual development of reptiles from proto-amniotes.... In order to picture things in this way, however, the nature of the proto-amniotes... would have to be thought of *differently* than materialists think of them. Evolutionists could never claim that, without having ever seen a reptile, they could derive the concept of reptiles, with all their features, from the concept of proto-amniotes. (pp. 185–186)

Steiner's intention here is to show that the idea of evolution, when understood correctly, does not contradict the fact that individuals, as moral beings, produce their own meaning. Here, the underlying principle of the theory of knowledge gains significance for our inner exercises when applied to future stages in the evolution of human consciousness.

This is the turning point from *created* (and dying) nature to the *creating* human being—the miracle of growing freedom. Here, indeed, it is good to understand that human beings carry within them the impulse to evolve, that human life is actively concerned with the growth of this impulse; but what will evolve will be known only when we have in fact reached those particular stages of higher development. As an analogy to the example given from *Intuitive Thinking as a Spiritual Path*, we cannot deduce from the concept of a person of ordinary consciousness, the concept of one of a higher consciousness. After such development has been accomplished, however, it is subsequently possible to understand such a transition from a lower to a higher stage. Thus, we must firmly maintain that whatever we can know of a human being developing to higher stages and individual experiences of higher worlds must largely arise initially from the actual evolution to which Steiner's life itself bears witness.

Epistemological remarks of this kind may be difficult to follow, and they appear to contradict much of what is said throughout Steiner's work and in our previous studies; nevertheless, if we go over such thoughts in our minds, such contradictions will be resolved as they develop. We must sharply distinguish between the knowledge we may gain about the actual evolution spoken of by Steiner, and the valuable experience resulting from one's active work in relation to individual evolution; knowledge derived from Steiner's descriptions will then provide immense help.

There are many in our time who are conscious of the spirit's call to attaining knowledge of higher worlds; such people constitute the anthroposophic movement—those who turn to the spiritual spring that flows from Steiner's research. Such investigations themselves are rich material for exercises within the soul, which bring an ascent into spirit realms. Certain goals for individual human evolution have been shown by Steiner's research; they are goals that conform to knowledge—the *intuitions* of moral imagination, for example, which are spoken of in *Intuitive Thinking as a Spiritual Path*. The actual practice of meditation, however, must completely refrain from prying into any such goal, insofar as this is not the result of active, meditative experience. This is the truly moral element, where Steiner demands three steps before one step can be taken toward higher knowledge. With serenity and patience, we must await the effects of inner development—what it is and when it may appear. This constitutes the *practice* of evolution, as opposed to a *theory* of evolution, as mentioned.

Intuitive Thinking as a Spiritual Path provides a training in knowing; it contributes powerfully to a selfless attitude and offers absolute protection from a dreamy or mystic confusion. Impatience in attaining our goal through inner work leads to sensationalism and superstition in relation to miracle. Indeed, amid the grievous emotions of the soul, this must prove to be illusion. Genuine selflessness, inner serenity, and patience lead us to a fresh understanding of *grace*; as in our previous study, we acquire a new attitude toward *miracle*. Grace attained through our own activity corresponds to the miracle experienced through knowing.

The specifically Christian concept of *grace* has come a long way since the time of the early Christian fathers. Some of the most violent spiritual battles were waged over this concept, and the most violent soul struggles sought its truth. Steiner showed the point from which the Christian concept of grace arose: "Of His Fullness we have all received grace upon grace" (John 1:16). About this sentence of the Gospel, he says:

> There are many who call themselves Christians—those who pass over the word *fullness*, thinking that nothing very special is intended. *Pleroma* in Greek means "fullness".... What then is *Pleroma*, or fullness? Only they can understand it who know that the ancient Mysteries referred to *Pleroma*, or fullness, as something very specific.... They distinguished between *Jahweh*, the individual God, the reflector, and the fullness of the Godhead, "Pleroma," which consists of the six Elohim. Since they understood that the full consciousness of the Sun Logos means the *Christ*, they called Him the "fullness of the gods."[1]

In the cosmic and earthly event of Christ's descent into a human body, grace came as visible cosmic being. Although the faculty for such sight was still weak at that time, John the Baptist—from whom this testimony came—possessed it. Steiner continues with regard to the next sentences in the Gospel: "For the law was given through Moses. Grace and truth have come into being through Jesus Christ" (John 1:17):

> Thus Christ is the bringer of the impulse of freedom from the law, that good may be done not because of the compulsion of any law, but as an inherent impulse of love within the soul. This impulse will still need the whole remaining Earth period for its full development.... The soul's capacity for doing right, out of the essential self, was referred to as *grace* in the Christian sense. Grace and an inner recognition of truth came into being through Christ. (ibid., pp. 75–77)

Redemption from the law through grace is the beginning of freedom. Then, in the time that followed, the relationship between grace and human freedom was one of the most important questions; indeed, the concept of grace was thus increasingly removed from its original meaning. In particular, since Augustine connected the concepts of grace, original sin, and predestination, every conceivable dogma combining these concepts has arisen. Thomas Aquinas alone

---

1   *The Gospel of St. John*, pp. 74–75.

rose above this conflict in his proposal to rescue the impulse of freedom. A common characteristic runs through all these struggles; an institutionalized church cannot tolerate redemption from the law, since it includes freedom. The concept of grace thus had to be combined in some way with the Father-principle, and, because of this, a very valuable portion of the Christ impulse would necessarily be lost.

For those who strive spiritually in our time, Steiner suggests a practice of the cultivation of grace.

> Because we wish to come gradually to a deeper characterization of Christianity, we must pay special attention at this juncture to a person's inward attitude toward the spiritual world.... Thus, even if we do not speak much of the concept of grace, we must make great use of it in practice. Every esotericist today understands clearly that the concept of grace must be a part of life's inner practice to a very special degree.... Everything, however, that relates to a certain lust for knowledge...will lead, if not to complete error, certainly to a distortion of the truth.... For there is a golden saying that applies especially to the esoteric researcher: *Have patience and wait, until you no longer wish to understand the fruits of your own efforts, but they come to you.*[2]

Active effort toward knowing serves to form higher organs of perception; the point, however, is then to have patience that the grace of truth may be imparted. This is the grace attained by being active.

---

2   *From Jesus to Christ*, pp. 70–71.

THE MICHAELIC NATURE OF
RUDOLF STEINER'S PHILOSOPHY OF FREEDOM

Intuitive Thinking as a Spiritual Path: A Philosophy of Freedom accompanies us further yet through the leading thoughts, especially through the letters. It is not accidental that the connection was already apparent between the methods of *Intuitive Thinking as a Spiritual Path* and Michael's mission. We may recall that, when Rudolf Steiner announced these great facts concerning Michael's mission (study 47), he was also in the midst of publishing the most important chapters of his *Autobiography* in the weekly magazine *Das Goetheanum*. Indeed, they are the very chapters that have the most to say about the origin of *Intuitive Thinking as a Spiritual Path*. In looking back over the course of his own life, Steiner showed us the direction we should take in our own development, but from the perspective arising from everything he gave humanity after writing *Intuitive Thinking as a Spiritual Path*. Thus, in the sense of a new myth (Study 44), his *Autobiography* can, with good reason, appear to us as symbolic.

We may now ask ourselves: What was it that Steiner, through *Intuitive Thinking as a Spiritual Path*, intended to incorporate in everything he gave later as concrete spiritual investigations and as paths to higher knowledge? It was very clearly not in order to solve certain philosophical problems as such; rather, it was for the sake of a soul attitude that strengthens consciousness so that it cannot stray from the paths of truth, for the temptation to do this is especially strong in our time. In his letter "The Human Experience of Michael–Christ," Steiner directly indicates the content of *Intuitive Thinking as a Spiritual Path*, which he always intended to integrate with the whole of his work, without which a firm support is lacking for all spiritual scientific efforts.

Above all, a deep earnestness and precise attitude of consciousness speaks to us in the letter concerning the human experience of Michael–Christ. In the previous leading thoughts and letters, Michael's mission was traced from the cosmic realms of a primeval past to our own period in a world of *finished work*. Now we are shown

> the true understanding of how this world is to be understood by human-
> kind—a world that is neither the *Divine Being*, nor the *revelation*, nor the
> *activity*, but *finished work* of the gods. To look with knowledge into this
> world is to be confronted by forms and formations that speak aloud of the

Divine; nevertheless, it is a world where—if we have no illusions about it—independent, living Divine Being cannot be found. (*Anthroposophical Leading Thoughts*, p. 86)

Thus, Steiner describes the situation into which *Intuitive Thinking as a Spiritual Path*, as a new beginning, eventually had to be brought. Throughout this book of education and initiation, Steiner considers a world stripped of the Divine. Furthermore, everything that he later presented as spiritual revelations had to begin in the world of *finished work*. No matter how much knowledge we may have gained through spiritual research, we must repeatedly return to the starting point and, from there, renounce all imaginary participation in the spiritual world and search out the steps of inner development. The dangers that otherwise threaten are vividly described in this letter as *luciferic* and *ahrimanic*.

Rudolf Steiner carried within him when he began *Intuitive Thinking as a Spiritual Path* a true experience of the spiritual world, in contrast to the illusory realm of *finished work*. Nevertheless, to move our whole evolutionary epoch of *finished work* one step forward, he had to sacrifice himself by immersing himself completely in this world stripped of the Divine. Indeed, we may be deeply moved by reflecting on the parallels between the passages in his *Autobiography* that refer to the origin of *Intuitive Thinking as a Spiritual Path* and the letters of the same time. From this, too, we may understand what was felt by many who approached *Intuitive Thinking as a Spiritual Path* from conventional circles, whether with astonishment or irritation. There is a certain abruptness with which everything of a traditional religious nature—all metaphysical or dualistic matters, although Christian—are dismissed in this book. And in the 1918 edition, this abruptness is not in any way softened in relation to these matters, though perhaps slightly in some of the expressions used. With this in mind, it is well to recall certain passages from *Intuitive Thinking as a Spiritual Path*, for they come like a strong wind blowing away what is outlived.

> For us, neither a human, personal God, nor force, nor matter, nor even a will empty of ideals (Schopenhauer) may be considered the universal element of the world. All these entities belong only to a limited arena of our observation. We perceive a humanly limited personality only in ourselves (p. 85).... The God derived through abstract inference is only the human being displaced to the Beyond (p. 236).... Just as Monism cannot employ supernatural creative thoughts to explain living creatures, so likewise it cannot derive the ethical order of the world from causes lying beyond the world of experience. For monism, the moral essence of someone's will is never fully explained by tracing it back to some continuous supernatural influence or ethical life (divine world rule from without), to a specific temporal revelation (transmission of the ten commandments), or to the appearance of God on Earth (Christ). What happens in a human being and to a

human being by means of these becomes ethical only if appropriated in human experience by individuals who make it their own. (pp. 188–189)

It would, of course, be incredibly foolish if we tried to conclude from these words—expressed even more abruptly in the first edition—that Steiner was at the time a kind of materialist. It is more a matter of recognizing that all of this, which he discarded, has a spirituality not in harmony with the time. It is a spirituality that, in ancient times, belonged to the realm of experience; and in future evolution, Steiner predicts that it will belong to the realm of conscious spirit vision. In the meantime, however, there is a time of the world of *finished work*, during which humankind must come to self-knowledge.

An anachronistic spiritual truth that is carried unchanged from the past into the present "is to be understood, in the purely technical sense of the concept, as *luciferic*."[1] In the letter before us (in relation to Leading Thoughts 115–117), this is made very clear through the example of Michael; and, from this, we can find the cosmic foundation of the abruptness shown in *Intuitive Thinking as a Spiritual Path*.

> For those who truly feel Michael's Being...it can never happen that the human view of nature will be led into the fantastic through the impressions received from Michael; nor will they be inclined thereby to shape their moral and practical life in this world—Divine as it is in form, but devoid of Divine life—as though impulses could be present there that did not require the moral and spiritual sustenance of human beings themselves.... If it were otherwise—if Michael acted in such a way that he carried his activities into the world, which humankind must presently know and experience as physical—human beings would now learn of the world, not the phenomena *presently* within it, but what *was* in it. This illusory concept of the world, when it occurs, leads the human soul away from the reality suited to it and into another—into the luciferic. (*Anthroposophical Leading Thoughts*, pp. 86–87)

Michael works differently; it is true that he brings a divine element of life from the past to humankind; nevertheless, "he keeps himself with all his activity within in a suprasensory realm—one that nonetheless borders the physical world in its present evolutionary phase" (ibid., p. 86). Before birth (or conception), before the entrance into the *finished* world, human beings are able to experience Michael's *activity*. Between birth and death, they carry it hidden within the depths of their own *being*. It will be awakened properly on the paths of *Intuitive Thinking as a Spiritual Path*, and the soul attitude depicted there must be sought again and again. The impulse of this work, as a disposition, can also exert an influence through soul exercises; though not expressly connected with its contents, through inner activity they lead to a

---

1   *Gegenwaertiges und Vergangenes im Menschengeiste* ("Present and Past in the Human Spirit"), lecture 12 (CW 167); unavailable in English.

"path into the suprasensory world" (ibid., p.89). There, Michael works to illuminate thoughts experienced in a warmth of heart.

In *Intuitive Thinking as a Spiritual Path* and in relation to this book in his *Autobiography*, Steiner speaks of the experience of a truly spiritual, eternal reality in contrast to the transitory. The experience of the eternal within thinking and willing proves a continuation of a *past state of the world*. This may be found not in the *finished* world, but in one that immediately borders it. This experience of the past, which works as eternal reality in humankind is, for this very reason, not connected with Lucifer, but with Michael.

In his *Autobiography* (chapter 39), Steiner summarizes what he said about *Intuitive Thinking as a Spiritual Path*:

> One goal of *Intuitive Thinking as a Spiritual Path* was to show that, in truth, the sensory world is spiritual, and that the human being, as a soul being, lives and weaves in spirit reality by apprehending the truth of the sensory realm. Another goal was to demonstrate that the moral realm is a sphere that is approached in freedom, because its existence shines for us when we experience the spiritual world with awareness. Consequently, human moral nature must be sought through an entirely individual and conscious union with the ethical impulses of the spirit world. (pp. 127–128)

We find, in these and similar statements, the Michaelic nature of *Intuitive Thinking as a Spiritual Path*.

STUDY 53

HOW CAN LIFE BE FILLED WITH CHRIST?

The dualistic worldview of our time documents a fear of confronting the world of *finished work*, a world forsaken by the gods. It is a mental reservation, a restriction of thought, when confronted by the inevitability of the facts and, thus, fundamentally dishonest. A Christianity, too, that wishes to preserve a separate realm for itself alongside or above the realm of today's scientific consciousness must be rejected by the soul attitude of *Intuitive Thinking as a Spiritual Path: A Philosophy of Freedom*. Such an attempt merely tries to hold on to ancient, anachronistic consciousness and, consequently, must be understood, in the purely technical sense, as *luciferic* (Study 52). Life cannot be Christ-filled by means of dualism.

The question of how life may be Christ-filled is evoked by another question: How is thinking made Christian? This question was handed down to us from the departing Middle Ages; it is answered, in fact, by Rudolf Steiner's method of guiding our thinking (Study 49). The first question, however, turns from the present to the future and can be answered only through what we *do*; Steiner liberally scattered the impulse for this as seed into the earthly realm of modern consciousness, furrowed with a sharp "thought plow." This is the question asked in the second part of the letter titled "The Human Experience of Michael–Christ," whose very wording has an influence. "It will become possible for life to be filled with Christ, when Christ is perceived as the Being who gives to the human soul the knowledge of its own suprasensory nature."[1]

We will first continue the parallel noted in our previous study. In *Intuitive Thinking as a Spiritual Path*, Steiner vehemently rejects all dualistic worldviews in whatever form they may appear—whether as the phantom of the *thing in itself* or in acquiescence to the *limits of knowledge*. Later, there were groups that wished to work out a dogmatic worldview for a primarily materialistic pseudo-monism. It must be firmly understood, however, that those same circles had previously been unsuccessful in understanding monism in such a way that spiritual experience could be created from the world of the given.

Continuing the monism of *Intuitive Thinking as a Spiritual Path*, Steiner established Spiritual Science, which enters the spiritual realm as a result of the soul attitude of this philosophy. In the second part of the letter mentioned, the phenomenon of the modern, dualistic worldview is considered from the summit

---

1   Anthroposophical Leading Thoughts, p. 88.

of spiritual scientific knowledge. The starting point, as in *Intuitive Thinking as a Spiritual Path*, is shown here from the spiritual history of world evolution as the final point reached by humankind—the *finished* world.

> Nature must be known and experienced in such a way that the gods are absent from it. Consequently, human beings no longer experience themselves through this relationship to the world. To the degree that they are suprasensory beings, the position of the human "I" in relation to nature, in accordance with our time, yields nothing regarding the human being. If human beings hold only this view, they cannot live a truly human, moral life.... [As a result] a sphere of *revelation by faith*, apart from science or above it, is set up in contrast to the sphere of what is knowable.[2]

This shows the position of the customary dualism of today.

These two poles—world and human being—as we have discussed them, have the factual result that human beings themselves stand amid the *finished* world, stripped of the Divine. Human beings certainly belong to this world themselves; but are they themselves also merely a *finished work*? The experience of initiation shown in *Intuitive Thinking as a Spiritual Path* is indeed based on an explicit "yes" to this question; in Steiner's letter, this is referred to as the *Michael experience*.[3] There is "the right road in relation to the world surrounding human beings, in order that they know and become active within it."[4] Nevertheless, to the degree that our surroundings are spiritually sustained by the spirit light of Michael, "the inner world of the soul, in its life of feeling realization, will be experienced as one illuminated by the light of spirit."[5] This is the *Christ experience*, the "gift of grace—the influx of the spirit into the human soul."[6] The word *grace* in this sentence may be understood in very much the same sense as that given in Study 51.

The *finished* world is adapted to contemporary humankind; this is pointed out in four different places in Steiner's letter; it makes human freedom possible. A necessary aspect of a correct training is that human beings come to understand themselves amid the world of *finished work*; it no longer contains divinity, but only preserves divine forms.[7] If a person seeks an active spiritual element in this world today, it can only be luciferic. Everything that has this tendency falsifies humankind's backward gaze to the ancient world (Leading Thought 115).

---

2   Ibid.

3   Ibid., pp. 86ff.

4   Ibid., p. 87.

5   Ibid., p. 89.

6   Ibid.

7   Ibid., pp. 81ff.

Michael carries the divine past into the present, but in such a way that human beings are allowed the freedom to accomplish their mission within themselves. The result of this is the Christening of *thinking.* In order that life may be *Christ-ened,* however, *feeling* and *willing* must be added. Since the Michael experience in our relationship to the world is permeated by feeling and will, the human soul is able to see its own suprasensory nature from the other side—from within. This is the Christ experience that leads us into the future.

Thus, there are two powerful soul exercises to enable humankind to find the right way into the world of *finished work*—renunciation of all atavistic clinging to past spiritual experience and the ability to wait for future revelations. Then, instead of a dualistic worldview, a unity of the Michael–Christ experience will result.

STUDY 54

THE QUESTION OF WORLD AND HUMAN BEING

We will come to understand the cosmic foundation of human freedom (presented in the letter that accompanies Leading Thoughts 118–120) only by pondering with increasing depth the recurring problems concerning *Intuitive Thinking as a Spiritual Path* in the letters and leading thoughts. The soul attitude of *Intuitive Thinking as a Spiritual Path* provides unassailable confidence when we are confronted by all the enticements and seductions along the path of knowledge; it is important to struggle for this soul attitude when confronted by the world of *finished work*.

This is the goal of the grand cosmic, spiritual evolution of Earth and humanity; it is only the beginning, however, for modern human consciousness. This is connected with living through the problems of world and humanity with the utmost intensity, problems we saw in relation to a previous letter.[1] It is in these two problems that we most clearly recognize the parallel already presented. In that earlier letter, this problem of world and human being is shown to be a soul exercise, inasmuch as it presents itself always afresh to us, demanding a solution that can lead to the certain understanding of Anthroposophy.

Briefly summarized, it may be said that, in pondering the world, human beings lose the world from their consciousness, and "I"-being enters; in experiencing the self, "I"-being is lost from consciousness, and the world enters.[2] In relation to the leading thoughts, this problem is left to meditative experience, but in modern spiritual life, not just in the battles over philosophy, it presents a sharp philosophical contrast. *Intuitive Thinking as a Spiritual Path* gives very important discussion to this problem. Perhaps it would go unnoticed, if nothing more were said, that we are dealing with the same views as those addressed in *Intuitive Thinking as a Spiritual Path* as *critical idealism* and *transcendental realism*.[3] Here, we will not go into the contrasting views of modern spiritual life by way of a philosophical discussion, but we will prove to ourselves in very simple terms that the spiritual experience of today has faded because of these problems; they are the same

---

1   *Anthroposophical Leading Thoughts*, pp. 37ff.

2   *A Way of Self-Knowledge*, first meditation.

3   The original translation uses the term *transcendental idealism*, but it is assumed that *critical idealism* is intended; see *Intuitive Thinking as a Spiritual Path*, pp. 69–72, 76–78. —ED.

problems that, when experienced in meditation, are able to rekindle a new anthroposophic spiritual life.

One of these problems has gained widespread significance in Schopenhauer's well-known formula, "The world is my representation (*Vorstellung*)."[1] In *Intuitive Thinking as a Spiritual Path*, Steiner showed the endless ingenuity that has been applied to support this statement, which renders all knowledge subjective. He certainly proved that every argument presented for its support collapse, one by one. Nevertheless, this statement has been absolutely devastating to all modern research in the field of knowledge; the *ignoramus, ignorabimus* ("I do not know, I will never know") is based on the assertion that it is impossible to approach reality through knowing, since, according to this view, our own representations will always stand in the way. Thus, in pondering the world, we lose sight of the world, and our own being spreads out over all phenomena. The result was an insurmountable mistrust of all knowing—especially thinking—and resignation in terms of our own soul needs. Because of this, the spiritual force of thinking died away.

The second of these two problems, in particular, has natural scientific matters in its grip. We can formulate it briefly as "universal, uninterrupted, mechanical causality." If the first problem annihilates knowledge of the world and affirms universal subjectivity, the second annihilates the significance of humankind, who is subjected to the world in conformity to law. Human freedom becomes merely an illusion. Humankind is nothing, and the laws of nature are all. This resulted in an appalling paralysis of all that belongs to human will and moral experience. Consequently, the spiritual force of willing died away.

It is clear that these two statements very radically contradict each other. In the true cultural life, they are an antinomy operating in the Kantian sense, and this has been extremely destructive, since it is a real contradiction.[2] These two perspectives, however, constantly commingle, one being used to support the other. In *Intuitive Thinking as a Spiritual Path*, both are finally overcome—not, however, by abstract proofs, but by actual experience in the soul's life. From this perspective, too, we can understand in a new way the significance and mutual relationship between the two parts of *Intuitive Thinking as a Spiritual Path*. Part one solves the problem in terms of human *knowledge*; part two resolves the problem with regard to human *freedom*. This becomes possible, because Steiner follows both problems to their common source, where the human being and the world are truly united in pure thinking.

Now, let us take the lack of justification for each of these problems when presented as abstract, one-sided theorems, and compare that to the grounds

---

1   *Building Stones for an Understanding of the Mystery of Golgotha*, lecture 5.

2   *Antinomies* are statements that contradict each other, although either may be proved with equally good reasoning. —ED.

for solving them both in meditative experience.[3] In continuing our studies, we may now be clear about two facts: Human freedom is not only significant for humankind, but also for the world. Furthermore, the foundation for human freedom is laid not only in human beings, but also in the world.

---

3   See the letter that accompanies Leading Thoughts 62–68.

THE OTHER SIDE OF HUMAN FREEDOM,
PART ONE

Leading Thoughts 118 to 120 and the accompanying letter specifically go beyond the province of *Intuitive Thinking as a Spiritual Path*. We can recognize the sense in which this must occur through the polarity that exists between the human being and the world, which we must always keep in sight to avoid sinking into one-sidedness. Humankind is *finished work* in a world of *finished work*, and also spirit among spirits. We must, however, show ourselves as spirit *beings* in a world of *finished work*; otherwise we ourselves become increasingly a finished work, even among spirits.

Everything that takes place within human beings has its other side in the world. Human freedom is not merely an established fact created by the gods, somewhat the way they finished the world; it is a process that arises from human beings and even stands somewhat in opposition to the divine creation of the finished world. What position do the creative beings themselves adopt in relation to human freedom? This is the question that takes us beyond *Intuitive Thinking as a Spiritual Path*.

If we look back at our earlier studies, we may recall that the threshold of the spiritual world passes through humankind and, in fact, exists where the etheric and astral bodies unite and separate from each other. Indeed, this is expressed in waking and sleeping. Viewed cosmically, the physical and etheric bodies are in the world of finished work; the physical body is completely finished, whereas the etheric body exists as the body formative forces, so that it also represents something of the world of *activity*. The astral body and the "I"-being belong to the spiritual world; thus, in addition, they represent something of the world of *revelation* and of *being*.

Perhaps we can characterize the whole human being by saying that the etheric body is the *activity* on the *finished work* of the physical body, and the astral body is the *revelation* of the *being* of "I." With our consciousness, we exist completely in the finished world; cosmically, however, from the perspective of the various hierarchies, special aspects must arise.

Let us recall that, according to Leading Thoughts 69–71, the realm of the influence of the First Hierarchy reaches to the physical body, that of the Second Hierarchy to the etheric body, and that of the Third Hierarchy to the astral body. It follows, therefore, that the physical body is the world of finished work for the beings of the Third and Second hierarchies, the etheric body for those of the Third Hierarchy; human beings—as physical, etheric, and astral bodies—belong to the world of finished work. From the "I," however, new being can be poured by humankind into the various human principles when, in the future, we will have created for ourselves the astral body as *revelation* (Spirit self), the etheric body as *activity* (Life spirit), and the physical body as *finished work* (Spirit human being).[1] The following sentence points to this: "There can be no freedom except through the "I"; and the astral body must be able to vibrate in harmony with the free activity of the "I," so that it may be able to transmit it to the physical and etheric bodies" (*Anthroposophical Leading Thoughts*, p. 91).

The sentences and paragraph following this statement are worded in a very difficult way; we can say with Capesius, "Alas! I've read a hundred times the words which follow now...."[2] In the difficulty of wording of these sentences, the fact is expressed that "this does not refer to my *Intuitive Thinking as a Spiritual Path: A Philosophy of Freedom*, which is based on the purely human faculties of cognition" (ibid.), but the human being is regarded from cosmic perspectives. In the construction of the sentences, indeed, there appears to be a contradiction, but this is solved when we consider that the relative sentences have not a humanly subjective, but a *spiritually objective*, meaning. They can then be comprehended as clearly expressed thoughts concerning Michael's mission, as presented in relation to the attitude of spiritual worlds toward human freedom.

In Leading Thought 118, the condition for a free act is expressed in the simplest terms—that no process of nature participates either within or outside human beings. The one side of this is clear; an action, if it is free, must depend not on the physical and etheric bodies through which participates in the external events of nature; in this way, external nature would influence that act. The other side is much more difficult; the physical and etheric bodies may also be influenced by the spirit, bypassing human freedom. The spirit no longer works from outer nature as such, because this is still only the world of *finished work*. Spirit works from the inner human being, from the unconscious, or subconscious, continuing what first began in divine *being* and *revelation*. Nor must an action, if it is to be free, depend on this spirit (nature working from within). If this spiritual element were to continue its work, then "the unconscious and subconscious elements that develop beneath the sphere of freedom unite more and more strongly with the world of matter" (ibid., p. 92). Thus a person would indeed preserve a "cosmically predestined character" (Leading

---

1   See *Theosophy*, "The Essential Nature of the Human Being" (especially the footnote, p. 54).

2   *The Four Mystery Dramas*, "The Soul's Probation," p. 14.

Thought 119). But, as Steiner stated in other contexts, humankind would lead something like an automatic existence.

This side cannot be understood from *Intuitive Thinking as a Spiritual Path*, but only after it has had its effect. It provides exercises so that the powers of cognition can operate "in the field of the spirit.... [then, however] something like an inner conversation with beings to whom we have opened up the way" will be the result of this same path.[1] As it proceeds, this letter gives wonderful statements on this subject, as a reward, so to speak, for the immense difficulties of the first part.

118. An action is free only when no process of nature, either within or outside the human being, plays an active role.

119. There is also the other pole, however—the opposite aspect of this truth. Whenever the human being works freely, a natural process is suppressed within that individual. In an unfree action, this process of nature would indeed be present, giving cosmically predestined character to that human being.

120. This character is not granted by means of nature to those who, with their own life and being, truly participate in the past and future stages of world evolution. It comes rather by way of the spirit when human beings unite with Michael, whereby they also find the way to Christ.

---

1   Ibid., pp. 91,92.

THE OTHER SIDE OF HUMAN FREEDOM,
PART TWO

The line of thought followed in the first part of the letter is an example of the way the most important events of the spiritual world may be expressed in thoughts.[2] It is clear that "inner conversation" with beings of other worlds cannot be disclosed by means of logical thinking; nevertheless, spiritual investigations, as revealed here, necessitate that they be expressed in thoughts arising from the modern state of human consciousness, which is characterized in the following passage from the letter:

> Humanity's relationship to the world will in the future become increasingly incomprehensible, unless people are prepared to recognize—in addition to their connections to natural beings and processes—relationships such as these to the Michael mission. (ibid., p. 92)

The emphasis in this sentence is on the word *recognize*, because only insight through thinking leads to the inner soul attitude of true recognition with reverence.

We are now concerned with a problem that no philosophical thought has yet been able to understand, because the solution cannot flow from the thinking life alone. To a certain extent, it is still possible to review the question of human freedom in terms of external influences, whereas the inner compulsion of the will has remained an insurmountable problem until the appearance of *Intuitive Thinking as a Spiritual Path: A Philosophy of Freedom*. It has revealed a path of knowledge through which the solution becomes accessible to human experience. Schiller had a particularly strong experience of this aspect of the problem of freedom, and he freed himself from it through his artistic soul attitude. The longing for deliverance through art in the difficult questions of inner (moral) freedom is a significant phenomenon of our age. But, in more recent times, art itself needs deliverance, and this can come only from the same spiritual sources that enable human beings to experience "inner conversation" with beings of other worlds.

In earlier considerations, we arrived at a perspective that may be expressed in this way: *The other side of nature is the moral world*. Here we stand before a kind of inversion, to the degree that what is known philosophically

---

2   *Anthroposophical Leading Thoughts*, pp. 91ff.

as "categorical imperative," or inner, moral necessity, is presented here as a higher, cosmic activity of nature. Humankind must stand aloof from this, in order to have the ability to reveal the impulse of freedom; and this is expressed "for inner perception" as "the consciousness of activity in freedom" (ibid., p. 92). In answer to this human process—that is, the repelling of cosmic forces—the cosmos and its beings act in a similar way, so to speak. Human beings free themselves from these impulses of the spirit beings, who can thus in turn apply freedom in their own way with regard to humankind; such cosmic freedom is expressed in the encroachment of Lucifer and Ahriman.

Now a true cosmic counterpart to *Intuitive Thinking as a Spiritual Path* can rise before us, for this is an epoch of the world not only for humanity, but also for the gods. Their common ground appears as an "inner conversation with a form of being" (true *inspiration*). The sentences and exercises of *Intuitive Thinking as a Spiritual Path* constitute human questions to the spiritual world; the mission of Michael provides the answers. We have already seen, in the first part of *Intuitive Thinking as a Spiritual Path*, the connection between this and the Michael experience. Isn't it as though Michael had continually sought the human experience since the remote past? Hasn't the Christ sought and overcome the completed human experience—human death? The second part of *Intuitive Thinking as a Spiritual Path* corresponds for us to the Christ experience. Just as the first part provides *knowledge*, the second part demands *action*. Thus, Michael's human experience is the right guide toward the act of the Christ (Leading Thought 120).

Feeling and the will lead *thinking* in the first part of *Intuitive Thinking as a Spiritual Path* to *life* in the second part. This indicates something completely new—after all, the old life of feeling and will, based on tradition, was set aside and rejected in the first part. There must be compensation for this obsolete, anachronistic relic of the past in *Intuitive Thinking as a Spiritual Path*. From the spiritual world, this may be seen as the effect of Michael's appearance on behalf of the natural activities of the cosmos repelled by humankind. "He devotes himself...to the task of bringing to humanity, from the spiritual part of the cosmos, forces that can replace those from the realm of nature, which have been suppressed" (ibid., p. 93). Thus humanity acquires a higher, spiritual nature, which is presented to us most impressively in the letter through images of light and warmth. It would be presumptuous to add anything explanatory to these pictures, since they are truly capable of inspiring a new art; here, experience alone is of value. Nevertheless, wonderful flashes of thought break through from these living pictures, which, enkindling light and warmth, can fill us with enthusiasm.

Again, follow the references to Lucifer and Ahriman. The soul attitude of *Intuitive Thinking as a Spiritual Path* assures us in our ordinary consciousness when confronted by these cosmic powers. Thus, the letter closes with a reference to the "certainty of soul and Spirit" that, for the other side of human freedom, flows from the Michael–Christ experience of another—a cosmic *Philosophy of Spiritual Activity*.

STUDY 57

THE HUMAN EXPERIENCE
OF SPIRITUAL BEINGS, PART ONE

The life of thought is the most social of elements that unite human beings. Through this element, Rudolf Steiner places himself on the same footing with all humankind, though he is raised much higher when he speaks of human beings as viewed by the hierarchies. When, however, he speaks to us about the beings of the spiritual world, he appeals to an element that unites humankind and the gods, connected from the beginning with the thought life, while, at the same time, cosmically visible.

This is shown in his letter through the image of light and warmth.[1] Light and warmth are powerful forces, and they are the primeval forces in the evolution of the world ever since Old Saturn and Old Sun.[2] They are *revelations* of spiritual beings, who today are perceived by humankind only externally as the cosmic activity of nature, since the cosmic beings have withdrawn behind them.[3] On the paths of the thinking life that leads to communication among human beings, light and warmth can again become heralds of primordial being, messengers of Michael and Christ.

In various letters, Steiner, in effect, stated that when humankind entered the world of *finished work*, Michael kept something of primordial being with human beings—that is, the light and warmth of thinking.[4] We must repeat here what was said in Study 35, beginning with the words: "Under Michael's banner, we are concerned with the effort to explain thinking" (page 132). The purpose of this was to enter the letter, "At the Dawn of the Michael Age."[5] It shows how Michael releases the thoughts from the region of the head, and frees the way for them to the heart. This is the precondition for the fact that now, as the letters develop further,[6] the direct spiritual counterpart can be given to what was the object of human striving in earlier times.

---

1   *Anthroposophical Leading Thoughts*, p. 93.

2   *The Spiritual Hierarchies and the Physical World*, lecture 3; *Genesis: The Secrets of Creation*, lecture 5; *Inner Experiences of Evolution*, lecture 3.

3   *Egyptian Myths and Mysteries*, lecture 4.

4   *Anthroposophical Leading Thoughts*, the letters beginning on pages 66, 76, 81, 91, and 97.

5   Ibid., pp. 51ff.

6   Ibid., pp. 51ff, pp. 56ff

Again and again, we may indeed be filled with reverence for the possibility of speaking to modern consciousness about the beings of the spiritual world, as is done in the letters and leading thoughts about Michael's mission. Steiner can speak in this way, because he has infinitely aided human life of thought. It is our task, on the other hand, to learn to listen more and more closely to this same language of the thought life, and not be afraid of making the necessary effort by actively exercising our ability to understand it. Since modern human beings perceive thought life to be their own, they separate themselves from cosmic thought reality. We experience one side of this separation directly; but, whereas we experience our reality from one side, we must just as readily grasp it spiritually from the other side. Again, however, this is not a matter of logical revelation. There is something else at the root of this separation.

In the previous study, we spoke with a certain audacity of Michael's human experience; but there are also other beings of the spiritual world who have sought human experience. Earlier in our studies, we were reminded by Steiner's investigations that Angel beings have sought an ever closer union with earthly humankind through the intellect. Those beings have remained with humanity; they are the messengers (Angels) who inform Michael of human affairs[7]; for Michael seeks human experience in relation to humanity as a whole. Ahriman, too, in a similarly comprehensive sense, has sought human experience—not, like Michael, in light and warmth, but on paths of the darkness and coldness of thought life. Our goal must now be to look out beyond the thought life to the great *imaginations* Steiner shows us in the next letter.[8] This is like a cosmic meditation that gives us the possibility of distinguishing between light and darkness, warmth and cold, so we may also recognize good and evil.

Out of feeling and the will—in contrast to thinking—human beings must develop this question into a capacity to distinguish, with which that letter begins: "How are these spiritual powers [Michael and Ahriman] related to each other in the cosmic sense, since both are active in unfolding the forces of intellectuality."[9] "We must also look for and try to recognize those beings from whom it arises" (Leading Thought 121).

Steiner has indeed brought such distinctions to our attention in human social life. He constantly insisted on the ability to distinguish, and he sharply denounced its lack in his image of "Baron-Distinguishing Ability" (*Freiherr von Unterscheidungsvermögen*).[10] He referred, for example, to judgments pro-

---

7 Ibid., pp. 91ff

8 Ibid., pp. 97ff.

9 Ibid., p. 97.

10 *Das Schicksalsjahr 1923 in der Geschichte der Anthroposophischen Gesellschaft: Vom Goetheanumbrand zur Weihnachtstagung* (The Year of Destiny, 1923 in the History of the Anthroposophical Society; CW 259), pp. 449–451; unavailable in English.

nounced by Hermann Grimm and Woodrow Wilson that were alike, almost word for word, in order to show that we cannot depend only on the abstract meaning, but on the individual's whole attitude toward life, efforts of will, and general disposition. Steiner presented another example to us many years ago in a most impressive way: "We must be clear that what may be compressed into a few words...may have great significance—and they may say nothing at all."[1] The same is true in terms of the indication that St. John the evangelist, at the end of his life when he had reached a great age, expressed the whole essence of Christianity in these words of truth: "Children, love one another!" And what a great difference when these same words are used by a mediocre human being. How much remains to be done among us before the ability to distinguish truly becomes a social factor.

> 121. In terms of the universe, we cannot fully understand the significance of something that is active there—for example, cosmic thoughts—as long as we stop short at the thing itself. We must also look for and try to recognize those beings from whom it arises. Thus, for the cosmic thoughts, we must see whether it is Michael or Ahriman who carries them into and through the world.

> 122. Proceeding from the one being—by virtue of his relation to the world—the same thing will work creatively and wholesomely; proceeding from another, it will prove fatal and destructive. Cosmic thoughts carry human beings into the future when they are received from Michael; cosmic thoughts lead away from a future of salvation when Ahriman has power to give them to humankind.

> 123. Such reflections lead us increasingly toward overcoming the idea of an undefined spirituality, conceived pantheistically as ruling at the root of all things. We are led to a concept that is definite and real, able to clarify ideas about the spiritual beings of the hierarchies. Everywhere, this reality is a reality of *being*. Whatever is not *being* in it, is the activity that arises from the relation of one being to another. This, too, may be understood only when we can turn our gaze to active beings.

---

1   *From Jesus to Christ*, lecture 6.

THE HUMAN EXPERIENCE
OF SPIRITUAL BEINGS, PART TWO

Rudolf Steiner has stated many times that, due to definite events or specific periods of evolution, humanity has been raised "half a stage." We may inquire about the significance of this expression *half a stage*. Whole stages are found when one great epoch passes into another—transitions provided for in the plan of world evolution; half stages, on the other hand, indicate the work of beings other than normal spirits. Now, in terms of our immediate future, we are given a hint at the close of a letter about the meaning of *half a stage*.[2] Indeed, modern human beings can, only with difficulty, find a fitting place in the world; we saw references to this in four different places in a previous letter.[3] It is like an unstable balance, and we must take hold of the world that exists just above humankind so that we do not risk sinking into the world just below us. Such a *hold* on to the next higher world can enable us to understand the meaning of *half a stage*.

The unstable element in our age is *intellectuality* itself, since it is placed on the summit of "I"-being. Thus it vacillates between an effort toward the superhuman (metaphysical) and the sub-human (materialistic); it can maintain itself only within the truly human element if it is morally permeated by the "I." Pointing to this moral element is Michael's earnestness, so strikingly presented in the letter.[4] He summons human beings to awareness of the confidence that can be given them through the selflessness of thinking and the love of action. *Intuitive Thinking as a Spiritual Path* also shows the appropriate soul attitude for this; it leaves human beings free to follow the call, the purpose of which is to raise their real humanity half a stage. The human outlook is freed in this direction as we view what Steiner shows us as the *Michael imagination*.

In the other direction, however, because of the unstable balance of the human "I"-being in our modern cultural phase, human beings have sunk half a stage into the domain of Ahriman. This is the illusion of intellectuality as a personal possession, whereas, in truth human beings lapse into *automatism*, which, as a spiritual element, is ruled by Ahriman. For this, too, the letter gives a corresponding imagination. The opposition between Michael

2   *Anthroposophical Leading Thoughts*, pp 97ff.

3   Ibid., pp 86ff.

4   Ibid., pp 97ff.

and Ahriman is essentially this: "Ahriman appropriated intellectuality to himself, [whereas] Michael has never appropriated intellectuality to himself," but administers it.[1] The words in the accounts of this letter are, as always, intended to be taken quite literally.

We may notice that *automatism* is mentioned twice in this letter in relation to the link between human thinking and Ahriman. It refers to something different from the automatism described in Study 55.[2] Here, again, as in Study 55, we can comprehend the polarity between the physical and the etheric bodies, on the one hand, and, on the other, that of the "I" and astral body. The physical body and etheric bodies—the two oldest human principles, which originated in Saturn and Sun—today form the instruments of intellectual development; they possess a degree of perfection expressed through intellectual capacity. Human beings would become "thinking machines" if the astral body and "I"-being were not included. These two, as younger principles, originated during the Moon and Earth stages; they carry the moral impulses.

Now, without the evolution of freedom, the moral element—which still works as a seed in an infant's "I"-being—would lead to a kind of automatism on the part of the normal creative spirits (this is what Study 55 meant). Human beings, however, sink into the automatism of the physical and the etheric bodies if the astral body and I do not apply moral impulses; for that is when Ahriman enters these organs of intellectuality. This then leads to the "world that humankind pictures as nature."[3] That world lies *half a stage* below the world fitting to human beings themselves.

Here, we look into the depths of a cosmic battle taking place on the stage of human consciousness; it is humanity's task to become conscious of this battle, for, otherwise, no decision can be reached. The imaginations of Michael and Ahriman (given in the letter) are the means used to enkindle this awareness. Earlier, we saw that powerful thinking will ward off Ahriman, but such thinking must be fully conscious. When such awareness in absent, "intellectuality pours forth from Ahriman as a cold and freezing, soulless cosmic impulse [bringing] a logic that seems to speak for itself alone, void of compassion and love."[4]

The thought exercises, on which human thinking depends, are contained in such words and in many others in this letter. These imaginations also provide unfailing gauges that we may use to test the source of the thinking of people we encounter. Compare, for instance, the cold cleverness that simply overwhelms another—one that really requires a certain darkness for its own light to shine—with the pure wisdom, which produces light and warmth in others.

---

1   Ibid., p. 98.

2   *The Karma of Materialism,* lecture 9.

3   *Anthroposophical Leading Thoughts,* p. 100.

4   Ibid., p. 98.

The problem of *world* and *human being* is thus solved in a living way—the problem that confronts humankind in the world of *finished work*. In Study 54, we found this in a philosophical and scientific way; now we learn to view beings, out of whose realm this problem comes to humankind: by seeking ourselves, we lose ourselves; we find ourselves not by seeking ourselves, but by uniting ourselves with the world—with willing in love.

STUDY 59

THE NATURE OF HISTORY

Questions of time and space are related to the most difficult problems, especially when we are not trying to understand them abstractly, but in their real being. This kind of understanding was the basis for Rudolf Steiner's "Goethe as Thinker and Investigator," where we find: "We see here that time first arises where the *essential being* of something comes to *outer manifestation* (*Erscheinung*)."[1] This passage is noticed far too seldom. This "being" has nothing to do with time, but may be understood by ordinary consciousness only from its inner conditions, which we previously termed *causality*. When this *essential being* reveals itself, time appears.

There is also a passage where Steiner explains space and time in a remarkable way in terms of good and evil.[2] According to this, we must picture to ourselves a living duration, a kind of primeval space, represented by the zodiac circle that endured throughout Saturn, Sun, and Moon, the ancient evolutionary stages of the Earth. This, in its essential being, is raised above time and space and above good and evil. "As soon as this (which, as I have said, is permanent, eternal, and having nothing to do with time) passes into time, it divides itself into good and evil."[3] In this connection, the relationship between seven and five replaced the number twelve; thus, "space divides into good and evil when it forsakes its sphere of eternity and takes into itself created things that run their course in time."[4] Seven is then the "good" number in terms of all that is concerned with time.

We can now compare time and space with the two imaginations of Michael and Ahriman as described in the letter.[5] Seven of the twelve *beings of duration*, who comprise primeval space, belong to a light world; five belong to a dark world. Thus, Michael rules in the light world through the course of time, maintaining the union with primeval Divine Being. On the other hand, it is said of Ahriman that, in his course, he would "wring *space* from time." This is not *primeval* space but, as we read in the previous quote, the creations that primeval space receives into itself and run their course in time. Thus, the

---

1   *Nature's Open Secret: Introductions to Goethe's Scientific Writings* (CW 1), p. 213.

2   *The East in the Light of the West*, lecture 9.

3   Ibid., pp. 201–202.

4   Ibid.

5   *Anthroposophical Leading Thoughts*, pp. 97ff.

imaginations in the letter accord with the revelations in this lecture cycle; this last passage closes:

> Do not imagine at this point that this is very difficult to understand; realize instead that the world is very profound and that there must be meanings in things that are very hard to fathom. We have a whole eternity before us so that we may understand everything there is to be understood in the world.[6]

In this way, we can find the transition to the great historical statements that begin Steiner's letter, where we see Michael traveling through the course of time. Perhaps, of all that we have considered about the mission of Michael, we can get an overall impression in one comprehensive sentence: *Michael is not only the protector of humanity, but he also protects the rule of the creative, primal beings.*

We have considered history from various perspectives (for example, Leading Thoughts 50 to 52). Now we have come to a point where, in the letters and leading thoughts, history is treated in terms of the age of the consciousness soul; the letter is titled "At the Gates of the Consciousness Soul." Here we will recall how we have designated short aphoristic sentences as "letters of the alphabet" from the language of the consciousness soul (see Study 30); now we may add similar sentences related to history.

57. We must understand the arising of history out of humanity's development, and then history's influence on modern human beings (Study 26).
58. From the perspective of uninterrupted natural causality, there is no history (Study 26).
59. Biographies form the higher explanatory science in contrast to the descriptive science of anthropology: that is history (Study 26).
60. Ancient humanity had no history; the essential occurrences took place in the spiritual world (Study 26).
61. The Old Testament is not merely a descriptive history, but points to a future goal; that goal became reality—historical fact—in the Mystery of Golgotha (Study 26).
62. The Apocalypse sets the new goal—Christ's reappearance (Study 26).
63. True history consists of this: what occurred in earlier times as completely spiritual became human and earthly; true history is that of human consciousness (Study 26).
64. Only selflessness in relation to our own destiny will lead to the investigation of real history (Study 27).
65. The substance of history grows from the etheric body, which vanishes into the Akashic Record after death (Study 27).

---

6   *The East in the Light of the West*, p. 202 (the last sentence was omitted from the book's translation).

66. Morality in history grows from the astral body's experiences after death in relation to the judgment of life (Study 27).

67. In the world of purpose, the "I" participates after death in the foresight that is active in history (Study 27).

68. By actually experiencing this history of human consciousness through an inner repetition, the today's human being becomes a coworker in the affairs of the higher hierarchies (Study 35).

69. Rudolf Steiner's victory, through thinking, over the materialistic *nominalism* of science gave the human soul the capacity to push its way through to a new *realism* of Spiritual experience (Study 35).

70. To throw the warmth of the heart's thoughts and the chill of the head's thoughts into the same vessel is, historically speaking, to confuse *nominalism* with *realism* (Study 36).

71. Spiritual history is due to the reign of spiritual beings through successive epochs; human history and the evolutionary facts of human beings are its outer manifestation (Study 42).

STUDY 60

THE LAW OF REPETITION

There are now four letters and the leading thoughts that accompany them in which Rudolf Steiner provides vivid historical images of the transition to modern times.[1] Those pictures are given in relation to spiritual history, with the reign of the beings in the spiritual world. Such images will never cease to stimulate historical research in the sense of one of the letters: "What spiritual observation is able to discover is in every way confirmed by external evidence."[2] It is a matter of historical events, over which lies a mysterious veil. We are concerned with raising that veil, which may be accomplished only by bringing the history of human consciousness into our present consciousness by repeating it inwardly. The historical investigator must also do this when examining external evidence.

We are quite familiar with the shortened repetitions, which, in short, consist of this: each new period of evolution briefly recapitulates all those that have gone before. Thus, Old Saturn is recapitulated at the beginning of the Old Sun evolution, then both are repeated in the first part of the Old Moon, and the same applies to Earth's evolution.[3] The individual smaller periods again represent a repetition of earlier conditions, until the new epoch in each case is able to appear. Thus, each post-Atlantean civilization is also a shortened repetition of the ancient epochs.[4] They are eventually repeated in the course of the evolution of the more modern peoples. This principle, however, does apply only to the formative forces active in evolving humanity, but also to the forces of consciousness. Thus, in *The Riddles of Philosophy*, Steiner states, in particular, that the whole development of human thinking, from antiquity to modern times, was repeated in the nineteenth century.

Thus, it may be good for us to reflect on this principle in the historical transition to the age of the consciousness soul. Here it must reveal itself in the whole attitude of soul as it is confronted by the world. With this in mind, if we dwell on the historical images in the letters mentioned, then we may experience, in the rise of the new evolutionary stream of the consciousness soul, the reverberation of the soul attitude of ancient civilizations. We must notice,

---

1   *Anthroposophical Leading Thoughts*, pp. 103–131.

2   Ibid., p. 103.

3   *Rosicrucian Wisdom*, lecture 11; *The Gospel of St. John in Relation to the Other Three Gospels*, lectures 3 and 4.

4   *Universe, Earth and Man*, lecture 2; *Egyptian Myths and Mysteries*, lecture 2.

however, that such repetitions do not simply follow one another in time but also interpenetrate. It is definitely possible, however, to compare the characteristic features of the centuries immediately preceding the rise of the consciousness soul with those of the various post-Atlantean civilizations. Italian art in particular is connected traditionally with the various centuries, and much may be gained by comparing, for example, the fourteenth century, with its aloofness from the world, with the ancient Indian civilization; whereas, when we go on to the sixteenth century, we find a correspondence to the features of Greece and Rome.

Steiner often described the soul mood of the ancient Indian civilization.[1] That time involved looking back to the ancient spirituality of Atlantis; consciousness had a dreamy clairvoyant quality—the physical world did not yet present itself sharply and clearly to the senses, and it was despised as illusion. There was a deep longing to revive the old Atlantean consciousness, and Yoga was the path. But when Steiner described old Atlantis, he always pointed to the dense masses of fog, out of which water had not yet separated. He made wonderful references to the rainbow, which could arise only when the fog had condensed and thus caused the great flood.[2] At the Easter Conference of 1927, Albert Steffen chose to begin his lecture by describing the first rainbow and how its colors illuminated the various civilizations that followed.

Our studies of the letters and leading thoughts have often shown that the words that are repeated many times may help to guide our understanding. It is therefore not without reason that one letter uses the word *fog* three times in describing the mood expressed by tales, sagas, and poems.[3] This gives us the clue to the first post-Atlantean civilization. "Stepping out of a fog" is naturally not meant in a physical sense; it is repeated in a belated way. As beautiful as the images are in these stories—the tale of Good Gerhard, the saga of Duke Ernest, the story of Roland, and the saga of the world of the Nibelungs—they bear witness to the longing for an old type of consciousness, for *Nifelheim*. Such longing indicates a Luciferic activity. In this letter, Steiner especially reminds us that these tales do not simply use subjects from the East, but describe phenomena of consciousness and longings, which are certainly connected with the Crusades. Perhaps it is also important, however, to notice that the Crusades themselves followed the same direction as the old migrations of the peoples, which started from Atlantis, and that they inaugurated a repetition of the old post-Atlantean civilizations before the

---

1   *Rosicrucian Wisdom*, lecture 12; *The Gospel of St. John*, lecture 8; *Universe, Earth and Man*, lecture 9; *The Apocalypse of St. John*, lecture 3; *The Gospel of St. John in Relation to the Other Gospels*, lecture 6.

2   *The Gospel of St. John*, lecture 8; *The Apocalypse of St. John*, lecture 6.

3   *Anthroposophical Leading Thoughts*, pp. 103ff.

arrival of the consciousness soul; conversely, the migrations of the peoples that began in the fourth century followed from east to west, thus taking the same course as the successive post-Atlantean civilizations themselves.

When we consider the brief repetition of the post-Atlantean civilizations before the age of the consciousness soul, we will understand Michael's activity from the spiritual world before he entered his office as leader in 1879. When we take to heart the descriptions in the letter—those relating the ancient Indian civilization, which later reappeared as *soul moods*—the activity of Michael may well be apparent also from this viewpoint. It's as though he himself repeated his work of former times before actually entering his mission in our time as leader of the new epoch of the consciousness soul.

124. The dawn of consciousness (the age of the spiritual soul) during the fifteenth century was preceded by a heightened luciferic activity during the twilight of the age of the intellectual (or mind) soul, which continued for some time, even into the new epoch.

185. This luciferic influence tried to preserve the ancient forms of thinking pictorially of the world in a wrong way. It thus tried to prevent human intellectual understanding and human entry into the fullness of life in the physical existence of the world.

126. Michael unites his being with human activity in such a way that the independent intellectuality may remain with the Divine and the Spiritual—not as luciferic, but in the right way—from which it is inherited.

HISTORY AND INITIATION

We have studied the tragedy of the ancient initiates from other view-points. The reason for this tragedy was that old principles of initiation were no longer appropriate nor effective. We may approach this tragedy from another aspect as well; the old principles of initiation were, in fact, connected deeply with the principle of repetition, which was, in turn, connected with what issued from the places of initiation for the further human evolution. The initiates of old Atlantis, for example, brought about in themselves and in their students a higher human form, reaching all the way into physical corporeal-ity, which, at that time, was still pliable.[1] This happened, because the content for their meditation was the oldest spiritual stages of Earth's evolution (if the upward striving of that time can be so called for the sake of comparison). As a kind of repetition of their work on Earth during those very ancient times, they thus maintained their union with the creative beings of the spiritual world, who were now able to continue their creative work on humanity.

An ancient, cosmic evolutionary process thus becomes meditation for a later epoch. This, in turn, was repeated.[2] The events of the first so-called "root race" (the *Polarian* epoch) became the principle of initiation during the ancient Indian epoch. And the same is true subsequently; the events of the *Hyperborean* epoch—especially the separation of the Sun from the Earth—became the principle of initiation for the ancient Persians; the events of the *Lemurian* time—the departure of the Moon from Earth—became the principle of initiation for Egypt; and the *Atlantean* world reappeared in the Mysteries of ancient Greece. After that, this sequence was necessarily exhausted, since there was nothing else of like nature to be repeated. Instead, it became neces-sary that what now follows should itself become the principle of initiation.

This was the effect of the Mystery of Golgotha, which began a new creation; and Earth received her future goal through the appearance among humanity of the Spirit who leads all of evolution. Since that time, the progressive activities, the principles of initiation, are no longer a repetition of the past but anticipate the future. Nevertheless, this work toward the future should be understood as the polar opposite of the past; thus, the Christ impulse, as the impetus of initiation, proposes to penetrate everywhere, transforming old conditions and legacies. Naturally, in this way, a kind of repetition of old processes again

1   *Egyptian Myths and Mysteries*, lecture 3.

2   Ibid., lecture 5; *The Spiritual Hierarchies and the Physical World*, lecture 1.

appears; but it is distinguished in essence from the pre-Christian repetitions. The old impulses, which depended on repetition, are still effective, because the spiritual beings who have remained behind will intervene and continue their previously legitimate activity at a later time. These are, of course, the *luciferic beings*. Thus, a battle arises between old and new activities.

Human beings, as we saw earlier, have inherited an enormous past. We bear within us the older forms of humanity—the old Atlantean, Indian, or Roman. These forms have become a hindrance in us today; they oppose our heart's acceptance of the Christ; they are enemies within us, and the historical confusion is an expression of battles such as these. By learning to see how these things affect historical events, they can train the consciousness soul. This is where the new principle of initiation is expressed—that the Mystery secrets of ancient times and their human guidance are entrusted to individual human beings. In this way, the ancient forms—otherwise merely disturbing elements in the subconsciousness—are raised to awareness and, in this way, released. Through the emergence of the age of the consciousness soul, the historical consciousness of humanity frees itself from the old forms.

The individual activities of several historical personalities currently incarnated must find their way into modern historical life, as the evolution of the consciousness soul dawns. For such personalities, the approaching age is distinguished by the appearance of intellectuality as individual, inner human activity; human beings begin to experience themselves as the creators of their thoughts.[3] Michael will work to inspire human thought forces when the time has come. Before then, however, the ahrimanic temptation enters into individual activity so that powerful historical conflicts arise—the individual tragedy of historical personalities.

The coming of the Christ impulse through Michael takes place in a way that cannot be understood by the consciousness of those historical epochs—it is all pure miracle. Our contemporary understanding, as it arises from the consciousness soul, is directed both toward the flow of historical events and toward the work of historic personalities. This is exemplified for us in Leading Thoughts 124 to 130; from them, we may clearly sense that past luciferic dangers are related more with the experience of nations, the general consciousness; and future ahrimanic dangers are connected more with individual personalities and a more intellectual consciousness.

Rudolf Steiner reveals the secrets of these historical processes to our modern consciousness; consequently, Michael's mission can be accepted in our time by individual human beings and, therefore, the path of Christ's work for all humankind can be shown. The principles of initiation for the present are thus shaped as the historical impulse of the future.

---

3   See *Anthroposophical Leading Thoughts*, pp. 76ff.

127. At the beginning of the age of consciousness, humankind had evolved the intellectual forces of the soul to only a small degree. Thus, a gap arose between what the human soul in unconscious depths longed for, and what the forces from the region of Michael's abode could give to human beings.

128. Due to that gap, there was a greater possibility for luciferic powers to hold humanity back in the forces of cosmic childhood, thus furthering human evolution, but not on the paths of the Divine spiritual powers with whom human beings were united from the beginning, but on the paths of Lucifer.

129. Furthermore, there was a greater possibility for ahrimanic powers to tear humankind from the forces of cosmic childhood, thus dragging human beings down, in terms of further evolution, into their own domain.

130. Neither of these dangers was realized after all, since Michael's forces were at work. But the spiritual evolution of humanity had to take place under those resulting hindrances; and in this way it has, in fact, became what it is.

HISTORICAL DECISIONS

The mood of transition that our previous study was intended to express is again presented in the first paragraph of the next letter.[1] The historical events described in this letter are ruled by a completely different mood from that of the more dreamy impulses presented in the previous letter.[2] In these letters (and in the next two), which are all related, we are concerned now with historic events and experiences of consciousness that occurred from around the thirteenth to sixteenth centuries. In the present letter we read of the most significant facts, such as the war between France and England, which lasted more than a hundred years, and the intervention of the Maid of Orleans.[3] Furthermore, in terms of the processes of consciousness, we read of the philosopher Descartes, who is compared to Augustine. There is also an important reference to the Crusades, which brought the impulses of ancient Eastern worldviews to the West—a kind of incentive to recapitulate the old civilizations before the age of the consciousness soul dawned.

According to this understanding of the situation, the mood of this letter is comparable to that of the ancient Persian civilization, to the degree that we can know it; by this time, however, we are viewing a distorted image, and the ancient impulses appear as hindrances. One such "hindrance" is the war between France and England. The beginning of the work of the consciousness soul was given to counter the dreamy mood, or "fog." Instead of working culturally, however, as indicated in the case of Chaucer, the war of conquest came along. The consciousness soul led humanity to seize the physical plane, to work at conquest—to repeat what had taken place, in a spiritual sense, in the ancient Persian age.

In that age (5,000 years before the Trojan War), the impulse to conquer the physical world led to the great War, which lasted for many centuries between Iran and Turan.[4] At that time, the more advanced Iranians opposed the backward Turanians, who had remained at the Atlantean stage of consciousness, representing a decadent counterpart to the even more ancient Indian civilization. In this War, the Iranians' battle for the physical plane was against the representatives of ahrimanic forces. In the conquest of the physical plane,

---

1   *Anthroposophical Leading Thoughts*, pp. 112ff.

2   Ibid., pp. 103ff.

3   Ibid., pp. 113ff.

4   *According to Matthew*, lecture 1.

through the consciousness soul in modern times, Ahriman threatens to tear humanity away from the physical plane.

In opposition to such a possibility—which could hinder or destroy the evolution of the consciousness soul—Michael intervened through the Maid of Orleans. Through her being, the power of Christ was obliged to overcome and transform the luciferic forces.[1] In terms of history, however, her task was to repel the overwhelming power of Ahriman. Luciferic powers also led to her death, but her activity in opposition to Ahriman continued after her death. Here we speaking of an anticipation of activities that really become possible only from our time on. This anticipation of future events is the impulse to initiation experienced by the Maid of Orleans.

In his letter Steiner asks: "What would have happened in the fifteenth century had there been no Maid of Orleans?"[2] He has, in fact, repeatedly answered this question himself.[3] The physical efforts of the British nation should have been directed toward conquests in the West. Had a separation of the British from the French not taken place through the intervention of the Maid of Orleans, the deepening of the cultural life of Europe—which arose a little later through the French people—would not have taken place. "For, at that time, everything happening in the will impulses, in the brains of physical heads, had the tendency to cover Europe, so to speak, with a view of a state that would flatten and reduce to nothing all the individualities of the peoples."[4] The reference to political thinking in the current letter also points to this in the passage that mentions the year 1215. That was the year King John of England signed the Magna Charta, which guaranteed individual freedom, but also inaugurated government by Parliament.

Perhaps it is possible to look at the later appearance of Descartes (and Spinoza) from the viewpoint of the actions of the Maid of Qrleans, and they would then appear in the realm of spiritual life as the counterpart to the historical events. This is not an attempt at a detailed philosophical discourse, nor, on the other hand, is it a detailed historical investigation; it is instead an insight into the mood caused by the approach of the consciousness soul. Steiner, in his *Riddles of Philosophy*, described the opposition between Descartes and Bacon of Verulam, with particular reference to the way in which the human "I" struggles against doubt. In his letter, the connection with Augustine is placed before us; and, in keeping with this—even in continuity—direct reference is made to ancient Persia, which had to be overcome. For Augustine could

---

1   *The Destinies of Individuals and of Nations*, lecture 5 (CW 157).

2   *Anthroposophical Leading Thoughts*, p. 114.

3   *The Destinies of Individuals and of Nations*, lecture 4; *Gegenwaertiges und Vergangenes im Menschengeiste* ("Present and Past in the Human Spirit"), lecture 3 (CW 167), unavailable in English.

4   *Occult History*, lecture 2.

accomplish his task only by overcoming traditional (not esoteric) Manicheism, which originated in Persia.

Scotus Erigena established a connection between the time of Augustine and that of Descartes; Steiner said of him that the same inspiring being stood behind both Scotus Erigena and the Maid of Orleans.[5] He also belongs to those through whom Michael prepared his later mission from the spiritual world.

---

5   Ibid., lecture 2.

STUDY 63

PROOFS OF THE EXISTENCE OF GOD

We can comprehend the mood we are led into by the next letter as we view the repetition of the Egypto-Chaldean civilization before the consciousness soul assumed its task in modern times.[1] It should be noted once again that such repetitions do not adhere to a simple succession in time; rather, they interpenetrate and occupy the whole of the thirteenth to the sixteenth century. Taking the facts in their entirety, our individual studies stress only the general mood of the transition according to the various viewpoints of earlier civilizations.

Everything that has come down to us through tradition—from religious forms of worship and worldviews—originated in the civilizations of the Near East. Because it is tradition, however, it opposes the impulses of the consciousness soul. The ancient Egyptian and Chaldean living within us are also our opponents. In Egypt in particular, the soul was chained to the physical world, into which divine intelligence was nevertheless brought from cosmic spheres.[2] In the transition to the consciousness soul, humankind is threatened by such bondage to materialism—not just as concept, but as reality.

The letter is titled "Hindrances and Helps to the Michael Forces at the Dawn of the Age of the Spiritual Soul." *Hindrances* arise through worldviews that are bound to the physical; *helps* arise through overcoming that bondage. Let us begin by considering the hindrances.

First, we need to consider, as a whole, the following: the appearance of the *proofs of the existence of god*; the denial of the traditional religious representations; the proceedings at the Councils of Constance and Basel; and the soul condition of Nicholas of Cusa. The common origin of all these events may be found in the spiritual realm. Michaelic forces are connected with the intellectuality that flows down to humankind, but Michael himself remains in the spiritual world. Those, whose intellectual soul forces were no longer in harmony with the times, perceived that the active downward stream of intellectuality (which had been going on for centuries) was connected with their most difficult problems. They center around the question of the Holy Spirit, and this matter may arise for earthly consciousness as a result of looking at the aforementioned facts as a whole.

---

1   *Anthroposophical Leading Thoughts*, pp. 118ff.

2   *Universe, Earth and Man*, lecture 1.

In contrast to earlier views, Anselm of Canterbury offered the *proof of the existence of god*, which was supported by human thinking in its own nature. This is the so-called ontological proof of God, and it really signifies the search for the divine in an individual's own human thinking, to the degree that one tries to prove the divine through concepts. Nicholas of Cusa, as a mystic, did not see such divinity through *knowing*, but through the *ignorance* that, of course, had to be *learned*—that is, it exists beyond common knowledge. In this search for the divine in thinking—through freeing Aristotelian, scholastic concepts—it is possible to recognize a search for the Holy Spirit. Questions arose in relation to the identity of being and thinking. The old concept of "being" can only be that of the Father principle. Thus, the problem of the identity of being and thinking is the same as the asking whether or not the Holy Spirit proceeds from the Father and is equal with Him.

The oldest *proofs of the existence of god* (which were really no proofs) began with the Father; they belong to the attainments of the ancient civilizations of Asia Minor. Kant introduced instead his refutation of the ontological proof of God, and the moral principle (categorical imperative!); this is a regression to Old Testament times, a resignation of knowledge in favor of simple faith in the Father. The *proof of the existence of god* through the Son lies in the Divinity of Christ in a human body; this was given for the true witnesses of the Mystery of Golgotha. It is therefore possible to point out successive ways of apprehending the human relationship to the divine as *proofs of the existence of god* through the Father, the Son, and the Holy Spirit.

The Christian Catholic Church disagreed over the question of the Holy Spirit (the Filioque Controversy), and the organization of the Councils of Constance and Basel should have helped to reunite the Churches in the East and West. At the Council of Basel, Nicholas of Cusa acted as follows: in the conflicts between the Popes—which played an important role at both Councils—he stood for the belief that, if the Councils were composed of the best representatives of the Church and if they assembled with right purpose in solemn session, the Holy Spirit would be able to speak through their resolutions. The depth of this reasoning of Nicholas of Cusa could not be maintained, although both Councils placed themselves above the Popes; rather, the whole problem sank into awful decadence. Rome carried the dogma into effect by degrees—that the Holy Spirit speaks through the assembled College of Cardinals, especially in the choice of the Pope, and finally in our time (1870), came the dogma of an infallible Pope in matters of faith. According to this, the Holy Spirit was to speak through the Pope as an individual. Thus, the whole problem has become the greatest hindrance, a counterpart to the third post-Atlantean civilization—the Pope replaced the Father. Only the genuine Michael Fellowship allows the Holy Spirit to be active in our time in human communities.

Now there is still something more to be said about furthering the Michael forces; this is shown to us in the letter—the activity of the true Rosicrucians. The following passage shows us that this activity also is deeply connected with the third post-Atlantean civilization:

> This wondrous harmony between the Egyptian remembrance in wisdom and the Christian impulse of power is found in Rosicrucian spiritual teaching. So the ancient seed laid down in the Egyptian period reappears, not merely as a repetition, but differentiated and at a higher level."[1]

True Rosicrucians promote the Michael forces, as well as the impulses allowed to pass into modern times from the second post-Atlantean civilization. Thus, they are also those who transmit true Manicheism for the future.[2]

The letter describes how the true Rosicrucians furthered the Michael forces by means of a remarkable dualism between external life on Earth and the inner life of the soul. In the complete separation of the two was the path that enabled them to repeat the genuine impulses of those ancient civilizations prior to the rule of Michael, so that they would not become a hindrance but a help and, in particular, not fall into materialism. Today, the Rosicrucian impulses are united with the Michael stream in Anthroposophy.

> 131. In the beginning of the age of the spiritual soul, the intellectuality now freed in humanity wished to be occupied with the truths of religious faith and ritual. The life of the human soul thus fell into uncertainty and doubt. People tried to prove, through logic, spiritual realities that were previously experienced directly in the soul. They tried to understand—and even determine by logical deduction—the content of sacred ritual, which may be taken hold of only in inspired *imaginations*.

> 132. All of this is related to the fact that Michael is determined to avoid any kind of contact with the present earthly world, which humanity *must* enter. Nevertheless, at the same time, it is still his task to guide in human beings the cosmic intellectuality that he administered in past ages. Thus, a disturbance in the cosmic balance arises through Michaelic forces—a disturbance that is necessary, however, for the progress of world evolution.

> 133. Michael's mission was made easier for him by certain individuals—the true Rosicrucians—who arranged their outer life on Earth in such a way that it did not interfere in any way with their inner soul life. Thus, they were able to develop forces within them that enabled them to work together in spiritual realms with Michael, without the danger of entangling him in present earthly events, which would have been impossible for him.

---

1   *Universe, Earth and Man*, lecture 11.

2   *The East in the Light of the West*, lecture 9.

THE OTHER SIDE OF THE CONSCIOUSNESS SOUL

The letter (with Leading Thoughts 134 to 136) begins with the transition to a repetition of the fourth post-Atlantean civilization before the consciousness soul entered its present task. The ideas of Copernicus, Galileo, and especially those of Kepler are still a part of the dawning age of Egyptian wisdom. Similarly, in a greater rhythm, our whole modern era—the fifth post-Atlantean civilization—is a renewal of the third.[3] We see in its effects, however, that the great explorers express the impulses of the repetition of the fourth post-Atlantean civilization as was shown in our previous studies. Nevertheless, this is really the final possibility for a repetition of this kind, since everything has by then come to an end, so to speak.

It is illuminating that this final repetition—the Greco-Roman civilization in modern times—has shown the most telling after-effects; for it is, at the same time, the real transition from the fourth to the fifth post-Atlantean civilization. In this meeting between the ancient, decadent remains emerging from the past and the real transition, a genuine tragedy arises—it is not perceived very well by humankind (as it was in ancient Greece), but it was experienced more so by the spiritual world, and most strongly of all by Michael. This is Michael's sorrow over humanity's evolution prior to the time of his earthly activity.

Again, we will trace briefly how the description in Rudolf Steiner's letter points to the nature of the repetition of the fourth post-Atlantean civilization up to our time.

In many places, Steiner describes the Greco-Roman civilization in the wonderfully beautiful expression of a "marriage" between the spiritual and the physical.[4] In it, forces originating from earlier civilizations are combined as a polarity.[5] Such forces, however, also originate from the oldest streams of evolution. The current letter describes the time when the consciousness soul began as this kind of polarity. In the fourth civilization, the harmony of spiritual and physical, or cosmic and earthly, could be clearly seen; now, however, we are more concerned with the arising of something having a twofold nature, in accord with the overlap indicated above.

---

3   *Universe, Earth and Man*, lecture 11; *Egyptian Myths and Mysteries*, lecture 12; *Manifestations of Karma*, lectures 1 and 8; *The Mission of the Folk-Souls*, lecture 1.

4   *Universe, Earth and Man*, lecture 9.

5   *According to Luke*, lecture 8.

The spirit-soul element (active on Saturn and Sun) appears as physical-etheric; in addition, the later physical and etheric appear, originating from the Moon and Earth. Furthermore, there is the spirit-soul element, now transformed through the evolution of the Moon and Earth.[1] Consequently, human beings consist of only *finished work* and *activity*—no longer Divine Spirit itself. In other words, there is no longer a harmonious marriage, but complete bondage to the physical and etheric "in order to draw forth the spiritual [consciousness] soul."[2] (Hence, the newly born consciousness soul even acts at first more like a changeling than like a real child.) The Mystery of Golgotha took place at the time of the true marriage in the Greco-Roman age, but Michael first had to enter his reign before that event could find its way into modern human consciousness.

In keeping with this, there is a wonderful remark in the letter that could easily be overlooked—that Michael "has preserved for humanity the image of humankind and the gods together."[3] We find a parallel to this in the divine images of ancient Greece, which were memories of the old Atlantean world of the gods, with which humanity was closely connected at that time.[4] In contrast to this human divine image, a "search for the knowledge of the human being" begins during the repetition in modern times. That is *humanism*, which is expressed in the character of Faust. The descriptions in the current letter show how ancient Greece, when it is repeated, can also become an opponent within us.

Ancient Greeks found themselves in the physical world and loved it; but there was a widespread fog of fear in relation to life after death.[5] A counterpart to this begins when humanism appeared; human beings lose their own being, and, in its place, the experience of death intrudes with overwhelming force. This occurs in the form of natural science, which has become increasingly interested in the lifeless. This is where the hidden Greek is active in modern consciousness; "in the direction where it [*spiritual rebirth*] should be sought, there are impotence, illusion, and bewildered consciousness."[6] An element that furthers the Michael forces may be found most recently in the art of the Renaissance (the word itself points to a return to antiquity).

Thus, everything accumulates until the transition in our time, as though the highest tension must be reached before the consciousness soul can break through. Consequently, as this whole evolution comes to a close, we are led

---

1   *Anthroposophical Leading Thoughts*, p. 125.

2   Ibid., p.126; (see also *An Outline of Esoteric Science*, pp. 46–50).

3   Ibid.

4   *Universe, Earth and Man*, lecture 2; *Egyptian Myths and Mysteries*, lecture 2.

5   *Egyptian Myths and Mysteries*, lecture 10; *The Gospel of St. John and Its Relation to the Other Gospels*, lecture 6; *From Jesus to Christ*, lecture 6.

6   *Anthroposophical Leading Thoughts*, p. 127.

to the other side of the consciousness soul.[7] Its first achievements on this side (the ordinary side) are to provide a picture of nature, out of which the image of human beings should be formed. In Michael's sight, however, this is nothing. This kind of soul nothingness, however, is the place where ahrimanic forces can penetrate. They pierce through the human consciousness soul, from the physical into the spiritual world, and there they cooperate with luciferic beings, who are already on the other side. There, Michael, who is full of concern, must battle the *dragon*.

The anxiety of Michael and his tragic position are the *other side* of the consciousness soul. Michael is alone in this battle, for he is obliged to keep himself above the physical world of humankind. He may not, through the human consciousness soul, break through from the other side to this side. Luciferic beings, consequently, do so all the more, and thus they are also able to cooperate with ahrimanic forces on this side. Thus, the human soul itself gradually becomes the battleground, although human beings, in their conditions of satisfaction, know nothing about the *solid* ground. This solid ground is ahrimanic: "The solid Earth do I make hard and fast," says Ahriman in the mystery play *The Portal of Initiation*; the satisfaction, on the other hand, is luciferic.

Thus, Rudolf Steiner's achievement can also be estimated—how, from this side of the consciousness soul, he assisted Michael in his battle with the dragon. He showed the way that the consciousness soul—in itself, through its own nothingness—can break through into the spiritual world. This process may therefore be compared with a turning inside out. Steiner enlists auxiliary fighters among us for Michael's battle with the dragon.

> 134. In the very earliest time of the evolution of the spiritual soul human beings began to feel that they had lost the picture of humanity—the image of their own being—which had previously been given to them in *imagination*. Still powerless to find it in the spiritual soul, they looked for it through natural science and history. They wanted that ancient picture of humanity to arise within them again.

> 135. Human beings do not become fulfilled in this way. Far from being filled with the true being of humanity, they are led only to illusions. But human beings are unaware of this; they think that such illusions have real power to sustain humanity.

> 136. Thus, during the time before his activity on Earth, Michael had to witness with anxiety and suffering the evolution of humanity. For, during that time, human beings shunned any real contemplation of the spirit, and consequently severed all links that connected humanity with Michael.

---

7   Ibid., pp. 103–131.

STUDY 65

THE MISSION OF THE CONSCIOUSNESS SOUL

The *Mystery of the Logos* brings to a close Rudolf Steiner's historical considerations in his letters.[1] This culminates the first year of the leading thoughts (December 28, 1924) and encompasses all that has preceded it. When we include in Steiner's Spiritual Science everything he said of the Mystery of Golgotha and its infinite greatness, this mystery always appears as the highest consummation, not an obvious point of departure. We may ask ourselves why the Mystery of Golgotha is not viewed, in general, as a self-evident truth by those searching for a modern worldview. Steiner often pointed out that, according to the modern views of science and history, the life of Jesus Christ cannot be thought of as a historical event. The efforts of Christian churches—especially the Protestants—to preserve the Gospels as historic documents has had the opposite result. Indeed, in terms of materialistic history, it is only honest to deny the life of Jesus historically.

When Steiner first wanted to explain Christianity in terms of modern consciousness, he interpreted it as *mystical fact*. In his book of that title, he clearly showed that the Gospels were not intended as historical biography. Christianity, in its essential nature as *mystical fact*, is presented as an experience of the consciousness—that a certain process of human consciousness guarantees the reality of the Mystery of Golgotha. Contemporary human beings must learn to work toward such a process in consciousness. Consequently, the Mystery of Golgotha exists now not at the beginning of such knowledge, but at the end. Scientific experiences as they can be gained in genuine natural science, however, prepare the way. Thus, Steiner's letter places transformations of consciousness before us with an eye, in fact, toward the consciousness soul of contemporary humanity.

This does not diminish the immense importance that we have the ability to comprehend the Mystery of Golgotha as a historic event. Nevertheless, this view cannot be gained from physical documentation; rather, it arises when we continue along the mystic path to spiritual scientific investigation. By developing our consciousness, we can enter the true events of history (akashic record), and thus sense how history *is* the development of human consciousness.

Let us look back to the historic events at the dawn of the consciousness soul—how, in their mood, they appear as a kind of final repetition of ancient civilizations. In the change of consciousness in modern times, a preparation

---

1   *Anthroposophical Leading Thoughts*, pp. 132–140.

for the *Mystery of the Logos* can be repeated. The way past historic facts were brought together so that the life of Jesus Christ, historically, should be made possible. In diverse ways, the whole outer and inner history of pre-Christian antiquity can be comprehended as a plan with a view toward that unique, central event.

We have seen how the older, even more cosmic stages of Earth's evolution became the principles of initiation in later civilizations. Then, however, what the neophytes of older civilizations experienced became an event in history through the Mystery of Golgotha.[2] Thus, Christianity can also appear as a confluence of various ancient views of the world.[3] Steiner, however, provided a detailed description of how the history of Jesus' childhood was an extraordinary repetition of those paths taken by more ancient civilizations—not merely one that was *typical*, in a general sense, of a pre-Christian initiate.[4] Why has all this been removed completely from ordinary, modern human consciousness? Why is it impossible to know of it directly from historical documents—that is, without the research of Spiritual Science? This points to an all-important mystery in human history.

The Mystery of Golgotha was the most free of all the acts of Christ.[5] Consequently, Christ may be found only through a free act, enacted in the consciousness soul. Archetypal being sank into the Earth and became nature; human spirituality succumbed to death and became the forces of knowing nature. Therefore, human beings can enkindle the freedom of the consciousness soul and, from this, learn the "letters." If done with courage—even unto death—those letters themselves form the Word, or *Logos*.

In this way, the consciousness soul attains its mission in history—that of opening the way once again into the spiritual world. This mission takes place within the sphere of the soul when history becomes mystical. In considering the historic processes during the appearance of the consciousness soul, we are thus concerned with bringing about a convergence of repeated ancient civilizations in individual consciousness. Thus, the final effect of the past evolution of human consciousness is in fact repeated in the human individual. In this way, the consciousness soul is prepared to approach the Christ event in our time— the significant event of *future* history. This mystical event becomes history, because, as a result of the series of generations as well as the series of incarnations, individual human beings are heirs to the past. Those of the present

---

2   *According to Luke*, lecture 10; *From Jesus to Christ*, lecture 4; *Background to the Gospel of St. Mark*, lecture 8.

3   *According to Luke*, lecture 2; also see Andrew Welburn's introduction to *Christianity as Mystical Fact*.

4   Ibid., lecture 5.

5   *From Jesus to Christ*, lecture 10; *The Being of Man and His Future Evolution*, lecture 8.

day who alone can rightly enter this heritage may overcome within themselves the inner hindrances created by the past, and thus transform ancient forms of humanity within themselves into the image of God. Those are the paths of knowledge in Anthroposophy.[1]

137. Due to the forces of Michael, the activity of world and human evolution repeats itself *rhythmically*—although in forms that constantly change and progress—both before and after the Mystery of Golgotha.

138. The Mystery of Golgotha is the greatest event, occurring only once in human evolution. In this there can be no question of rhythmic repetition; for, whereas human evolution also exists within a grand cosmic rhythm, still it is *one*—one vast member in a cosmic rhythm. Before it became this *one*, humanity was essentially other than humanity; afterward, humanity will again be something different. Thus, there are many Michaelic events in human evolution, but there is only one occurrence of Golgotha.

139. Divine Spiritual being descends into the depths of Earth to permeate natural processes with spirit; this process is accomplished through the quick, rhythmic repetition of annual seasons. Thus, nature is ensouled with the *forces* of beginning and eternity, which must remain active, just as the descent of Christ ensouls humanity with the *Logos* of beginning and eternity, whose effort toward human salvation will never cease.

---

1   For further reading on the Mystery of the Logos, see Rudolf Steiner, *Christianity as Mystical Fact*; and Andrew Welburn, *The Beginnings of Christianity* and *Gnosis: The Mysteries and Christianity*.

STUDY 66

SURVEY, PART 1

It is no doubt obvious that the leading thoughts are given in rhythmic sequences; here, too, as in all spiritual matters, they create their form from the spirit that lives within them—they grow organically. There is a wonderful artistic charm in trying to enter such forms. Between the lines, even concealed in the words, we touch deep secrets. Once, many years ago, Rudolf Steiner proved this by what he said to me about such forms in his book *Theosophy*. He said that they are really present—not, of course, in an abstract way but, when the thoughts are true, arising as if on their own from the realm of spirit. One who has artistic, creative capacity will perceive the same in other areas. In Steiner's descriptions, *Logos* wisdom is revealed through human consciousness, for the substance of thought is adapted to free formation by spirit. This is said only as an indication.

It is obvious that the leading thoughts may be arranged in certain ways and, in previous studies, we have tried repeatedly to notice when changes occur, especially in the soul attitude intended; for, when considering the meditative character of the leading thoughts, it is the subtle shades of meaning that are important. Beyond this, however, there is also an arrangement according to facts, primarily concerned with thought content, as it were— the matter to be thought. Their meditative nature cannot be revealed anew until the essential facts have been accepted by our inner being. At the beginning of the previous study, it was stated that everything that had gone before appears comprehensively in the letter that accompanies Leading Thoughts 137 to 139. We shall see how the leading thoughts of the first year lead to this conclusion.

The leading thoughts are presented in groups of two to four. Furthermore, in a regular sequence, we find six to seven of these groups, which, taken together, deal with a particular subject. We will try to characterize these collections of groups in short sentences. There are seven groups of leading thoughts along with letters (Leading Thoughts 1 to 19).[2] They speak of spirit knowledge and the human being. The relationships between these two shape knowledge of experiences after death and before rebirth; this is expressed in the three kinds of suprasensory research and imprinted in the threefold nature

---

2   These letters may be found in *The Foundation Stone/The Life, Nature, and Cultivation of Anthroposophy*, pp. 24–41.

of the human being. That is again the content of seven groups in the following letters (Leading Thoughts 20 to 40).

Six groups follow in Letters 20 to 25 (Leading Thoughts 41 to 58).[1] These may be denoted by the single word *destiny*. Nevertheless, it also became clear how the influences affecting the human being on the other side of birth and death are expressed in destiny. Such influences are guided by the beings of the three hierarchies, to whom Leading Thoughts 59 to 81 (in seven groups and letters) are devoted.[2] The beings of the hierarchies are now also active in ordinary human experience, which, for this very reason, is revealed in its spiritual background. This is shown in the next seven letters (Leading Thoughts 82 to 102) in waking, dreaming, sleeping, and in thinking, feeling, willing.[3] In their spiritual background, the activity of Michael appears, and our line of thought advances in the next group of seven letters (Leading Thoughts 103 to 123) into cosmic and spiritual development and events; the mission of Michael dominates these groups.[4] Its activity is reflected as human history at the dawn of the age of the consciousness soul. This is described in the next group of letters (Leading Thoughts 124 to 139; Leading Thoughts 140 to 143 also belong to the same subject, making it six groups in all).[5] Now follow two groups of seven Leading Thoughts, which we shall provisionally denote with the words *macrocosm* and *microcosm*.

We must now look for the transition from the letter and Leading Thoughts 137 to 139,[6] of the first year, to the second year (1925). As a result of surveying the facts presented in the earlier leading thoughts, we may be led to a practice of meditation. First, an objection may be raised here. The letter and leading thoughts in question were presented by Steiner during Christmas, 1924 (a year after the laying of the Foundation Stone) to provide a festival mood for the benefit of those who had, at the time, participated in working on the leading thoughts. We might feel scruples about arranging a discussion such as ours apart from the time of year and its festival, since this may run counter to the purposes of these leading thoughts and their author. Spiritual laws are at work there, however; meditation content that has spiritual effects cannot be elaborated at the same time through thinking. Whereas it is best to meditate in relation to a definite rhythm, it is precisely because of this that it is valuable to ponder the content of meditation at another time. Thus, in

---

1   Ibid., pp. 61–65; and *Anthroposophical Movement* (the weekly news for English-speaking society members), pp. 1–24.

2   Ibid., pp. 25–80.

3   Ibid., pp. 81ff.

4   *Anthroposophical Leading Thoughts*, pp. 66–102.

5   Ibid., pp. 103–149.

6   Ibid., pp. 132ff.

the yearly rhythm, Christmas is the right time for meditating the *Mystery of the Logos*; aside from this time, everything can be acquired that will give the right mood of consecration to the Christmas meditation.

This is what is meant in the letter (with Leading Thoughts 137 to 139) about the *cosmic Christmas* being "celebrated every year in remembrance.... For the spiritual [consciousness] soul, which first receives the element of intellectuality, is strengthened by allowing true life to enter this coldest element of the soul."[7] To this end, it is necessary that, during the natural course of a year, the rhythmic revelation of nature (the myth of Persephone) be seen anew in the element of light. Thus, it is necessary to understand everything in this letter in two ways; for not until all the past has been laid out upon the consciousness soul can it then turn to the future by meditating the Mystery of the Logos in freedom. This letter speaks of a past that reveals nature and history as a unity. This leads us into the next letter, "Heavenly History—Mythological History—Earthly History: The Mystery of Golgotha," and the accompanying leading thoughts:

> 140. The cosmic process into which human evolution is interwoven— reflected in human consciousness, as "history" in the broadest sense— reveals these successive epochs: a long epoch of heavenly history; a shorter epoch of mythological history; and the relatively very short epoch of earthly history.

> 141. Today this cosmic process is divided into the activities of divine spiritual beings in free *intelligence* and *free will*—which none can calculate— and the "calculable" process of the world body.

> 148. Luciferic powers stand opposed to the calculable order of the world body; ahrimanic powers oppose all that creates in free intelligence and free will.

> 143. The event of Golgotha is a free, cosmic act that springs from universal love; it is intelligible only through human love.

---

7   Ibid., pp. 139.

STUDY 67

SURVEY, PART 2

This survey, especially in relation to our previous studies, shows us that all past must be transferred to the consciousness soul. We found ancient spirit forms—images from ancient history—from which modern human beings must be delivered. Alternatively, they are a disturbing element and become the enemies of humankind, who have inherited an immense past, both in terms of nature and spirit. If, however, this past is dammed up within the consciousness soul, we ultimately become our own enemy. This is the final effect of the repetitions that has engaged our attention in relation to the dawning consciousness soul. Here is the greatest danger for contemporary human beings, who thus find only Lucifer and Ahriman as the spiritual aspects of the consciousness soul. This is the egoism and abstract character of our civilization, and it can lead only to the war of all against all.[1]

Is there not the law, however, that whatever disappears into the center reappears in the circumference? The statements made by the newer synthetic (projective) geometry can become true symbolism. If opposition to oneself is transformed by meditative experience, does that not signify the seed of a new human being? This is where the purpose of the Logos Mystery can be accomplished. In the current letter we are shown how the spirit of nature comes to the Earth and, in human development, disappears, as it were, into the center of the Earth. The Logos then enters into the Earth from the circumference of the cosmos and, correspondingly, the spirit of nature rises to the Earth's surface. This presents a balance in the polarity between Earth's center and the cosmos. This may be shown by the line of the circle in the polarity between inner and outer in a common figure of projective geometry:[2]

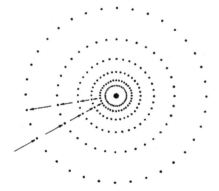

1   *The Apocalypse of St. John*, lecture 8; *The Effects of Esoteric Development*, lecture 8.

2   Olive Whicher, *Projective Geometry: Creative Polarities in Space and Time*, London: Rudolf Steiner Press, 1971, p. 188.

On the surface of the Earth, the Logos meets the spirit of nature and *becomes flesh*; thus, Christ walked the Earth as a man. The heart of modern human beings can unite with the mystery of His death and resurrection and, in this way, be released by the Christ from self-opposition; then, the ancient spirit forms inherited by humanity may gain redemption. And now Michael's gesture points humankind toward the vast nature of the circumference—to the cosmos. There, the resurrection of humanity should be achieved. In this way, we are led to the contents of the letter.

"In the spatial cosmos, there is the contrast of the cosmic expanse and Earth's center."[3] This is the first sentence, and it appeals to an understanding of everything in earlier letters and leading thoughts through the heart. If this does not happen, then much of this letter would only seem to be a further development of earlier statements. The unity of heavenly and earthly history, of the spirit of nature and humanity, can be experienced in the living soul of today only in a way that corresponds to the spiritual purposes of this letter. This is because each sentence and phrase is arranged in such a way that the great cosmic panorama on the horizon of the consciousness soul may be surveyed as a single whole. This is supported by a *new* power of proof, completely unique in all of today's so-called evidence in an intellectual sense. We can refer to this new capacity as the faculty of *surveying*. It is an experience today of what ordinary consciousness divides into past and future.

The key to this letter (whose actual wording must certainly be left unchanged) is given in the following sentence: "What is thus *of the past* in the shining of the stars, is *present* in the spirit world. And human beings, in their essential being, live in this *present* spirit world."[4] From another perspective, the word *calculable* is especially illuminating. It expresses human understanding of the work of the gods in the past and, indeed, through the spirit's power, the way humankind participates with the creative beings. The fact that natural phenomena can be calculated is one of the "proofs" against human freedom. Thus, again we encounter the central question of freedom, which, in the realm of Anthroposophy, never really leaves us.

The current letter is concerned with three grand cosmic epochs, which also play an important role in following letters and leading thoughts. These three epochs, despite their vast extent, are not like the one described in Leading Thought 138 as a "grand cosmic rhythm," during which the whole evolution of humanity takes place. This cosmic progress of the whole of human evolution—in which the Mystery of Golgotha is the single "greatest event"—reaches from ancient Saturn to Vulcan, while the three epochs now being considered occur in the middle of those planetary evolutions. What this means is Earth's development out of the cosmos (*manvantara*) and its return to the

---

3   *Anthroposophical Leading Thoughts*, p. 141.

4   Ibid., p. 142.

next intermediate condition (*pralaya*) and, within this, again, the central part, which begins with the Polarian epoch.[1]

Thus, since humanity is completely different before and after the passage through the Saturn through the Vulcan epochs (Leading Thought 138), the possibility of *calculation* applies only to the central epochs of Earth's evolution—that is, those being considered here. Accordingly, it cannot be used as a proof against human freedom, since it is not absolute; rather, it arose and will pass away. The power of proving, with which we should unite here, is in no way based on absoluteness of intellectual thinking. Rudolf Steiner once pointed out that modern science recognizes that the intensity of light and gravity decreases in proportion to the square of the distance; from this, it is concluded that such scientific thinking also decreases in proportion to the square of the distance from the place where it was valid—that is, from the Earth's surface.

---

1   *Founding a Science of the Spirit*, lecture 10; *Cosmic Memory*, chapters 8 and 9.

THE LIGHT OF THE SPIRIT SELF

The fact that the cosmos is calculable is related in a special way to human freedom, not with any lack of freedom. In calculations—or at least in the soul attitude from which they are computed—modern human beings experience the creative thoughts of primeval times; creation, as planned by the creating beings, is repeated in human thoughts. Thus, to humankind, the *past* creation of the universe becomes *present*. That not only refers to the expanses of the universe, but also to nature that enters human beings from below. Nature and history are polar opposites; they become one only when seen cosmically. Now, if human beings train their inner being toward participation in the divinity of the past by studying what is calculable in nature and cosmos, the meaning of what is *incalculable* in the history of Earth and heaven may become clear. Only through conscious participation in the development of human history can freedom become real. Conversely, every truly free act forms a part of true spiritual history. From this, there rises once again the *proof* for the most free accomplishment between Saturn and Vulcan—the deed of the Christ.

Nature and history stand in contrast to each other, and the same contrast is found in the polarity of life between birth and death and life between death and a new birth. The calculable element leads the human being to birth; the incalculable leads back into the spiritual realm. Everything that has been said about the rhythm of birth and death gains fresh meaning here by becoming a subject for meditation. In the current letter, Lucifer and Ahriman are also presented in terms of this same polarity between the calculable and the incalculable.[2] It will now help—after discussions such as those in the previous studies—to immerse ourselves once again in the precise wording of this letter, since our studies will be useless if they do not lead us back, in continually new ways, to the actual words of Rudolf Steiner.

In the next letter and leading thoughts,[3] and in those that immediately follow, the light of a new power of proving, which is contained in the faculty of surveying, illuminates more and more of the areas where microcosm and macrocosm take shape. It falls gradually on all the subjects that have been treated previously in the letters and leading thoughts. In Study 67, we were shown the new power of proving contained in the faculty of surveying; this has arisen

2   *Anthroposophical Leading Thoughts*, pp. 141ff.

3   Ibid., pp. 150ff.

because the ability to understand nature and history was transferred to the consciousness soul. It is thus able to bring light to the knowledge of the future that was made possible to humanity by the redeeming power of the Mystery of Golgotha, under Michael's guidance.

Such knowledge of the future belongs to the *spirit self*; it is therefore the light of the spirit self that, like a searchlight, illuminates those various spheres. Steiner once said in a very important passage:

> In developing the sentient soul, the intellectual soul, and the consciousness soul, human beings develop something that corresponds to the flower of their being, lifting it to receive the influx of Divine Spirit from above. By thus receiving the spirit self, we may rise to ever greater heights of human evolution.[1]

The disciples of the Christ, who stood around Him, understood this to mean that, in association with Him, they had this new power of proving contained in the faculty of surveying, at a time before there was as yet a consciousness soul for the ordinary person.

In this letter, the light of the spirit self again falls on a threefold epoch existing within that one reaching from the Polarian time to the end of this period—in fact, at the center of it, or perhaps somewhat earlier. The middle period of this epoch is described with its extremes, with one in the latest Lemurian time and the other in the Atlantean time. We must bring before our minds that the first period reaches far into the past, and the third far beyond our time into the future. It is important to be as clear as possible about the epochs mentioned in the letters and leading thoughts, so that we may find our way through a more precise study with the help of Rudolf Steiner's *Outline of Esoteric Science.*

In descriptions such as those given in these letters, we may now accompany Steiner on his path, as it were, while investigating past earthly lives, even as far back as to those remote times when human life on Earth (between birth and death) and human life in the cosmos (between death and a new birth) had not yet separated. Here, it will help to verify the survey that arises from the fact that a cosmic memory of that distant past has remained in modern humankind.[2] In terms of the paths taken in this kind of research, we can imagine that through the practice of entering ancient cosmic memories in our soul life, as it is today, a view of the past opens before us. On the other hand, reviewing those cosmic creative processes—after Steiner has investigated them—is the best inner training for soul development. Here we are shown how cosmic memories are expressed in the three stages of evolution through thinking, feeling, and willing; and we have their foundation, created in primeval times, in

---

1   *According to Matthew*, lecture 11.

2   *The Effects of Esoteric Development*, lecture 4.

the human three-fold system. Thus, nothing abstract is intended here, but rather a living soul experience of one's self as the student. Furthermore, we are told in this letter how during the time between death and a new birth, as it runs its course for contemporary human beings, these cosmic memories return to their source.

The will represents the part of this cosmic evolution that still persists today; therefore, the study of cosmic creation is carried on into the immediate present in the will—that is, directly into our own experience. The whole study thus leads to the actuality of today's consciousness. The letter closes by again pointing to the Christmas Mystery, the truth of which is expressed in the saying, "Unto you is born this day a Saviour." *This day,* not just 2,000 years ago! Finally, therefore, awakening the spirit self depends on the will. Beginning with the will, the transformative power of Anthroposophy will lay hold of the whole human being; it demands those of good will.

144. Looking back into a human being's repeated lives on Earth, we find three distinct stages. In a remote past, humankind did not exist as individuated beings, but as seeds in the divine spiritual realm. As we look back into this stage, we find not yet a human being, but divine spiritual beings—the archetypal forces of Principalities and Archai.

145. This was followed by an intermediate stage. Humanity existed with individuality of being, but was not yet loosened from the thinking, willing, and being of the divine spiritual realm. At this stage, human beings did not yet have the present personality with which they appear on Earth as completely self-possessed beings, loosened from the divine spiritual realm.

146. The present state is the third and latest. Here human beings experience themselves in human form and figure, loosened from the divine spiritual realm; the world is experienced as an environment with which human beings stand face to face, individually and personally. This stage began in Atlantean time.

STUDY 69

COSMIC INDIVIDUATION

In the present letter, previous lives in the period between death and new birth are used as the carriers of retrospective knowledge of the cosmos.[1] It speaks of the same epochs as in the previous letter, since, in terms of time, it makes no difference whether the retrospect concerns the life between birth and death or that between death and rebirth, provided it reaches the point where they are no longer distinguishable. There is, however, one essential difference; in esoteric research this depends, when meditating, on the starting point from which the spiritual gaze is directed toward the past. Different spheres are affected by the light of the spirit self according to what serves to carry the research. Of course, this does not imply that such spiritual investigation is subjective; rather, the path of spiritual evolution leads beyond subjectivity and objectivity, or a dependence on subject or object.

The retrospect into repeated earthly lives reveals more of what frees human beings—and with them the Earth—from fellowship with the beings of the hierarchies; the retrospect into previous lives between death and a new birth, on the other hand, reveals more of what concerns those spirit beings themselves. This second viewpoint proves to be the more important, which is shown to modern humankind by the fact that earthly lives are short compared to the lives between death and new birth.

The significant feature in these two letters[2] is that they show us how the cooperation of the hierarchies is introduced. Here, too, becoming and changing may be found. Let us try once again to comprehend the new teaching that Rudolf Steiner gave here compared to his descriptions in *An Outline of Esoteric Science*, as well as in lectures. At that important point in time when earthly life and the life between death and rebirth become distinguishable, it is the activity of the Archai that especially stands out. "And, indeed, if we trace back the life of one human being, we find not one divine spirit being but all the beings that belong to that Hierarchy."[3]

All of the Archai work together to fashion the figure of humankind from all that has been brought about by all of the higher hierarchies in the cosmos since primeval times; that figure is conceived as *spiritual being*, which is the goal of the gods: the *human being*. This is the other new element presented to

---

1   *Anthroposophical Leading Thoughts*, pp. 155ff; part one of a study in two parts.

2   Ibid., pp. 155–166.

3   Ibid., pp. 155.

us—the cosmic figure, or macrocosmic form, that is not the physical nor the etheric human body; rather, the later physical body was stamped into the multiplicity of matter according to this divine image as the Earth became physical. "Divine spirit beings hold the balance, one with another, in the cosmos. The visible expression of this mutual balance is the form of the starry heavens. What they are there, all together, they willed to create as a single unity as human being."[4]

Here again is a pointer! The old question of individuation (which has already occupied us) appears in a macrocosmic form. As the unity of the foundation of the cosmos was differentiated into the multiplicity of stars, so the figure of macrocosmic humankind—Adam Kadmon—changed into a multitude and became the phantom that fashions human bodies when the grain of sand—Earth—separated in its material aspect from the cosmos.[5] The next letter also deals with this subject.[6] In answer to the stirring question of how many individual human beings there are on Earth, is it now too bold to say that they number the same as there are stars?

The creation of the human form is the one side of individuation, the nature of which is sharply delineated in Leading Thought 148. It is suggested in Leading Thought 149 that the other side is the path of humanity, which is presented in the letter that follows those leading thoughts.[7] During the second epoch of former lives between death and new birth—through the power of the Archangels on the etheric body of the evolving human being—the element of movement belonging to the heavens comes into the human form, which is turned toward Earth. This is related to individuation, which works toward the inner human being. This is expressed when, during the third epoch, the activity of the Angels on the astral body develops the individual element to the degree that the human "I" can awaken gradually to consciousness. At the time of this transition to our own epoch, cosmic memory becomes active. We must imagine to ourselves that outer and inner individuation go hand in hand.

The influences of Lucifer and Ahriman are now active, in which we can recognize an essential factor in human individuation. Finally, there is divine tragedy at the foundation of the development of humanity toward individuality. This echoes ancient sagas—when the primal human became too haughty, the gods were obliged to divide the human into separate beings. Thus, in the mystery of the strife in heaven, the division of single, individual heavenly bodies into the multitude of planetoids is the effect of the agency of those

---

4   Ibid., p. 157.

5   *The Spiritual Hierarchies and the Physical World*, lecture 9; *The Temple Legend*; and *From Jesus to Christ*, lecture 6.

6   *Anthroposophical Leading Thoughts*, pp. 167ff.

7   Ibid., pp. 160ff.

beings who have fallen behind.[1] Human individuation may be thought of as a means whereby the creative gods can master the opposing forces. In this connection, we find the brief statement in the current letter (part two) that the Archai, who originally united to create the human form, later appeared individually as the Spirits of Time and races. (This applies only to later times. In the Atlantean time, when the concept of race had a particular significance, the Spirits of Form were the leaders of the races.) The Archangels, who during that second epoch still united to work on the etheric body, later appeared individually as leaders of nations.[2] Finally, the Angels in their epoch—the third—bring the sacrifice of working as individuals on individual human beings. When one's own nature is recognized from the remote past, the single individual can again turn in freedom toward the primal forces through the strength of thinking; by uniting oneself with Michael's mission and receiving redemption from the evil of individuation through the Christ, the purpose of cosmic individuation is fulfilled. This, too, is indicated in part two of the letter, which describes the descent of thinking to sense perception, and the corruption of the primeval human spirit into the illusion of freedom.

147. Human lives between death and rebirth also show three distinct periods. In the first, human beings lived entirely within the Hierarchy of the Archai, who prepared the human form and figure to be borne thereafter in the physical world.

148. Thus, the Archai prepared the human being to subsequently unfold free self-awareness. For this self-awareness can evolve only in beings who can display it in the form and figure that was created from an inner impulse of the soul.

149. We see in this how human qualities and forces manifesting in the current cosmic age were placed in the seed of ages long past. We see how the microcosm grows from the macrocosm.

150. In a second stage of evolution of the lives between death and a new birth, humankind entered the domain of the Archangeloi. The seed of later human "I"-consciousness—prepared for, in the first period, in the formation of the human figure—was now implanted in the nature of the human soul.

151. During this second period, luciferic and ahrimanic influences drove humankind more deeply into the physical than would have happened without their intervention.

---

1   *The Spiritual Hierarchies and the Physical World*, lecture 5.

2   *Universe, Earth and Man*, lecture 3; *Egyptian Myths and Mysteries*, lecture 6; *Spiritual Beings in the Heavenly Bodies and in the Kingdoms of Nature*, lecture 3.

152. In the third stage, humankind enters the domain of the Angeloi, who wield their influence, however, only in the astral body and the "I." This is the current stage; but what took place in the two previous ones still lives in human evolution and explains the fact that in the nineteenth century—within the age of the spiritual [consciousness] soul—humankind stared into the spiritual world as though into a dark void.

STUDY 70

THE COSMIC TURNING POINT

Out of all that has been gathered from the work of Rudolf Steiner, one of the greatest achievements in his Anthroposophy is the knowledge that the Earth and human beings cannot be considered separately. Thus, what we are told about the Earth in this next letter must—in keeping with all our studies—also take hold of our humanity with cosmic strength.[1] The microcosm is not the little everyday individual with what that requires, but the cosmic turning point. Our consciousness, experienced as a point, is nothing compared to the cosmos; it is an opening through which the cosmos itself passes in the backward swing of its grand rhythm from Saturn to Vulcan. Nevertheless, human beings could never learn the powerful language of the cosmos with its overwhelming super-objectivity if they did not experience themselves as points.

The image of the Earth as a grain of dust arose initially when the consciousness soul experienced itself as a point. This picture expresses an infinite feeling of loneliness. This growth of loneliness and homelessness is the result of the cosmic forces engraved upon human beings as the hierarchies worked together; that was the cosmos becoming human. Consequently, the Earth arose at the same time—and not only the Earth, but mineral, plant, and animal as well. Humanity has indeed placed the kingdoms of nature outside itself; concealed and spiritually active in those realms is what human beings did not need to become points themselves. As beings of nature, they are turned toward Earth and serve humanity; as beings of spirit, they are turned toward the cosmos and serve the revelation of the spirit in the future. As human beings, the decision is ours; our task is to free those beings from bondage to nature, to further Christ's work of redemption. That is the germinating force of the human "I"-experience—to produce love out of loneliness as the counterpart of the love-filled cooperation of the hierarchies. *Loneliness is the medium between love and freedom.* It is the human being becoming the cosmos.

To attain such love, we must walk the path that imbues all thinking related to the dead past with the *will*—the seed cell of the future; this is the path of inner transformation. *The old cosmos dies and the new one germinates because it passes through the human being.* This is presented in the form of a grand meditation in the rhythm of human life from birth to death and from

---

1   *Anthroposophical Leading Thoughts*, pp. 167ff.

death to new birth. As a result of looking back at these facts and surveying them, Rudolf Steiner derives this line of thought in the present letter: Death is only the transition that accomplishes the purpose of life—the human being becomes the cosmos. The great turning point, however, is the *cosmic midnight*, when the cosmos begins to become human. The cosmic day (which spans one earthly life and the time between two earthly lives) can be seen in its entirety only at the midnight hour of existence. One "should try to make the thought of these things fully living in oneself, and thus feel what such a thought may signify for the human heart and mind."[2] *The purpose of individuation is accomplished in the germinating spirit self.*

The significance of such considerations is still further strengthened when, in the next letter,[3] they are applied to waking and sleeping. Here we are shown how, in Spiritual Science, one thought is always supported by another. This may be demonstrated by comparing what Steiner said at various times and places. In this way, the strongest testimony to the survey is offered; for truth itself rules there. Through his research, Steiner has already proved what can then be understood with conviction as truth through our ordinary consciousness. The coherence of his investigations does not depend on remembering facts; rather, there is a living principle of spiritual knowledge at work. Every new addition to knowledge freshly illuminates all that is already known (see Study 2).

The rhythm of waking and sleeping recapitulates the cosmic rhythms (the connection with previous studies can be clearly seen). When falling asleep, a human being plunges into the primal past, passing through the dream world, the stage of animal consciousness, and unites with the spirit of the plants in sleep. One even contacts the spiritual realm of the minerals at the rhythm's turning point in the experience of midnight, from which the *cosmic midnight* of the greater rhythm of repeated Earth lives derives its name. (The present letter ends with a reference to this.) Now, in order to thoroughly understand what the cosmos has formed in the human being through waking and sleeping, we are once again concerned with making full use of our human experience. If this were all that is active, the dying cosmos could not rise to new life, since the work of the cosmos was directed toward humanity as its goal. This is expressed as follows in the letter:

> Such is the rhythm of the present moment of cosmic time: when the rhythm of human earthly existence is outside the *inner being* of the world, one's own being is experienced in consciousness; and when one's existence is within the *inner being* of the world, consciousness of one's own being is extinguished.[4]

2   Ibid., p. 170.

3   Ibid., pp. 171ff

4   Ibid., p. 173.

The same is true of the greater rhythm of repeated earthly lives. According to certain teachings of the East, they would roll on cosmically, constantly repeated without the advent of anything new, unless, through such earthly lives, one's own cosmic impulse is grasped. This new element can be effective in repeated lives on Earth only when the dead point in the rhythm of sleeping and waking is overcome. We have already asked: Can freedom be given? Here we see how the cosmos awaits on us to use the freedom given to us, because, for the cosmos, humanity is an end. The path is that of *Intuitive Thinking as a Spiritual Path: A Philosophy of Freedom*, and, in its continuation, that of meditation practice. In this way, ordinary waking consciousness will become permeated with what we ordinarily experience of the cosmos only in sleep; and, conversely, a higher awakening will be introduced into the realm of sleep. This letter closes in a deeply tragic mood: "What is present in dreams as only a sun-abandoned glimmer, lives transfused with spiritual sunlight in the spirit realm, awaiting the beings of the higher hierarchies; or humankind shall summon it in the creative work of shaping new life forms."[1] If humanity fails, and the hierarchies must exert their power alone, then the cosmic hour is missed.

153. In the beginning of the age of the spiritual [consciousness] soul, it became customary to pay attention to the physical, spatial greatness of the universe. Impressed most of all by this immensity of physical appearance, human beings speak of Earth as a mere speck of dust in the universe.

154. To the consciousness of the seer, this speck of dust, the Earth, is revealed as the seed and beginning of a newly arising macrocosm, whereas the old macrocosm appears as a thing whose life has died away. The old macrocosm had to die so that human beings might sever themselves from it with full self-awareness.

155. In the cosmic present, human beings, with the thought forces that make them free, participate in the dead macrocosm; they participate with the will forces, whose essence is concealed from them, in the germination of this Earth existence—the macrocosm newly springing to life.

156. In waking life, to experience themselves with full and free self-awareness, human beings must forego a conscious experience of reality in its true form, both in their own existence and that of nature. From the ocean of reality, human beings lift themselves, so that in their shadowy thoughts, they can fully experience their own "I"-being.

157. In sleep, human beings live within the life of their earthly environment; but this very life extinguishes their self-awareness.

---

1   Ibid., p. 174.

158. In dreaming, the powerful cosmic existence flickers up into self-awareness, from which the human being is woven and from which human beings build the body in their descent from the spirit world. In earthly life, this cosmic existence, with its potent forces, is put to death in human beings; it dies into the shadows of their thinking. Only in this way can it become the basis for a humankind that is self-aware.

STUDY 71

CIVILIZATIONS AS POLAR OPPOSITES

In the letter (with Leading Thoughts 153 to 155) there is an important remark about thinking during the second of the two epochs discussed—that thinking and perception, which had formed a unity, began to divide during that epoch (the Atlantean time).[1] This was significant for human individuation. The single spiritual life of previous times became the infinitely differentiated— sense perceptions separated, in contrast to which thinking presented a unified, dead image. In the following letter, we find: "Human beings *think* within the sphere of those very forces that enable them to grow and live; nevertheless, they cannot become thinkers until those forces die."[2] The reunification of sense perception and thinking is the original impulse of *Intuitive Thinking as a Spiritual Path: A Philosophy of Freedom*, which is mentioned in the letter as "a bridge leading from the depths of thinking "I"-being to the depths of nature's reality."[3]

Now, we must now consider the contents of the following letter[4]; the third post-Atlantean civilization, the Egypto-Chaldean, is a repetition of the old Lemurian time.[5] And ours, the fifth post-Atlantean civilization, is a kind of reflection of the third.[6] In this way, we are provided a momentous impulse in the polarity between *Gnosis and Anthroposophy; this is presented in the present letter. First, we find how ancient epochs are repeated in the transition from the second to the third and fourth post-Atlantean civilizations, except that all that was previously macrocosm has become microcosm. This time of the unfolding of the sentient soul "was the age when the Gnosis really originated and had its life."[7] The Gnosis known to history still existed during the fourth post-Atlantean civilization and was then destroyed.*

---

1   *Anthroposophical Leading Thoughts*, pp. 160ff.

2   Ibid., p. 172.

3   Ibid., p. 173.

4   Ibid., pp. 175ff.

5   *The Spiritual Hierarchies and the Physical World*, lecture 8.

6   Ibid., lecture 6; *Universe, Earth and Man*, lecture 1; *Manifestations of Karma*, lecture 8.

7   *Anthroposophical Leading Thoughts*, p. 176.

The accounts given—especially of the transition to this period—shed new light on what Rudolf Steiner said in other books and lectures of the Egypto-Chaldean civilization. We found in our studies that these civilizations created cults that are still with us today. The wording of the letter's descriptions should not be altered; but, as a meditative mood, we are offered further help in the contrast to the historical revelations regarding the unfolding consciousness soul.[8]

In Rudolf Steiner's *Theosophy*, and in other places in his writings, we find that *sentient soul* and *sentient body* belong together, as do *consciousness soul* and *spirit self* [*Manas*].[9] The actual center of the human soul being is the *intellectual soul*, or mind soul. The sentient soul is fashioned from the sentient body, and the consciousness soul receives the growing spirit self. This must be followed by a corresponding polarity in the post-Atlantean civilizations, characterized historically through the development of the soul principles. Actual history goes back just far enough to include the development of these soul principles; what was previous to that and what will come after has a different nature and belongs to spiritual events.

Now, in the historical studies of the time when the consciousness soul was dawning, we saw how all of the past had to be transferred to the consciousness soul so that the spirit self could germinate therein. That, then, is the transition of our time, during which Anthroposophy is able to arise. The opposite occurred during the third post-Atlantean civilization. Then the sentient soul was released from the sheath of the soul body, and that was the time when Gnosis was able to arise.

We now learn to recognize this powerful spiritual stream from its esoteric side—a chapter in suprasensory cosmic history. We can gain a strong impression, which may affect us deeply, that all spiritual life of ancient times then had to be held back toward the spiritual world. Angelic beings again had to take up what had been previously given to humankind. This is expressed in the cult of that time; in it, the feeling content of ancient spirituality was bestowed upon human beings in their loneliness, whereas the *content of the image of the universe*, or primal thought, was preserved in the spiritual world. The Mystery of Golgotha occurred during the transition to our time, the fourth post-Atlantean civilization. If esoteric Gnosis could bring a reasoning, and not merely a feeling comprehension, to the greatest impulse in earthly human evolution, this would be seen as a process in the spiritual world, from where this Mystery was beheld. In our day, the dam should be broken down as it were; the store of spiritual treasure can and must flow over the consciousness soul in order to permeate it with the spirit self.

---

8   In the letters, ibid., pp. 103–131.

9   *Rosicrucian Wisdom*, lecture 2, pp. 26–29.

Angels preserved the *precious store* of spiritual knowledge; in the cult, spirit beings distributed the *feeling content*; and now that Rudolf Steiner, as a human being, out of the forces of loneliness, has broken through the dam through his work from below, Michael, the greatest of the Archangels, steps forward and gives an impulse to the *will content* of the Mystery of Golgotha.

159. The Gnosis, in its appropriate form, evolved during the age of the sentient soul (from the fourth to the first millennium before the Mystery of Golgotha). It was an age when the Divine was made manifest to human beings as a spiritual content within their being. During the preceding age (that of the sentient soul), however, it had revealed itself directly through the sense impressions of the external world.

160. During the age of the intellectual (mind) soul, human beings could experience only in a more vague way the spiritual nature of the Divine. The Gnosis was strictly guarded within hidden Mysteries. When human beings could no longer preserve it—since they could no longer enkindle the sentient soul to life—spirit beings carried over not the knowledge content, but the feeling nature of Gnosis into the Middle Ages (as indicated in the legend of the Holy Grail). At the same time, the esoteric Gnosis, which penetrated the intellectual (mind) soul, was ruthlessly exterminated.

161. Anthroposophy cannot be a revival of Gnosis, because Gnosis depended on the development of the sentient soul, whereas Anthroposophy must develop a new understanding of Christ and the world through the spiritual soul in the light of Michael's activity. When the Mystery of Golgotha occurred, Gnosis, as preserved from ancient times, was the way of knowledge most capable of bringing that Mystery to human understanding.

THE NATURE OF MEMORY, PART 1

If one considers things in an unbiased way, the strongest proof for the spiritual nature of the universe may be found in the human capacity for remembering. Because contemporary science refuses to hear such testimony to the spirit, all the various phenomena of memory present great difficulties to the intellectual capacity of modern consciousness. We find many details about memory and remembering in the work arising from Rudolf Steiner's spiritual research, which explains it spiritually to ordinary consciousness. His book *Theosophy* presents the nature of memory as being connected with the life of the soul: The soul "mediates between the present and the permanent. It preserves the present for remembrance, wresting it away from perishability and giving it a place in the permanence of its own spiritual nature" (p. 64). In the same place, it is also shown how the bodily organization would allow all impressions to sink back again into nothingness. In other passages, in his lectures, Steiner speaks of "I"-consciousness being closely knit with the continuous threads of remembering.[1] In another context, he shows how the "I" is related to the forces of the etheric body—that, through this, memory arises. When this first happened, the colossal memory of the Atlanteans arose (which is the main epoch treated in the last Letters).[2] This was repeated during the intellectual soul's development; this may be characterized precisely by saying that the "I" lives in the forces of the etheric body.[3] Steiner also spoke in various places of cultivating and transforming memory into the capacity to see the Akashic Record, so that the faculty of remembering increases until it reaches pre-birth experience.[4] Conversely, after death memory becomes the cosmic sight of thoughts.[5]

In three different letters, Steiner speaks at length about remembering and memory.[6] This is especially valuable in clarifying much that arises from our earlier studies. The first sentence of the first of those letters reminds us specifically of its relation to previous letters (ibid., p. 181). There we can realize

---

1   *Forming of Destiny and Life after Death*, lectures 1 and 5.

2   *The Apocalypse of St. John*, lecture 1.

3   *The Mission of the Folk-Souls*, lecture 3.

4   *The Effects of Esoteric Development*, lecture 3.

5   *The Inner Nature of Man and the Life between Death and Rebirth*, lecture 5.

6   *Anthroposophical Leading Thoughts*, pp. 181ff; pp. 186ff; pp. 201ff.

the vital importance of what we encountered in the last letters in regard to cosmic memory (Study 68). Even in a much earlier letter, we were shown how, in a cosmic sense, the past becomes present.[1] This is also the meaning of the principle of repetition, which has repeatedly come before. Thus, it is comprehensible that cosmic memory, as a principle of knowledge, is directed toward its own nature. In other words, the principle of investigation (in the previous letters) itself becomes the object of this same investigation. This applies to one of the present letters[2]; with this, something new is in fact given along with Steiner's previous statements on remembering and memory, although this principle was certainly already active in the background.

Thus we are shown the cosmic origin of remembering and memory, and it is clearly revealed that this occurs in forms that may be called *epistemological*. With this, the nature of epistemology in general gains new meaning. For one who bears this in mind, it is possible to understand the tremendous value Rudolf Steiner always placed on permeating all processes of knowledge—including suprasensory knowledge—with epistemological understanding. The transition from the ancient cosmos to the new is expressed in seemingly abstract statements, as Steiner himself so often used; statements based on a theory of knowledge or, rather, a *science* of knowledge. One letter in particular is an example of this, a prototype that can enrich anthroposophic work well into the future.[3] That letter closes by pointing to the "abyss of nothingness" over which we must leap. Every grain of knowledge in ordinary consciousness is a leap of this kind over the abyss of nothingness; this can be experienced in thinking.

Now, there is an argument that should be considered against the thinking about thinking in *Intuitive Thinking as a Spiritual Path: A Philosophy of Freedom*. It states that we can never grasp present thinking but only make past thought, which is remembered, into an object of fresh thinking, which again we cannot grasp as such. According to this, the whole effort of thinking about thinking must be set aside, since it can only lead repeatedly to endless retrogression, inasmuch as present thinking would escape and succumb to the past. As long as people theorize in this way, they cannot attain what is meant in *Intuitive Thinking as a Spiritual Path*; this can be done only when it is actually practiced. Then it becomes apparent that, when entering a state of meditation, present thinking, by coming to a standstill, grasps itself. At this point, the will enters and changes thinking into *imagination*; indeed, it is memory that is taken hold of through this transformation.

In this same letter, we may pursue this line of thought and see a corresponding process for *observation*, which is the polar opposite of thinking. Actual

---

1   Ibid., pp. 141ff.

2   Ibid., pp. 181ff.

3   Ibid.

perceiving also cannot really be grasped in that moment, for a mere staring does not imply comprehension; rather, perceiving, in its essence, escapes consciousness. Memory alone gives duration to the percept; what would otherwise fall into the past is lifted into the present by a spiritual process. We are concerned here with a spiritual process, because there is no fundamental difference between the process of remembering and that of perceiving—except that, in place of an external process, one appears from a past event, which has been active "in the more hidden portions of the soul's life."[4] The truly spiritual process, however, is the same as that of thinking about thinking—observing or perceiving also may be grasped in its essence only when it enters the state of meditation.

162. In forming mental images, humanity lives not in being, but in image of being—in a realm of non-being—with the conscious, spiritual soul. Thus one is freed from living and experiencing with the cosmos. Pictures do not compel. Being alone has power to compel. And if human beings direct themselves according to images, doing so is independent of them, in freedom from the universe.

163. At the moment of such representation, one is joined to the being of the universe only by what has become through that individual's past: through former lives on Earth, and lives between death and new birth.

164. One can achieve this leap across the gulf of non-being in relation to the cosmos only through Michael's activity and the Christ impulse.

---

4   Ibid., p. 182.

STUDY 73

THE NATURE OF MEMORY, PART 2

The present letter has infinite significance but, since we considered it in our previous study, a purely epistemological examination may in fact be enough.[1] This letter, however, contains still more—mainly the important epistemological distinction between *image* and *being*. In the treatment of the "I," we found its pictorial character in Leading Thoughts 11 to 13, 14 to 16, and then again in 35 to 37 and in another letter and its accompanying leading thoughts.[2] Even in that early context, in contrast to the pictorial nature of ordinary consciousness, there was an indication of the reality introduced by repeated Earth lives through karma. Whereas those considerations were concerned with an inner experience of an image, however, now external sensible existence is also brought before us to illuminate the pictures in our consciousness.

The act of remembering is not attached to such an image existence, but to another process at work in the unconscious. This is accomplished where the human etheric body is active and, through the rule of spiritual beings, is called into soul existence. The anticipation of such facts made it possible for the thought to arise: *The world is my representation.* This, however, is a luciferic temptation opposed by Michael. The consequences of such a statement lead to the denial of human freedom, whereas, in fact, it is just through the non-being of the images that we can be ourselves; "Pictures do not compel. Being alone has power to compel." This is the monumental expression of Leading Thought 162. The past holds us in being, the present in a void.

As in all the letters, so also in the present one; everything depends on the actual wording. We must approach it sentence by sentence. It will then become clear to the soul (and this is most important) that the past cosmos, with its spiritual activity, withdraw all true being from human consciousness and leave human beings to themselves within the realm of pictures. This—the new contribution to understanding the cosmic foundation of freedom—is an addition to Leading Thought 111. From the pictures of the world, we learn to take hold of our own being. This arises continually from epistemological statements; the meaning of pure thinking is to strive repeatedly from the image experience of the world toward "I"-being. In 1907, Steiner

---

1   *Anthroposophical Leading Thoughts*, pp. 181ff.

2   This letter is contained in the *Monthly News Sheet* of the Anthroposophical Society in Great Britain, pp. 56ff.

266

imprinted this in his mantric sentence: "In pure thinking you find the self that can hold itself."[3]

Now, however, a new cosmos and the spiritual beings of the world await what human beings will begin with their own being. Lucifer wishes to bind us to interior images, and Ahriman to the outer. Between them, Michael holds open the door, which allows free access to Christ's deed. The path of *imagination* is described afresh in the letter; the cosmos is prepared to receive human *imaginations*. We are concerned here with taking the same path, epistemologically, that we recognized in the previous study; there it became apparent that *cosmic remembering*, the cognitive principle of suprasensory investigation, leads to the application of that principle to itself. We can repeat this along with the knowledge that the image being of the world makes it possible for our own being to have its origin in freedom; this leads beyond mere theoretical knowledge.

We may ask ourselves: If pictures do not compel—if being alone compels—is it not possible that our own being, which we acquire in the presence of the image of the world, can itself become compulsion? Therefore, wouldn't the first act of true freedom be for the "I" to make itself into a picture as a final free continuation of ancient cosmic activity? If human beings make their own being into an image, the cosmic being of the future arises. "Human beings have the potential to become cosmic beings once again when, as earthly beings, they have become *themselves*."[4] Steiner continued the previous mantric expression of 1907 with this: "*Transform the thought into picture life, and you will know creative wisdom.*"[5]

When we change our own being into an image, we dare to leap over the abyss of nothingness. The moment is indicated in this mystery experience, (which Steiner describes in *How To Know Higher Worlds*) when the student is left entirely alone and feels forsaken, even by the guide. Destiny, however, which leads human beings out of the past into the present, thus places the student before the abyss of nothingness in order to gain enough courage to make the leap, unconcerned with the consequences; this is true freedom. In the historical development of our time, this decision has emerged as the karma of materialism, an ordeal every modern individual must experience in some way. In *A Way of Self-Knowledge* (first meditation), Steiner points to this ordeal in the context of speaking about the question of continued existence,

3   "Jachin and Boaz," the two pillars of the temple: "*J* —In pure thinking you find the self that can hold itself. / Transform the thought into picture life and you will know creative wisdom. *B* —Condense your feeling into light; formative powers are revealed through you. / Forge your will into acts of being; thus, you share in cosmic creation." *Verses and Meditations*, p. 153.

4   *Anthroposophical Leading Thoughts*, p. 183.

5   See also *How to Know Higher Worlds*, p. 145, paragraph 35.

independent of the body's dissolution; "You cannot even come close to a true understanding of the spiritual world without complete objectivity and a willingness to accept equally 'no' or 'yes.'" Thus, in Steiner's mystery drama *The Soul's Probation*, Capesius, whose experience of this mystery of our time is particularly strong, says:

> And if all wisdom were to unite in this,
> And if I were powerless to reject the claim
> That destiny demands of human beings
> That they lose the individual self
> And fall into the abyss of nothingness,
> Yet would I fearlessly venture forth.

Then, however, he continues:

> Such thoughts would be profanity today,
> For I now know I cannot win repose
> Until the spirit treasure in my soul
> Has been unveiled to the light of day.

This is the ordeal before everyone who has encountered Anthroposophy.

STUDY 74

THE THREEFOLD EARTH

During the final month of his life, Rudolf Steiner clothed *imagination* knowledge in forms of epistemology, which are continued until the letter entitled "The Apparent Extinction of Spirit Knowledge in Modern Times."[1] Indeed, it is remarkable to see the way he allows all the subjects discussed previously in the leading thoughts and letters to pass before us once again (this was indicated in Study 68). We are inclined to ask whether this expresses something like a farewell to Earth life—if he was including here the possibility of leaving the physical plane. Now that we are nearing the end of our work on the leading thoughts, after scrupulous examination we may say, "No, that is absolutely not the case! These communications in letters and leading thoughts have not come to a close." We can definitely sense that, in these final letters, Steiner's spiritual strength was especially concentrated toward giving a new, and even higher level to these revelations. Perhaps the direction planned for their continuation will yet be shown to us.[2]

In earlier studies,[3] we learned of a realm where Michael rules, which borders on the physical world. He remains in that realm and does not work directly into the physical world; that is his strength in opposition to Lucifer and Ahriman, and it is, at the same time, a test for humankind. In a another letter,[4] this world is shown to us in the light of *imagination* knowledge. The physical Earth and the spiritual Earth are polar opposites; mediating between them, however, is the *rhythmic* Earth—the sphere with which Michael has united without contacting physical Earth. Since human language is no longer adequate to express direct *imaginations*, such knowledge of the Earth and humankind is characterized through the light from those higher spheres (although forms of epistemology are also used). First, the human "I" is discussed, and, to understand what is said, we must work through very complicated interpretations; even the thinking of ordinary consciousness is rejected when considering these difficult statements.

---

1   *Anthroposophical Leading Thoughts*, pp. 206ff.

2   Ita Wegman, after Rudolf Steiner's death, attempted to continue the leading thoughts, but owing to pressure from others in the Anthroposophical Society, she discontinued them after September, 1925; see Ita Wegman, *Esoteric Studies: The Michael Impulse*, pp. 8–9, and 25–78.

3   For example, *Anthroposophical Leading Thoughts*, pp. 86ff.

4   Ibid., pp. 201ff.

Within the physical world, the "I" appears in ideation (thinking) to our ordinary consciousness. What is the "physical world" in terms of this letter? Here again, we must listen very closely. A distinction is made between *in* and *with* a certain realm. Let us take *in* to have a more spatial meaning and *with* a more causal sense. It thus follows that where *in* and *with* are used, humankind initially has no self-awareness—but only where *in* is really meant, not *with*, since self-awareness arises when human beings free themselves from causality.

Rudolf Steiner once defined the physical body as "something...that, when it is in a certain place, no other body can occupy that same place at the same time"[1] In the same connection, he speaks of the physical world as the place where the human "I" can maintain itself consciously. The first definition applies in the sense of the modern view of nature; the second is given through Spiritual Science. That is, *in* and not *with* the physical Earth. It is different in terms of the spiritual Earth, where the "I" is *in* and *with*—*in*, for it is "I"-being, and *with*, since it is essentially connected with this realm, but not in self-awareness. We can now try to summarize the facts presented in the letter "Where is Humankind as Beings Who Think and Remember."[2]

Self-awareness for the "I" *grows* from communion with the spiritual Earth; it is *experienced*, however, in the physical Earth. Thinking is accomplished in the physical world, but the power to think comes from the spiritual Earth. The "I" brings the results of previous earthly lives into the spiritual Earth, where it lives as a being of will in relation to destiny. Destiny, however, is *experienced* in the physical world and carried into the next earthly life as conscious activity.

Now these facts would sharply contradict one another—*I* and *not-I*—if not mediated by *memory*. Thus, memory, though certainly in a changed form, is seen as the true bearer of *imagination* knowledge. The experience of memories also occurs for human beings within the physical world; but whereas thinking strikes against the physical body (conscious of space), remembering is attached to the etheric body (conscious of time). In relation to this causality, "the forces of the spirit world, which we experience between death and new birth, flow" into the *astral body*. Thus, memory is active in the astral body, but conscious is active in the etheric body and serves the self-awareness of the "I." The participation (the *with*) into which we enter as beings gifted with memory is rhythmic; it is an oscillation in time between the physical and the spiritual.

It could be said that the above merely repeats what Steiner himself wrote in the letter. In attempting to return again to the wording of this letter, however, we find that the difficulties are still plenty. Working on them can lead to a path into the spiritual world, which Steiner points to as the appropriate path for modern humanity, rather than that of Indian yoga, for example. It is the

---

1   *According to Matthew*, lecture 8.

2   *Anthroposophical Leading Thoughts*, pp. 186ff.

path of Michael, and the discussions in the letter assume the perspective from which Michael exercises his activity.

165. Although as human beings we live in the realm of physical Earth, as thinking beings we do not enter into communion with it. As beings of spirit, we live in such a way that we perceive the physical; but we receive our forces for thinking from the *spiritual Earth* in the same way we receive our destiny—as the result of previous lives on Earth.

166. What we experience in memory is already present in the world where, in rhythm, the physical becomes half spiritual, and where spiritual processes take place such as those brought about by Michael in the present cosmic moment.

167. Those who realize the true nature of thinking and memory will also begin to understand how, as earthly beings, we do not become submerged with our whole being in the earthly realm, though we live within it. As beings from beyond Earth, we are seeking self-awareness through communion with the *spiritual Earth*—as the fulfillment of our "I"-being.

THE NATURE OF THE ASTRAL

The region from which Michael works for humanity belongs to the realm that, in keeping with earlier studies, we may call the threshold of the spiritual world. *Imagination* knowledge considers humankind and the universe from the perspective of this threshold realm. Here, too, in this context, we find a fact that follows from our earlier studies—that the threshold of the spiritual world passes right through the human being of today. The physical and etheric bodies have their being on this side, and the astral body and the "I"-being are on the other side of this threshold. In the previous letter,[1] the gaze of *imagination* is directed from the realm of the threshold toward the "I" and the astral body; the present letter[2] sheds more light on the conditions of the physical and etheric bodies. The finer details must, however, be carefully observed. The previous letter shows how *imagination* illuminates the "I" and astral body with the help of phenomena in the realm of consciousness experienced in the physical world—representations (*Vorstellung*) and memories. Now, in the present letter, the conditions of the physical, and particularly those of the etheric body, are characterized with the help of what flows in from the cosmos and the spiritual world.

For the "I" and the astral body, there is a polarity between earthly lives and the lives between death and new birth; likewise, for the physical and etheric bodies, there is a polarity between the center of the Earth and the starry periphery. Indeed, in both cases, it is a matter of which forces are active. Conversely, the center of the Earth is related by the physical body to "I"-consciousness, and the astral and etheric are brought to Earth from the starry periphery. The letter receives its own particular character from this fact, for *imagination* sight—which begins when one becomes conscious of the etheric body—reveals that there must be a further differentiation. Mineral and plant are in contrast to animal and humankind, and this relates to the inflowing astral. Thus, these conditions are extremely complicated, and the amazingly colorful description in these letters recalls the eternally changing picture world of knowing through *imagination*.[3]

In the physical world human beings are surrounded by witnesses to their own past—that is, mineral, plant, and animal. If the light of *imagination*

---

1   *Anthroposophical Leading Thoughts*, pp. 186ff.

2   Ibid., pp. 190ff.

3   *Rosicrucian Wisdom*, lecture 2; *According to Luke*, lecture 1.

illuminates these realms, there is again a special kind of remembering at work. *Imagination* invokes the past into knowledge as the present; it creates a realm of knowledge out of time. Thus, real activity of the past is revealed there in the present. In this way we encounter a secret of the astral sphere, which is disclosed in the present letter.[4]

In earlier studies, the astral was seen as the representative of a substantially causal element, clearly effective in itself. As such, it may be considered independent of space and time. Activity in time originates in the union of the astral and the etheric; activity in space originates in the union of the astral and physical. As a purely active force, it is very possible to picture the astral independently of space. Enigmatic actions at a distance, which cause such difficulties in physics, can be understood only by overcoming the images of space we make through thought. Cosmic forces are *astral* forces; it is clear from their name that they are the activity of the stars. According to a lecture by Rudolf Steiner in Dornach, there is a sense-perceptible manifestation of the cosmic astral element in the light of the stars; likewise, this manifestation is present in the light of Sun and Moon.

In the current letter we become more familiar with the astral activity that is independent of time. Thus, since there is direct cosmic light shining spontaneously from heavenly bodies—radiating from the sun and fixed stars and reflected cosmic light from the moon and planets—likewise, there is astral activity acting *immediately in the present*, and there is astral activity *reflected through time*, which appears to shine from the past into the present. This can also be expressed by saying that the old Moon, for example, is in no way *past* in terms of time, but is *present* where it is active.

In this way, we can follow what is presented to us in the letter. Mineral and plant are reached through the astral forces flowing in at the present time from the starry realms, because they themselves have nothing of past astral in them—that is, they possess a cosmic astral body, but not an earthly one.[5] The animal realm is reached through the astral forces of the ancient Moon, since that realm is connected with that period through its own past astral body. That is Jehovah's realm, to which human beings in the astral body also belong, to the degree that it is not transformed by the addition of the "I."[6] For this part of the human astral body, however, the present astral Sun's activity is added through the medium of the spiritual Earth. This is the realm of the other Elohim, which is connected with "I"-being from the past; it is the realm of the Christ to the degree it is connected with the spiritual Earth.

This study may be regarded as an attempt to show that "human beings once more gain the ability to experience the life of ideas within themselves,

---

4   *Anthroposophical Leading Thoughts*, pp. 190ff.

5   *Spiritual Beings in the Heavenly Bodies and in the Kingdoms of Nature*, lecture 8.

6   *The Gospel of St. John*, lecture 3; *The Mission of the Folk-Souls*, lecture 6.

even when they do not base their ideas on the world of the senses.... However, this signifies that they will become acquainted with Michael in his kingdom."[1]

168. At the beginning of the age of the spiritual [consciousness] soul, humankind's sense of communion with the cosmos beyond the Earth grew dim. On the other hand (and this was especially true of scientists), the sense of belonging to the earthly realm grew so intense through the experience of sense impressions that it became stupefying.

169. While thus stupefied, the activity of ahrimanic forces became extremely dangerous for human beings. For humankind lives with the illusion that the overly intense, stupefying experience of sense impressions is appropriate and represents true evolutionary progress.

170. Human beings must find the strength to fill their world of Ideas with light—to experience it in this way even when ideas are not based on the stupefying world of the senses. In this experience of the world of ideas—independent and thus filled with light—humanity's sense of communion with the cosmos beyond Earth will reawaken. In this way, the true foundation for festivals of Michael will arise.

171. The organization of the human senses does not belong to human nature; it is built into human nature by the outer world during earthly life. Spatially, however, it is within human beings but, in its true essence, the perceiving eye is *in the world*. Human beings with their soul and spirit reach out into what the world experiences in them through the senses. Human beings do not receive the physical environment into themselves during life on Earth, but grow out into that environment with their soul and spirit.

172. Likewise, human beings, through their thinking organization, grow out into the existence of the stars. They know themselves as a world of stars; they live and move within cosmic thoughts when, through the living experience of knowledge, they have set aside the organization of the senses.

173. When both the earthly world and the world of the stars have been set aside, human beings stand before themselves as beings of soul and spirit. At this point, human beings are no longer of the world but are truly human. Becoming aware of this experience is *self-knowledge*, just as awareness through the organs of the senses and thinking is *cosmic-knowledge*.

---

1   *Anthroposophical Leading Thoughts*, p. 194.

WHAT THE FUTURE HOLDS

Only when human beings have freed themselves from the sense organization through means of inner development will they see through false views of the physical world and their own role in it. Those false views arise through the stupefaction of our time and change truth into its opposite. In relation to this, Rudolf Steiner gave this meditative mantric thought through the whole substance of his final letters and reflections: "*Filled with ideas, the human soul experiences spirit light when what appears to the senses is as the echo of a memory.*"[2] Everything that has come before us in the previous few studies as epistemology—its significance striving upward beyond that form—is contained in this sentence. It points to continual, persistent work on soul development. After prolonged consideration, we may make such a thought our own; it is the beginning of true inner growth for an active soul. Once again, in this solemn close of that letter, the word as well as the nature of memory characterizes the transition from ordinary consciousness to higher consciousness.

After death, a person looks back at the experiences of earthly life, which has run its course. By stripping away the connection to the sense life, those memories are transformed into the essence of spiritual existence; and, without losing them, they are brought to the next earthly life in that individual's spirit being. Thus, in rising to *imagination* knowledge, human beings learn to look back at the sense world without losing sight of its essence. Steiner shows this in detail in the next letter, which reveals the true relationship between human beings and the sense world. *Memory* of sense perceptible existence is thus filled with reality, no longer the shadowy picture existence of ordinary memory; "Human beings preserve what they have gained through their earthly nature even when, *after having acquired it*, they divest themselves of it in the conscious activity of higher knowledge."[3] The description in this letter, given through the vision of *imagination*, considers human beings in relation to the sense organization and the outer world; and it can directly illuminate the epistemological aspect. There are, for example, wonderful polarities revealed here; as the results of suprasensory knowledge, it presents the same epistemological facts that Steiner frequently discussed elsewhere, especially in his *Intuitive Thinking as a Spiritual Path*. This clearly proves that pure thinking

2   Ibid., p. 194.

3   Ibid., p. 196.

is closely related to *imagination*; but, it would go beyond the scope of our considerations to develop this in greater detail.

Now, the next step is significant—stripping off not only the sense organization (physical body), but also the thinking organization (etheric body), which leads to experience in the astral body. There, we enter a way of observing that must be described as *moral*; this, too, accords with our earlier studies and is developed in a previous letter.[1] Much of what earlier letters and leading thoughts dealt with, however, is concentrated in this and the preceding letter. References to earlier letters, leading thoughts, and studies could be added to almost every sentence; the wording here by Steiner is supported by the extreme clarity and overwhelming power of the Survey (Studies 66 and 67).

The difference in this new approach is that, beyond *imaginative* sight, *inspiration* knowledge begins to come into play. The voice of conscience is an *inspirational* experience. Conscience is shown as the opposite pole of memory, but at the same time it is itself a new form of remembering—a divine spiritual *aftereffect*. When we picture to ourselves the transformation of this echo of sleep experience into a herald of future awakening, we are presented with the essence of genuine *inspiration* knowledge.

Because death tore the physical instrument away from Rudolf Steiner, here we may suffer deeply with the sense that his letters and leading thoughts come to an end. Just as we have been introduced into *imagination* knowledge, perhaps we also expect a similar introduction to *inspiration* and, possibly, *intuition* knowledge. We may realize that, if this had been presented to us, it would necessarily have had tremendous moral value.

The three letters and groups of leading thoughts that still follow were perhaps the prelude to such a continuation. We are clearly brought to the present through them, and in fact current phenomena appear as the moral concern of modern human beings. *Remembering* plays a tragic part today. In relation to the "dawn of the age of the consciousness soul," the description in the next letter speaks of the historical "necessity to connect the spiritual life of humankind, not with any living, present knowledge, but with knowledge gained in the past—with tradition."[2] The tragic element of the active *remembering* here becomes *guilt*, if the consciousness soul does not turn to the spirit self, to the power of knowledge that lives in the present and carries the future within it. This, however, is Anthroposophy as a "path of knowledge, intended to guide the human spirit to the cosmic spirit" (Leading Thought 1).

174. The human being is organized in spirit and in body from two different sides. First, from the physical and etheric cosmos. All that radiates from Divine spiritual being into this organization in human nature lives there

---

1   Ibid., pp. 201ff.

2   Ibid., p. 206.

as the forces of sense perception, the capacity for memory, and of the play of fantasy.

175. Second, human beings are organized from their own past lives on Earth. This organization is purely soul and spirit, and lives in human beings through the astral body and "I"-being. All of the life of Divine spiritual beings that enters the human being lights up there as the voice of conscience and everything related to it.

176. In the human rhythmic organization, there is a constant union of Divine spiritual impulses from the two sides. The force of memory is carried, through the experience of rhythm, into the life of will, and the power of conscience into the life of ideas.

177. In the age of science, when we view human evolution with the eye of the soul, a sorrowful perspective opens before us at first. Human knowledge grew in splendor in relation to the substance of the outer world. On the other hand, a feeling arose, as though knowledge of the spiritual world were no longer possible at all.

178. It seems as though such knowledge had the possession of only the ancients, and as though humankind must now be content—in all that concerns the spiritual world—merely to accept the old traditions as objects of belief.

179. From the resulting uncertainty, arising in the Middle Ages as to humanity's relation to the spiritual world, *nominalism* and *realism* proceeded. Nominalism is unbelief in the real spiritual aspect of human ideas; we have its continuation in the modern scientific view of nature. Realism is well aware of the reality of ideas, yet it finds fulfillment only in Anthroposophy.[3]

---

3   See chapter 4 in *Intuitive Thinking as a Spiritual Path*. The word *Idea* (*Idee*) refers to something more than an ordinary concept. "Ideas are not qualitatively different from concepts. They are only concepts with more content, more saturated, and more inclusive" (ibid., pp. 49–50).

STUDY 77

CROSS AND GRAVE

If Anthroposophy, as a path of knowledge, overcomes the limits of knowledge, it is extremely important to know the origin of those limits. Through
Rudolf Steiner's final letters to the members, we are, in a sense, placed again
at the beginning of our work on the leading thoughts. We may even discern it
as Steiner's bequest that, again and again throughout his work, he returns to
new beginnings; this is again true of the first paragraphs of the two current
letters.[1] Anyone who recognizes that a genuine path of knowledge proceeds in
spirals will certainly feel the need to go back to the beginning of the leading
thoughts and letters, after reaching the end brought about by Steiner's death.
Everything that one learns and becomes through such work contributes to this
fresh beginning. Thus, those who are transformed by knowledge advance to
further knowledge and development. By continuing to work in a living way on
the leading thoughts and letters, Steiner's words will echo again, not merely
from the printed text, but also from the hearts of those exerting the effort.
The path of *inspiration*, which Steiner was no longer able to develop in this
way, may therefore be realized in a harmonious striving toward knowledge.

The current letters are permeated with deep tragedy in their return to the
question of the limits of knowledge. We may well view this description of the
dawn of the *age of consciousness* in comparison to the corresponding descriptions in several previous letters.[2] In those letters, we became acquainted with
the origin of a history of humanity and its recapitulations until the present
time, directly from the viewpoint of Michael and his mission. Now, we learn
to recognize in particular how the power of Lucifer and Ahriman has penetrated the soul life of modern humankind, though the names of these beings
are never mentioned in these present letters.[3] The dualism that, even today,
still prevails had its precursor in the spiritual battle of the Middle Ages in the
form of *realism* and *nominalism*. It constitutes the dispute between progressive knowledge of the natural world and regressive spiritual tradition: "The
life of the human soul was torn in two."[4]

The course indicated here shows this split first as external, then as internal,
battles of entire groups of people. Today, this battle occurs in every human

---

1   *Anthroposophical Leading Thoughts*, pp. 206–215.

2   Ibid., pp. 51–59; pp. 66–102.

3   Ibid., pp. 206–215.

4   Ibid., p. 206.

soul. Let us refer to this as a split between intellect and mind; thus, we can easily perceive that it arose through the impact of the consciousness soul on what was originally the combined activities of the intellectual (mind) soul. That work was still combined when the intellectual soul had to be active within its own civilization—the pre-Roman period of the fourth post-Atlantean civilization. At first, the people of that time attempted to fight through to themselves in opposition to the aftereffect of the third post-Atlantean civilization. This is represented by the Trojan War. Then, however, a split in this civilization itself arose from the ruins of the third civilization carried over from East to West (Aeneas). Later, the East encroached again through Arabic influences, which to a great extent destroyed the work of the fourth civilization through the premature birth of the fifth. This provides a bold outline of the disruption that occurred during that important period of transition in an East–West orientation; it will continue noticeably until the future sixth post-Atlantean civilization.

In the current letter[5] another stream is added; it appears in more of a North–South orientation. The new impulse of the consciousness (spiritual) soul comes in contact with this split pertaining to ethnic migration, which, at the same time, thus becomes the dispute between inner and outer experience. Nevertheless, another stream appears, one worthy of notice and carrying the impulse of Christianity on mysterious paths from South to North, in order to transform the South from the North. The fact that these streams overlap is thoroughly characteristic. Through the endless battles between them, the new spiritual impulse has been crucified in humanity, having entered the human consciousness soul from the Mystery of Golgotha. Today, our modern achievements have grown to such an extent that this impulse is in danger of being crucified within every individual human soul; tragedy is thus transformed into guilt.

Historically, the split between the outer and inner manifested in the battles between the Roman Church and Mysticism; later it would be seen in the struggles of the Reformation. Does the anthroposophic movement have the capacity to settle the disputes of humanity? Will it transform the split into a higher unity or fall back into the battle between intellect and mind? This calls for a vital decision. The final letter[6] directs our attention to this. There a picture of today is presented that is a continuation of the crucifixion of the spiritual impulse. The demonic world of technology, the world of sub-nature, threatens to devour it. The grave follows the crucifixion; may Resurrection follow the grave.

180. The Greeks and Romans were the groups predestined by their very nature for unfolding the intellectual (mind) soul. They developed that stage of the soul to perfection. They did not carry within them, however,

---

5   Ibid., pp. 211ff.

6   Ibid., pp. 206ff.

the seeds of a direct unbroken progress to the consciousness (spiritual) soul. Their soul life sank in the intellectual soul.

181. During the time between the origin of Christianity and the age of the unfolding consciousness soul, a world of the spirit ruled and did not unite with the forces of the human soul. Human souls attempted to *explain* the world of spirit but could not experience it in living consciousness.

182. The groups of people advancing from the North and East in the great migrations encroached on the Roman Empire, and they took hold of the intellectual (mind) soul more through the inner life of feeling. Meanwhile, embedded in this element of feeling, the consciousness (spiritual) soul was evolving within those human souls. The inner life of those people was awaiting the present time, when the reunion of the soul with the world of spirit is again fully possible.

183. In the age of natural science, beginning around the middle of the nineteenth century, civilized human activities are gradually sliding downward, not only into the lowest regions of nature but even below nature. Technology and industry become sub-nature.

184. Because of this, it is urgent that humankind finds knowledge of the spirit through conscious experience. In this, human beings will rise as high above nature as they sink below it through sub-natural technological activities. Human beings will thus create within themselves the strength *not* to go under.

185. A past concept of nature still carried within it the spirit, which is connected to the source of all human evolution. Gradually, this spirit vanished altogether from human theories of nature. A purely ahrimanic spirit has entered and replaced that spirit, thus passing from theories of nature to a culture of technology.

STUDY 78

CONCLUSION ... OR NEW BEGINNING?

We have come to the close of these studies on the leading thoughts and letters from Rudolf Steiner to the members of the Anthroposophical Society. "Friend, it is indeed enough" (Angelus Silesius). We have wrung from the consciousness soul the sounds that are now able to serve the *Word* in selflessness; this Word will awaken in the spirit self. The following sentences further supplement those in Studies 30 and 59:

72. Anthroposophy is human beings asking and the spiritual world answering; but, we must constantly learn to ask questions and understand the answers (Study 31).

73. Every ascent into spiritual heights begins at the level of ordinary consciousness (Study 31).

74. Youth's experience that calls them to participate in Anthroposophy is an experience of death connected with inner destiny; it will transform itself into the forces of knowledge (Study 31).

75. The foundation of human thinking is laid on truth; individual human existence is based on a spiritual lie (Study 32).

76. Before true self-knowledge appears in human beings, the activity of the higher hierarchies is concealed behind our own being (Study 35).

77. The right approach to Michael is to walk the path of knowledge courageously and, at decisive moments, become aware of his cooperation (Study 35).

78. Under Michael's banner, we try to understand thinking (Study 35).

79. Thinking in thinking is the substance of the third Hierarchy and *imagination* (Study 38).

80. Feeling in feeling is the substance of the second Hierarchy and *inspiration* (Study 38).

81. Willing in willing is the substance of the first Hierarchy and *intuition* (Study 38).

82. Feeling in thinking is the Substance of logic—*inspiration* of thinking (Study 38).

83. Willing in thinking is the substance of conformity to law—*intuition* of thinking (Study 38).

84. Thinking in feeling is the substance of ideals—*imagination* of feeling (Study 38).

85. Willing in feeling is the substance of morality—*intuition* of feeling (Study 38).

86. Thinking in willing is the substance of moral fantasy—*imagination* of willing (Study 38).

87. Feeling in willing is the substance of love for the action—*inspiration* of willing (Study 38).

88. The kingdoms of nature arose from a cosmic analysis of humankind (Study 39).

89. Psychological considerations always contain something painful; thus, they must assume the form of exercises in inner experience (Study 39).

90. The religious approach is a real soul process that occurs when feeling is active in willing (Study 39).

91. The artistic approach is a real soul process that occurs when thinking is active in feeling (Study 39).

92. The scientific approach is a real soul process that occurs when willing is active in thinking (Study 39).

93. In the course of history, the religious element was overpowered by the artistic, the artistic element was overpowered by the scientific, the scientific element was overpowered by the religious (Study 40).

94. According to Anthroposophy, science is redeemed by art (*imagination*), art by religion (*inspiration*), religion by knowing (*intuition*) (Study 40).

95. There is no art of art and no religion of religion, but there is a science of science (Study 40).

96. In the will, the spiritual compulsion of destiny prevails; the seeds of future destiny are within thinking (Study 41).

97. The religious attitude prevailing in human willing brings about the Fatherhood of God, in feeling the Brotherhood of Christ, and in thinking the Fellowship of Michael (Study 41).

98. The shadow of an intuitive process appears in the concept, experienced in "I"-being; the shadow of an inspirational process appears in the judgment, experienced in the astral body; the shadow of an imaginative process appears in the conclusion, experienced in the etheric body (Study 42).

99. Anthroposophy is a path of knowledge leading from fettered thought to free thought (Study 43).

100. Thought becomes free when thinking stands still (Study 43).

101. Anthroposophy as a path of knowledge is justified by knowing, no longer only through believing (Study 45).

102. Love transfigures the individuality out of the universality of thinking (Study 47).

103. The greatest miracle ever is human freedom (Study 50).

104. A counterpart of the miracle experienced through knowing is the grace attained through activity (Study 51).

105. Human freedom is significant not only for humankind but for the world as well (Study 54).

106. Human beings free themselves from the impulse of spirit beings, who in turn acquire freedom in relation to human beings; this cosmic freedom is expressed in the infringement of Lucifer and Ahriman (Study 56).

107. Michael not only protects human freedom but also the reign of creative primeval beings (Study 56).

108. Contemporary human beings, who alone can properly enter the heritage of the historic past, are able to overcome within themselves the internal hindrances created in them by the past; human beings transform the ancient forms of humanity within themselves into the divine human image (Study 65).

109. Survey, as a force of knowledge, is a current experience of what is divided, for ordinary consciousness, into past and future (Study 65).

110. Nature and history are polar opposites; they become one only when seen cosmically (Study 68).

111. Divine tragedy is at the foundation of human individuation; it may be considered a means through which the gods can master the opposing forces (Study 69).

112. The purpose of human individuation is accomplished in the germinating spirit self (Study 70).

113. Unbiased consideration would find the strongest proof of the spirituality of the world in the human power of memory (Study 72).

114. The voice of conscience is an *inspiration* experience (Study 76).

115. All knowing transforms what is already known. (Study 70).

CITED WORKS BY RUDOLF STEINER

According to Luke: The Gospel of Compassion and Love Revealed, Great Barrington, MA: Anthroposophic Press, 2001; 10 lectures in Dornach, September 1909 (CW 114).

According to Matthew: The Gospel of Christ's Humanity, Great Barrington, MA: Anthroposophic Press, 2003; 12 lectures, Berne, Sep. 1–12, 1910 (CW 123).

Ancient Myths and the New Isis Mystery, Hudson, NY: Anthroposophic Press, 1994; 8 lectures, Dornach, 1918, 1920 (CW 180 & 202).

Anthroposophical Leading Thoughts: Anthroposophy as a Path of Knowledge: The Michael Mystery, London: Rudolf Steiner Press, 1998; written 1923–1925 (CW 26).

The Anthroposophic Movement, London: Rudolf Steiner Press, 1993; 8 lectures, Dornach, June 10–17, 1923 (CW 258).

Anthroposophy (A Fragment): A New Foundation for the Study of Human Nature, Hudson, NY: Anthroposophic Press, 1996; written 1910 (CW 45).

Anthroposophy and the Inner Life: An Esoteric Introduction, London: Rudolf Steiner Press, 1992; 9 lectures, Jan.–Oct. 1924 (CW 234).

The Apocalypse of St. John: Lectures on the Book of Revelation, Hudson, NY: Anthroposophic Press, 1993; 12 lectures, Nuremberg, June 17–30, 1908 (CW 104).

Aspects of Human Evolution, Hudson, NY: Anthroposophic Press, 1987; 8 lectures, Berlin, May–July 1917 (CW 176).

Autobiography: Chapters in the Course of My Life, 1861–1907, Great Barrington, MA: SteinerBooks, 2006; written 1924-1925 (CW 28).

Background to the Gospel of St. Mark, London: Rudolf Steiner Press, 1968; 13 lectures, Berlin, Munich, Hanover & Coblenz, 1910–1911 (CW 124).

The Being of Man and His Future Evolution, London: Rudolf Steiner Press, 1981; 9 lectures, Berlin 1908-1909 (CW 107).

The Bhagavad Gita and the West: The Esoteric Significance of the Bhagavad Gita and Its Relation to the Epistles of Paul, Great Barrington, MA: SteinerBooks, 2009; 5 lectures, Köln, Dec. 28-Jan. 1, 1913 (CW 142); 9 lectures, Helsinki, May 28–June 5, 1913 (CW 146).

Building Stones for an Understanding of the Mystery of Golgotha, London: Rudolf Steiner Press, 1972: 10 lectures, Berlin, March 27–May 8, 1917 (CW 175).

The Child's Changing Consciousness as the Basis for Pedagogical Practice, Hudson, NY: Anthroposophic Press, 1996; 8 lectures, Dornach, Switzerland, 1923 (CW 306).

Christ and the Spiritual World: And the Search for the Holy Grail, London: Rudolf Steiner Press, 2008; 6 lectures, Leipzig, Dec. 1913-Jan. 1914 (CW 149).

The Christ Impulse and the Development of the Ego-Consciousness, Gloucester, UK: Anthropsophical Publishing, 1926; 7 lectures, Berlin, Oct. 25, 1909–May 8, 1910 (CW 116).

Christianity as Mystical Fact: And the Mysteries of Antiquity, Great Barrington, MA: SteinerBooks, 2006; written 1902 (CW 8).

Cosmic and Human Metamorphoses, Great Barrington, MA: SteinerBooks, 2012; 7 Lectures, Berlin, Feb. 6–Mar. 20, 1917 (CW 175).

The Destinies of Individuals and of Nations, Hudson, NY: Anthroposophic Press, 1986; 14 Lectures, Berlin, Sept. 1, 1914-July 6, 1919 (CW 157).

Earthly and Cosmic Man, Blauvelt, NY: Garber, 1986; 9 lectures, Berlin, October 23, 1911-June 20, 1912 (CW 133).

Earthly Death and Cosmic Life: Anthroposophical Gifts for Life, Blauvelt, NY: Garber, 1989; 7 lectures, Berlin, Jan. 22-Mar. 26, 1918 (CW 181).

The East in the Light of the West / The Children of Lucifer and the Brothers of Christ (with Edouard Schuré), Blauvelt, NY: Garber Publications, 1986; 9 lectures, Aug. 23–31, 1909 (CW 113).

The Effects of Esoteric Development, Great Barrington, MA: SteinerBooks, 2007; 10 Lectures, the Hague; March 20-29, 1913 (CW 145).

The Forming of Destiny and Life after Death, Blauvelt, NY: Garber, 1989; 7 lectures, Berlin, Nov. 16–Dec. 21, 1915 (CW 157a).

The Foundation Stone / The Life, Nature and Cultivation of Anthroposophy, Rudolf Steiner Press, London, 1996; written 1923–1924 (CW 260 & 260a).

Founding a Science of the Spirit, London: Rudolf Steiner Press, 1986; 14 lectures, Stuttgart, Aug. 22–Sept. 4, 1906 (CW 95).

Four Mystery Dramas: The Portal of Initiation; The Soul's Probation; The Guardian of the Threshold; The Souls' Awakening, Great Barrington, MA: SteinerBooks, 2007; written 1910–1913 (CW 14).

From Buddha to Christ, Hudson, NY: Anthroposophic Press, 1978; 5 lectures, 1909–1912 (from CWs 58, 60, 109, 130).

From Jesus to Christ, London: Rudolf Steiner Press, 2005; 11 lectures, Karlsruhe, Oct. 4–14, 1911 (CW 131).

The Gospel of St. John, Hudson, NY: Anthroposophic Press, 1984; 12 lectures, Hamburg, May 5-31, 1908 (CW 103).

The Gospel of St. John and Its Relation to the Other Gospels, Great Barrington, MA: Anthroposophic Press, 1982; 14 lectures, Kassel, June 24–July 7, 1909 (CW 112).

The Gospel of St. Mark, Hudson, NY: Anthroposophic Press, 1986; 10 lectures, Basel, Sept. 15–24, 1912 (CW 139).

Guidance in Esoteric Training, London: Rudolf Steiner Press, 2001; lectures and writings, 1903–1922 (CWs 42, 245).

How to Know Higher Worlds: A Modern Path of Initiation, Hudson, NY: Anthroposophic Press, 1994; written 1904–1905 (CW 10).

Human and Cosmic Thought, London: Rudolf Steiner Press, 1991; 4 lectures, Berlin, January 20–23, 1914 (CW 151).

Initiation, Eternity, and the Passing Moment, Spring Valley, NY: Anthroposophic Press, 1980; 7 lectures, Munich, Aug. 25–31, 1912 (CW 138).

Inner Experiences of Evolution, Great Barrington, MA: Anthroposophic Press, 2009; 5 lectures, Berlin, Oct. 31–Dec. 7, 1911 (CW 132).

The Inner Nature of Man: And the Life between Death and Rebirth, London: Rudolf Steiner Press, 1994; 8 lectures and a short address, Vienna, April 6–14, 1914 (CW 153).

Intuitive Thinking as a Spiritual Path: A Philosophy of Freedom. Hudson, NY: Anthroposophic Press, 1995; written 1894 (CW 4).

The Karma of Materialism, Hudson, NY: Anthroposophic Press, 1985; 9 lectures, Berlin, July 31–Sept. 25, 1917 (CW 176).

Karmic Relationships: Esoteric Studies, vol. 8, London: Rudolf Steiner Press, 1975; 6 lectures, Torquay & London, Aug. 12–27, 1924 (CW 240).

Learning to See into the Spiritual World: Lectures to the Workers at the Goetheanum, Great Barrington, MA: SteinerBooks, 2009; 4 lectures, Dornach, June 28–July 18, 1923 (CW 350).

Life between Death and Rebirth, Hudson, NY: Anthroposophic Press, 1968; 16 lectures, various cities, Oct. 1912–May 1913 (CW 140).

Man in the Light of Occultism, Theosophy, and Philosophy, Blauvelt, NY: Garber, 1989; 10 lectures, Oslo, June 2–12, 1912 (CW 137).

Manifestations of Karma, London: Rudolf Steiner Press, 1995; 11 lectures, Hamburg, May 16–28, 1910 (CW 120).

The Mission of the Folk-Souls: In Relation to Teutonic Mythology, London, Rudolf Steiner Press, 2005; 11 lectures, Oslo, June 7–17, 1910 (CW 121).

A Modern Art of Education, Rudolf Steiner Press, London, 1981; 14 lectures, Ilkeley, England, August 5–17, 1923 (CW 307).

Nature's Open Secret: Introductions to Goethe's Scientific Writings, Great Barrington, MA: SteinerBooks, 2000; written 1883 (CW 1).

Necessity and Freedom, Hudson, NY: Anthroposophic Press, 1988; 5 lectures, Berlin, Jan. 25–Feb. 8, 1916 (CW 166).

Occult History: Historical Personalities and Events in the Light of Spiritual Science, London: Rudolf Steiner Press, 1982; 6 lectures, Stuttgart, Dec. 27, 1910–Jan. 1, 1911 (CW 126).

An Outline of Esoteric Science, Catherine Creeger, trans., Anthroposophic Press, Hudson, NY, 1998 (CW 13).

Philosophie und Anthroposophie: Gesammelte Aufsätze 1904–1923, Basel: Rudolf Steiner Verlag, 1984; collected essays (CW 35).

Psychoanalysis & Spiritual Psychology, Anthroposophic Press, Hudson, NY, 1990 (from CWS 143, 178, 205).

A Psychology of Body, Soul & Spirit: Anthroposophy, Psychosophy, Pneumatosophy, Hudson, NY: Anthroposophic Press, 1999; 12 Lectures, Oct. 1909; Nov. 1910; Dec. 1911 (CW 115).

The Redemption of Thinking: A Study in the Philosophy of Thomas Aquinas, Hudson, NY: Anthroposophic Press, 1983; 3 lectures, Dornach, May 22–24, 1920 (CW 74).

The Riddles of Philosophy: Presented in an Outline of Its History, Great Barrington, MA: SteinerBooks, 2009; written 1914 (CW 18).

Riddles of the Soul: The Case for Anthroposophy, Great Barrington, MA: SteinerBooks, 2012; Written 1917 (CW 21).

Rosicrucian Wisdom: An Introduction, London: Rudolf Steiner Press, 2000; 14 lectures, Munich, May 22–June 6, 1907 (CW 99).

Secrets of the Threshold, Great Barrington, MA: Anthroposophic Press, 2007; 8 lectures, Munich, Aug. 24–31, 1913 (CW 147).

Spiritual Beings in the Heavenly Bodies and in the Kingdoms of Nature, Great Barrington, MA: SteinerBooks, 2012; 10 lectures, Helsinki, Apr. 3–14, 1912 (CW 136)

The Spiritual Guidance of the Individual and Humanity: Some Results of Spiritual-Scientific Research into Human History and Development, Great Barrington, MA: SteinerBooks, 1991; written 1911, from 3 lectures, Copenhagen, June 1911 (CW 15).

The Spiritual Hierarchies and the Physical World: Zodiac, Planets & Cosmos, Great Barrington, MA: SteinerBooks, 2008; 10 lectures, Dusseldorf, April 13–22, 1909 (CW 110).

The Stages of Higher Knowledge: Imagination, Inspiration, Intuition, Great Barrington, MA: SteinerBooks, 2009; written 1905 (CW 12).

Theosophy: An Introduction to the Spiritual Processes in Human Life and in the Cosmos, Anthroposophic Press, Hudson, NY, 1994; written 1904 (CW 9).

True and False Paths in Spiritual Investigation, Rudolf Steiner Press, London, 1985; 11 lectures, Torquay, Aug. 11–22, 1924 (CW 243).

Truth and Knowledge: Introduction to Philosophy of Spiritual Activity, Great Barrington, MA: SteinerBooks, 2007; written 1891 (CW 3).

Truth-Wrought-Words: With Other Verses and Prose Passages, Spring Valley, NY: Anthropsophic Press, 1979.

Universe, Earth and Man, Rudolf Steiner Press, London, 1987; 11 lectures, Stuttgart, Aug. 4–16, 1908 (CW 105).

Verses and Meditations, London: Rudolf Steiner Press, 2005; a collection.

A Way of Self-Knowledge: And the Threshold of the Spiritual World, Great Barrington, MA: SteinerBooks, 2006; written 1912 and 1913 (CWs 16/17).

A Western Approach to Reincarnation and Karma: Selected Lectures and Writings by Rudolf Steiner, René Querido, ed., Hudson, NY: Anthroposophic Press, 1997.

Wonders of the World, Ordeals of the Soul, Revelations of the Spirit, Rudolf Steiner Press, London, 1983; 10 lectures, Munich, Aug. 18–27, 1911 (CW 129).

World History and the Mysteries in the Light of Anthroposophy, London: Rudolf Steiner Press, 1997; 9 lectures, Dornach, Dec. 1923–Jan. 1924 (CW 233).

The World of the Senses and the World of the Spirit, North Vancouver, BC: Steiner Book Centre, 1979; 6 lectures, Hanover, Dec. 27, 1911–Jan. 1, 1912 (CW 134).

CPSIA information can be obtained at www.ICGtesting.com
Printed in the USA
LVOW03s1757291114

416198LV00009B/314/P